THE CONSTITUTION
OF THE
UNITED STATES OF AMERICA

WITH BIOGRAPHIES OF THE FOUNDING FATHERS AND THE AMERICAN PRESIDENCY

WWW.FAIRHAVENPRESS.COM

MICHAEL J. HOLLIS, PH.D.

The Constitution of the United States of America: With biographies of the founding fathers and the American Presidency (3rd Hardback Ed)

ISBN: 978-1-62992-030-6

Published by
Fairhaven Press Inc.

Special thanks to: The White House, The White House Historical Foundation, The US National Archives, The University of Virginia and special contributors: Frank Friedel, Stephen Knott, C. James Taylor, Peter Onuf, J.C.A. Stagg, Daniel Preston, Margaret A. Hogan, Daniel Feller, Joel Silbey, William Freehling, John C. Pinheiro, Michael F. Holt, Jean H. Baker, William Cooper, Michael Burlingame, Hans Trefousse, Joan Waugh, Ari Hoogenboom, Justus Doenecke, Henry F. Graff, Allan B. Spetter, Lewis L. Gould, Sidney Milkis, Peri E. Arnold, Kendrick Clements, Eugene Trani, David Greenberg, David E. Hamilton, William E. Leuchtenburg, Alonzo L. Hamby, Chester J. Pach, Jr., David Coleman, Kent Germany, Ken Hughes, John Robert Greene, Robert A. Strong, Lou Cannon, Stephen Knott, Russell L. Riley, Carl M. Cannon, and Michael Nelson.

Printed in the USA, UK, EU and Australia.

www.FairhavenPress.com

CONTENTS

PREFACE IV

CONSTITUTION 1

FOUNDING FATHERS 39

US GOVERNMENT 117

AMERICAN PRESIDENTS 145

PREFACE

The Constitution of the United States is the most important document in the founding of our nation. It is the supreme law of the land but despite the importance of this document its interpretation is still frequently up for heated debates. The founding fathers put considerable effort into producing a document that would stand the test of time. It was written to be a living document that would always be relevant in the lives of American citizens.

It is important for all Americans to have, read, and regularly study the original document. It is equally important to understand the men who drafted this document in order to fully understand what their intentions were at the time of its drafting and ratification. A quick overview of the lives of these signers is included for this purpose.

The next section in this text is a brief overview of the three branches of government. As most already know, the three branches of government are the basis for a Constitutional Republic. The three branches are of equal power and can hold the others accountable through a system of checks and balances.

A section of this text on the biographies of United States presidents is also included. Any student of American history or government should study the history of the presidency to better understand how our government has evolved over the years. This book has been produced not only for my own students but to anyone who would like to know more about the U.S. Constitution, it's creators, and the 43 men who have held the office of U.S. President.

-- Michael J. Hollis, Ph.D., Editor

THE CONSTITUTION OF THE UNITED STATES OF AMERICA

We the People of the United States, in Order to form a more perfect Union, establish Justice, insure domestic Tranquility, provide for the common defence, promote the general Welfare, and secure the Blessings of Liberty to ourselves and our Posterity, do ordain and establish this Constitution for the United States of America.

ARTICLE I

SECTION 1

All legislative Powers herein granted shall be vested in a Congress of the United States, which shall consist of a Senate and House of Representatives.

SECTION 2

The House of Representatives shall be composed of Members chosen every second Year by the People of the several States, and the Electors in each State shall have the Qualifications requisite for Electors of the most numerous Branch of the State Legislature.

No Person shall be a Representative who shall not have attained to the Age of twenty five Years, and been seven Years a Citizen of the United States, and who shall not, when elected, be an Inhabitant of that State in which he shall be chosen.

Representatives and direct Taxes shall be apportioned among the several States which may be included within this Union, according to their respective Numbers, which shall be determined by adding to the whole Number of free Persons, including those bound to Service for a Term of Years, and excluding Indians not taxed, three fifths of all other Persons.[1] The actual Enumeration shall be made within three Years after the first Meeting of the Congress of the United States, and within every subsequent Term of ten Years, in such Manner as they shall by Law direct. The Number of Representatives shall not exceed one for every thirty Thousand, but each State shall have at Least one Representative; and until such enumeration shall be made, the State of New Hampshire shall be entitled to chuse three, Massachusetts eight, Rhode-Island and Providence Plantations one, Connecticut five, New-York six, New Jersey four, Pennsylvania eight, Delaware one, Maryland six, Virginia ten, North Carolina five, South Carolina five, and Georgia three.

When vacancies happen in the Representation from any State, the Executive Authority thereof shall issue Writs of Election to fill such Vacancies.

The House of Representatives shall chuse their Speaker and other Officers; and shall have the sole Power of Impeachment.

SECTION 3

The Senate of the United States shall be composed of two Senators from each State, chosen by the Legislature[2] thereof, for six Years; and each Senator shall have one Vote.

Immediately after they shall be assembled in Consequence of the first Election, they shall be divided as equally as may be into three Classes. The Seats of the Senators of the first Class shall be vacated at the Expiration of the second Year, of the second Class at the Expiration of the fourth Year, and of the third Class at the Expiration of the sixth Year, so that one third may be chosen every second Year; and if Vacancies happen by Resignation, or otherwise, during the Recess of the Legislature of any State, the Executive thereof may make temporary Appointments until the next Meeting of the Legislature, which shall then fill such Vacancies.[3]

No Person shall be a Senator who shall not have attained to the Age of thirty Years, and been nine Years a Citizen of the United States, and who shall not, when elected, be an Inhabitant of that State for which he shall be chosen.

The Vice President of the United States shall be President of the Senate, but shall have no Vote, unless they be equally divided.

The Senate shall chuse their other Officers, and also a President pro tempore, in the Absence of the Vice President, or when he shall exercise the Office of President of the United States.

The Senate shall have the sole Power to try all Impeachments. When sitting for that Purpose, they shall be on Oath or Affirmation. When the President of the United States is tried, the Chief Justice shall preside: And no Person shall be convicted without the Concurrence of two thirds of the Members present.

Judgment in Cases of Impeachment shall not extend further than to removal from Office, and disqualification to hold and enjoy any Office of honor, Trust or Profit under the United States: but the Party convicted shall nevertheless be liable and subject to Indictment, Trial, Judgment and Punishment, according to Law.

SECTION 4

The Times, Places and Manner of holding Elections for Senators and Representatives, shall be prescribed in each

State by the Legislature thereof; but the Congress may at any time by Law make or alter such Regulations, except as to the Places of chusing Senators.

The Congress shall assemble at least once in every Year, and such Meeting shall <u>be on the first Monday in December,</u>[4] unless they shall by Law appoint a different Day.

SECTION 5

Each House shall be the Judge of the Elections, Returns and Qualifications of its own Members, and a Majority of each shall constitute a Quorum to do Business; but a smaller Number may adjourn from day to day, and may be authorized to compel the Attendance of absent Members, in such Manner, and under such Penalties as each House may provide.

Each House may determine the Rules of its Proceedings, punish its Members for disorderly Behaviour, and, with the Concurrence of two thirds, expel a Member.

Each House shall keep a Journal of its Proceedings, and from time to time publish the same, excepting such Parts as may in their Judgment require Secrecy; and the Yeas and Nays of the Members of either House on any question shall, at the Desire of one fifth of those Present, be entered on the Journal.

Neither House, during the Session of Congress, shall, without the Consent of the other, adjourn for more than three days, nor to any other Place than that in which the two Houses shall be sitting.

SECTION 6

The Senators and Representatives shall receive a Compensation for their Services, to be ascertained by Law, and paid out of the Treasury of the United States. They shall in all Cases, except Treason, Felony and Breach of the Peace, be privileged from Arrest during their Attendance at the Session of their respective Houses, and in going to and returning from the same; and for any Speech or Debate in either House, they shall not be questioned in any other Place.

No Senator or Representative shall, during the Time for which he was elected, be appointed to any civil Office under the Authority of the United States, which shall have been created, or the Emoluments whereof shall have been encreased during such time; and no Person holding any Office under the United States, shall be a Member of either House during his Continuance in Office.

SECTION 7

All Bills for raising Revenue shall originate in the House of Representatives; but the Senate may propose or concur with Amendments as on other Bills.

Every Bill which shall have passed the House of Representatives and the Senate, shall, before it become a Law, be presented to the President of the United States; If he approve he shall sign it, but if not he shall return it, with his Objections to that House in which it shall have originated, who shall enter the Objections at large on their Journal, and proceed to reconsider it. If after such Reconsideration two thirds of that House shall agree to pass the Bill, it shall be sent, together with the Objections, to the other House, by which it shall likewise be reconsidered, and if approved by two thirds of that House, it shall become a Law. But in all such Cases the Votes of both Houses shall be determined by yeas and Nays, and the Names of the Persons voting for and against the Bill shall be entered on the Journal of each House respectively. If any Bill shall not be returned by the President within ten Days (Sundays excepted) after it shall have been presented to him, the Same shall be a Law, in like Manner as if he had signed it, unless the Congress by their Adjournment prevent its Return, in which Case it shall not be a Law.

Every Order, Resolution, or Vote to which the Concurrence of the Senate and House of Representatives may be necessary (except on a question of Adjournment) shall be presented to the President of the United States; and before the Same shall take Effect, shall be approved by him, or being disapproved by him, shall be repassed by two thirds of the Senate and House of Representatives, according to the Rules and Limitations prescribed in the Case of a Bill.

SECTION 8

The Congress shall have Power To lay and collect Taxes, Duties, Imposts and Excises, to pay the Debts and provide for the common Defence and general Welfare of the United States; but all Duties, Imposts and Excises shall be uniform throughout the United States;

To borrow Money on the credit of the United States;

To regulate Commerce with foreign Nations, and among the several States, and with the Indian Tribes;

To establish an uniform Rule of Naturalization, and uniform Laws on the subject of Bankruptcies throughout the United States;

To coin Money, regulate the Value thereof, and of foreign Coin, and fix the Standard of Weights and Measures;

To provide for the Punishment of counterfeiting the Securities and current Coin of the United States;

To establish Post Offices and post Roads;

To promote the Progress of Science and useful Arts, by securing for limited Times to Authors and Inventors the exclusive Right to their respective Writings and Discoveries;

To constitute Tribunals inferior to the supreme Court;

To define and punish Piracies and Felonies committed on the high Seas, and Offences against the Law of Nations;

To declare War, grant Letters of Marque and Reprisal, and make Rules concerning Captures on Land and Water;

To raise and support Armies, but no Appropriation of Money to that Use shall be for a longer Term than two Years;

To provide and maintain a Navy;

To make Rules for the Government and Regulation of the land and naval Forces;

To provide for calling forth the Militia to execute the Laws of the Union, suppress Insurrections and repel Invasions;

To provide for organizing, arming, and disciplining, the Militia, and for governing such Part of them as may be employed in the Service of the United States, reserving to the States respectively, the Appointment of the Officers, and the Authority of training the Militia according to the discipline prescribed by Congress;

To exercise exclusive Legislation in all Cases whatsoever, over such District (not exceeding ten Miles square) as may, by Cession of particular States, and the Acceptance of Congress, become the Seat of the Government of the United States, and to exercise like Authority over all Places purchased by the Consent of the Legislature of the State in which the Same shall be, for the Erection of Forts,

Magazines, Arsenals, dock-Yards, and other needful Buildings;—And

To make all Laws which shall be necessary and proper for carrying into Execution the foregoing Powers, and all other Powers vested by this Constitution in the Government of the United States, or in any Department or Officer thereof.

SECTION 9

The Migration or Importation of such Persons as any of the States now existing shall think proper to admit, shall not be prohibited by the Congress prior to the Year one thousand eight hundred and eight, but a Tax or duty may be imposed on such Importation, not exceeding ten dollars for each Person.

The Privilege of the Writ of Habeas Corpus shall not be suspended, unless when in Cases of Rebellion or Invasion the public Safety may require it.

No Bill of Attainder or ex post facto Law shall be passed.

No Capitation, or other direct, Tax shall be laid, <u>unless in Proportion to the Census or enumeration herein before directed to be taken</u>.[5]

No Tax or Duty shall be laid on Articles exported from any State.

No Preference shall be given by any Regulation of Commerce or Revenue to the Ports of one State over those of another: nor shall Vessels bound to, or from, one State, be obliged to enter, clear, or pay Duties in another.

No Money shall be drawn from the Treasury, but in Consequence of Appropriations made by Law; and a regular

Statement and Account of the Receipts and Expenditures of all public Money shall be published from time to time.

No Title of Nobility shall be granted by the United States: And no Person holding any Office of Profit or Trust under them, shall, without the Consent of the Congress, accept of any present, Emolument, Office, or Title, of any kind whatever, from any King, Prince, or foreign State.

SECTION 10

No State shall enter into any Treaty, Alliance, or Confederation; grant Letters of Marque and Reprisal; coin Money; emit Bills of Credit; make any Thing but gold and silver Coin a Tender in Payment of Debts; pass any Bill of Attainder, ex post facto Law, or Law impairing the Obligation of Contracts, or grant any Title of Nobility.

No State shall, without the Consent of the Congress, lay any Imposts or Duties on Imports or Exports, except what may be absolutely necessary for executing it's inspection Laws: and the net Produce of all Duties and Imposts, laid by any State on Imports or Exports, shall be for the Use of the Treasury of the United States; and all such Laws shall be subject to the Revision and Controul of the Congress.

No State shall, without the Consent of Congress, lay any Duty of Tonnage, keep Troops, or Ships of War in time of Peace, enter into any Agreement or Compact with another State, or with a foreign Power, or engage in War, unless actually invaded, or in such imminent Danger as will not admit of delay.

Article II

Section 1

The executive Power shall be vested in a President of the United States of America. He shall hold his Office during the Term of four Years, and, together with the Vice President, chosen for the same Term, be elected, as follows

Each State shall appoint, in such Manner as the Legislature thereof may direct, a Number of Electors, equal to the whole Number of Senators and Representatives to which the State may be entitled in the Congress: but no Senator or Representative, or Person holding an Office of Trust or Profit under the United States, shall be appointed an Elector.

The Electors shall meet in their respective States, and vote by Ballot for two Persons, of whom one at least shall not be an Inhabitant of the same State with themselves. And they shall make a List of all the Persons voted for, and of the Number of Votes for each; which List they shall sign and certify, and transmit sealed to the Seat of the Government of the United States, directed to the President of the Senate. The President of the Senate shall, in the Presence of the Senate and House of Representatives, open all the Certificates, and the Votes shall then be counted. The Person having the greatest Number of Votes shall be the President, if such Number be a Majority of the whole Number of Electors appointed; and if there be more than one who have such Majority, and have an equal Number of Votes, then the House of Representatives shall immediately chuse by Ballot one of them for President; and if no Person have a Majority, then from the five highest on the List the said House shall in like Manner chuse the President. But in chusing the President, the Votes shall be taken by States, the Representation from each State having one Vote; A quorum for this Purpose shall consist of a Member or Members from two thirds of the States, and a

Majority of all the States shall be necessary to a Choice. In every Case, after the Choice of the President, the Person having the greatest Number of Votes of the Electors shall be the Vice President. But if there should remain two or more who have equal Votes, the Senate shall chuse from them by Ballot the Vice President.[6]

The Congress may determine the Time of chusing the Electors, and the Day on which they shall give their Votes; which Day shall be the same throughout the United States.

No Person except a natural born Citizen, or a Citizen of the United States, at the time of the Adoption of this Constitution, shall be eligible to the Office of President; neither shall any Person be eligible to that Office who shall not have attained to the Age of thirty five Years, and been fourteen Years a Resident within the United States.

In Case of the Removal of the President from Office, or of his Death, Resignation, or Inability to discharge the Powers and Duties of the said Office, the Same shall devolve on the Vice President, and the Congress may by Law provide for the Case of Removal, Death, Resignation or Inability, both of the President and Vice President, declaring what Officer shall then act as President, and such Officer shall act accordingly, until the Disability be removed, or a President shall be elected.[7]

The President shall, at stated Times, receive for his Services, a Compensation, which shall neither be encreased nor diminished during the Period for which he shall have been elected, and he shall not receive within that Period any other Emolument from the United States, or any of them.

Before he enter on the Execution of his Office, he shall take the following Oath or Affirmation:—"I do solemnly swear (or affirm) that I will faithfully execute the Office of President of the United States, and will to the best of my

Ability, preserve, protect and defend the Constitution of the United States."

SECTION 2

The President shall be Commander in Chief of the Army and Navy of the United States, and of the Militia of the several States, when called into the actual Service of the United States; he may require the Opinion, in writing, of the principal Officer in each of the executive Departments, upon any Subject relating to the Duties of their respective Offices, and he shall have Power to grant Reprieves and Pardons for Offences against the United States, except in Cases of Impeachment.

He shall have Power, by and with the Advice and Consent of the Senate, to make Treaties, provided two thirds of the Senators present concur; and he shall nominate, and by and with the Advice and Consent of the Senate, shall appoint Ambassadors, other public Ministers and Consuls, Judges of the supreme Court, and all other Officers of the United States, whose Appointments are not herein otherwise provided for, and which shall be established by Law: but the Congress may by Law vest the Appointment of such inferior Officers, as they think proper, in the President alone, in the Courts of Law, or in the Heads of Departments.

The President shall have Power to fill up all Vacancies that may happen during the Recess of the Senate, by granting Commissions which shall expire at the End of their next Session.

SECTION 3

He shall from time to time give to the Congress Information of the State of the Union, and recommend to their Consideration such Measures as he shall judge necessary and expedient; he may, on extraordinary Occasions, convene both Houses, or either of them, and in Case of Disagreement between them, with Respect to the Time of Adjournment, he may adjourn them to such Time as he shall think proper; he shall receive Ambassadors and other public Ministers; he shall take Care that the Laws be faithfully executed, and shall Commission all the Officers of the United States.

SECTION 4

The President, Vice President and all civil Officers of the United States, shall be removed from Office on Impeachment for, and Conviction of, Treason, Bribery, or other high Crimes and Misdemeanors.

ARTICLE III

SECTION 1

The judicial Power of the United States, shall be vested in one supreme Court, and in such inferior Courts as the Congress may from time to time ordain and establish. The Judges, both of the supreme and inferior Courts, shall hold their Offices during good Behaviour, and shall, at stated Times, receive for their Services, a Compensation, which shall not be diminished during their Continuance in Office.

SECTION 2

The judicial Power shall extend to all Cases, in Law and Equity, arising under this Constitution, the Laws of the United States, and Treaties made, or which shall be made, under their Authority;—to all Cases affecting Ambassadors, other public Ministers and Consuls;—to all Cases of admiralty and maritime Jurisdiction;—to Controversies to which the United States shall be a Party;—to Controversies between two or more States;— between a State and Citizens of another State,[8]—between Citizens of different States,—between Citizens of the same State claiming Lands under Grants of different States, and between a State, or the Citizens thereof, and foreign States, Citizens or Subjects.

In all Cases affecting Ambassadors, other public Ministers and Consuls, and those in which a State shall be Party, the supreme Court shall have original Jurisdiction. In all the other Cases before mentioned, the supreme Court shall have appellate Jurisdiction, both as to Law and Fact, with such Exceptions, and under such Regulations as the Congress shall make.

The Trial of all Crimes, except in Cases of Impeachment, shall be by Jury; and such Trial shall be held in the State where the said Crimes shall have been committed; but when not committed within any State, the Trial shall be at such Place or Places as the Congress may by Law have directed.

SECTION 3

Treason against the United States, shall consist only in levying War against them, or in adhering to their Enemies, giving them Aid and Comfort. No Person shall be convicted of Treason unless on the Testimony of two Witnesses to the same overt Act, or on Confession in open Court.

The Congress shall have Power to declare the Punishment of Treason, but no Attainder of Treason shall work Corruption of Blood, or Forfeiture except during the Life of the Person attainted.

ARTICLE IV

SECTION 1

Full Faith and Credit shall be given in each State to the public Acts, Records, and judicial Proceedings of every other State. And the Congress may by general Laws prescribe the Manner in which such Acts, Records and Proceedings shall be proved, and the Effect thereof.

SECTION 2

The Citizens of each State shall be entitled to all Privileges and Immunities of Citizens in the several States.

A Person charged in any State with Treason, Felony, or other Crime, who shall flee from Justice, and be found in another State, shall on Demand of the executive Authority of the State from which he fled, be delivered up, to be removed to the State having Jurisdiction of the Crime.

No Person held to Service or Labour in one State, under the Laws thereof, escaping into another, shall, in Consequence of any Law or Regulation therein, be discharged from such Service or Labour, but shall be delivered up on Claim of the Party to whom such Service or Labour may be due.[9]

SECTION 3

New States may be admitted by the Congress into this Union; but no new State shall be formed or erected within the Jurisdiction of any other State; nor any State be formed by the Junction of two or more States, or Parts of States, without the Consent of the Legislatures of the States concerned as well as of the Congress.

The Congress shall have Power to dispose of and make all needful Rules and Regulations respecting the Territory or other Property belonging to the United States; and nothing in this Constitution shall be so construed as to Prejudice any Claims of the United States, or of any particular State.

Section 4

The United States shall guarantee to every State in this Union a Republican Form of Government, and shall protect each of them against Invasion; and on Application of the Legislature, or of the Executive (when the Legislature cannot be convened), against domestic Violence.

Article V

The Congress, whenever two thirds of both Houses shall deem it necessary, shall propose Amendments to this Constitution, or, on the Application of the Legislatures of two thirds of the several States, shall call a Convention for proposing Amendments, which, in either Case, shall be valid to all Intents and Purposes, as Part of this Constitution, when ratified by the Legislatures of three fourths of the several States, or by Conventions in three fourths thereof, as the one or the other Mode of Ratification may be proposed by the Congress; Provided that no Amendment which may be made prior to the Year One thousand eight hundred and eight shall in any Manner affect the first and fourth Clauses in the Ninth Section of the first Article; and that no State, without its Consent, shall be deprived of its equal Suffrage in the Senate.

Article VI

All Debts contracted and Engagements entered into, before the Adoption of this Constitution, shall be as valid against the United States under this Constitution, as under the Confederation.

This Constitution, and the Laws of the United States which shall be made in Pursuance thereof; and all Treaties made, or which shall be made, under the Authority of the United States, shall be the supreme Law of the Land; and the Judges in every State shall be bound thereby, any Thing in the Constitution or Laws of any State to the Contrary notwithstanding.

The Senators and Representatives before mentioned, and the Members of the several State Legislatures, and all executive and judicial Officers, both of the United States and of the several States, shall be bound by Oath or Affirmation, to support this Constitution; but no religious Test shall ever be required as a Qualification to any Office or public Trust under the United States.

ARTICLE VII

The Ratification of the Conventions of nine States, shall be sufficient for the Establishment of this Constitution between the States so ratifying the Same.

The Word, "the," being interlined between the seventh and eighth Lines of the first Page, The Word "Thirty" being partly written on an Erazure in the fifteenth Line of the first Page, The Words "is tried" being interlined between the thirty second and thirty third Lines of the first Page and the Word "the" being interlined between the forty third and forty fourth Lines of the second Page.

Attest William Jackson Secretary

done in Convention by the Unanimous Consent of the States present the Seventeenth Day of September in the Year of our Lord one thousand seven hundred and Eighty seven and of the Independance of the United States of America the Twelfth In witness whereof We have hereunto subscribed our Names,

G. Washington
Presidt and deputy from Virginia

Delaware
Geo: Read
Gunning Bedford jun
John Dickinson
Richard Bassett
Jaco: Broom

Maryland
James McHenry
Dan of St Thos. Jenifer
Danl. Carroll

Virginia
John Blair
James Madison Jr.

North Carolina
Wm. Blount
Richd. Dobbs Spaight
Hu Williamson

South Carolina
J. Rutledge
Charles Cotesworth Pinckney
Charles Pinckney
Pierce Butler

Georgia
William Few
Abr Baldwin

New Hampshire
John Langdon
Nicholas Gilman

Massachusetts
Nathaniel Gorham
Rufus King

Connecticut
Wm. Saml. Johnson
Roger Sherman

New York
Alexander Hamilton

New Jersey
Wil: Livingston
David Brearley
Wm. Paterson
Jona: Dayton

Penslyvania
B Franklin
Thomas Mifflin
Robt. Morris
Geo. Clymer
Thos. Fitzsimons
Jared Ingersoll
James Wilson
Gouv Morri

(Note: for more information on each of these signers please visit the section of this text immediately following the Bill of Rights)

1. see Amendment XIV
2. see Amendment XVII
3. see Amendment XVII
4. see Amendment XX
5. see Amendment XVI
6. see Amendment XII
7. see Amendment XXV
8. see Amendment XI
9. see Amendment XIII

The U.S. Bill of Rights

The Preamble to The Bill of Rights

Congress of the United States

begun and held at the City of New-York, on

Wednesday the fourth of March, one thousand seven hundred and eighty nine.

THE Conventions of a number of the States, having at the time of their adopting the Constitution, expressed a desire, in order to prevent misconstruction or abuse of its powers, that further declaratory and restrictive clauses should be added: And as extending the ground of public confidence in the Government, will best ensure the beneficent ends of its institution.

RESOLVED by the Senate and House of Representatives of the United States of America, in Congress assembled, two thirds of both Houses concurring, that the following Articles be proposed to the Legislatures of the several States, as amendments to the Constitution of the United States, all, or any of which Articles, when ratified by three fourths of the said Legislatures, to be valid to all intents and purposes, as part of the said Constitution; viz.

ARTICLES in addition to, and Amendment of the Constitution of the United States of America, proposed by Congress, and ratified by the Legislatures of the several States, pursuant to the fifth Article of the original Constitution.

(Note: The following text is a transcription of the first ten amendments to the Constitution in their original form. These

amendments were ratified December 15, 1791, and form
what is known as the "Bill of Rights.")

AMENDMENT I

Congress shall make no law respecting an establishment of
religion, or prohibiting the free exercise thereof; or abridging
the freedom of speech, or of the press; or the right of the
people peaceably to assemble, and to petition the
Government for a redress of grievances.

AMENDMENT II

A well regulated Militia, being necessary to the security of a
free State, the right of the people to keep and bear Arms,
shall not be infringed.

AMENDMENT III

No Soldier shall, in time of peace be quartered in any house,
without the consent of the Owner, nor in time of war, but in a
manner to be prescribed by law.

AMENDMENT IV

The right of the people to be secure in their persons, houses,
papers, and effects, against unreasonable searches and
seizures, shall not be violated, and no Warrants shall issue,
but upon probable cause, supported by Oath or affirmation,
and particularly describing the place to be searched, and the
persons or things to be seized.

AMENDMENT V

No person shall be held to answer for a capital, or otherwise
infamous crime, unless on a presentment or indictment of a

Grand Jury, except in cases arising in the land or naval forces, or in the Militia, when in actual service in time of War or public danger; nor shall any person be subject for the same offence to be twice put in jeopardy of life or limb; nor shall be compelled in any criminal case to be a witness against himself, nor be deprived of life, liberty, or property, without due process of law; nor shall private property be taken for public use, without just compensation.

Amendment VI

In all criminal prosecutions, the accused shall enjoy the right to a speedy and public trial, by an impartial jury of the State and district wherein the crime shall have been committed, which district shall have been previously ascertained by law, and to be informed of the nature and cause of the accusation; to be confronted with the witnesses against him; to have compulsory process for obtaining witnesses in his favor, and to have the Assistance of Counsel for his defence.

Amendment VII

In Suits at common law, where the value in controversy shall exceed twenty dollars, the right of trial by jury shall be preserved, and no fact tried by a jury, shall be otherwise re-examined in any Court of the United States, than according to the rules of the common law.

Amendment VIII

Excessive bail shall not be required, nor excessive fines imposed, nor cruel and unusual punishments inflicted.

Amendment IX

The enumeration in the Constitution, of certain rights, shall not be construed to deny or disparage others retained by the people.

Amendment X

The powers not delegated to the United States by the Constitution, nor prohibited by it to the States, are reserved to the States respectively, or to the people.

ADDITIONAL AMENDMENTS TO THE UNITED STATES CONSTITUTION

AMENDMENT XI

Passed by Congress March 4, 1794. Ratified February 7, 1795.

(Note: Article III, section 2, of the Constitution was modified by amendment 11.)

The Judicial power of the United States shall not be construed to extend to any suit in law or equity, commenced or prosecuted against one of the United States by Citizens of another State, or by Citizens or Subjects of any Foreign State.

AMENDMENT XII

Passed by Congress December 9, 1803. Ratified June 15, 1804.

(Note: A portion of Article II, section 1 of the Constitution was superseded by the 12th amendment.)

The Electors shall meet in their respective states and vote by ballot for President and Vice-President, one of whom, at least, shall not be an inhabitant of the same state with themselves; they shall name in their ballots the person voted for as President, and in distinct ballots the person voted for as Vice-President, and they shall make distinct lists of all persons voted for as President, and of all persons voted for as Vice-President, and of the number of votes for each, which lists they shall sign and certify, and transmit sealed to the seat of the government of the United States, directed to the President of the Senate; -- the President of the Senate shall, in the presence of the Senate and House of Representatives, open all the certificates and the votes shall then be counted; -- The person having the greatest number of votes for President, shall be the President, if such number be a majority of the whole number of Electors appointed; and if no person have such majority, then from the persons having the highest numbers not exceeding three on the list of those voted for as President, the House of Representatives shall choose immediately, by ballot, the President. But in choosing the President, the votes shall be taken by states, the representation from each state having one vote; a quorum for this purpose shall consist of a member or members from two-thirds of the states, and a majority of all the states shall be necessary to a choice. [And if the House of Representatives shall not choose a President whenever the right of choice shall devolve upon them, before the fourth day of March next following, then the Vice-President shall act as President, as in case of the death or other constitutional disability of the President. --]* The person having the greatest number of votes as Vice-President, shall be the Vice-President, if such number be a majority of the whole number of Electors appointed, and if no person have a majority, then from the two highest numbers on the list, the Senate shall choose the Vice-President; a quorum for the purpose shall consist of two-thirds of the whole number of Senators, and a majority of the whole number shall be necessary to a choice. But no person constitutionally ineligible to the office of President shall be eligible to that of Vice-President of the United States.

*Superseded by section 3 of the 20th amendment.

AMENDMENT XIII

Passed by Congress January 31, 1865. Ratified December 6, 1865.

(Note: A portion of Article IV, section 2, of the Constitution was superseded by the 13th amendment.)

SECTION 1

Neither slavery nor involuntary servitude, except as a punishment for crime whereof the party shall have been duly convicted, shall exist within the United States, or any place subject to their jurisdiction.

SECTION 2

Congress shall have power to enforce this article by appropriate legislation.

AMENDMENT XIV

Passed by Congress June 13, 1866. Ratified July 9, 1868.

(Note: Article I, section 2, of the Constitution was modified by section 2 of the 14th amendment.)

SECTION 1

All persons born or naturalized in the United States, and subject to the jurisdiction thereof, are citizens of the United States and of the State wherein they reside. No State shall make or enforce any law which shall abridge the privileges or immunities of citizens of the United States; nor shall any State deprive any person of life, liberty, or property, without due process of law; nor deny to any person within its jurisdiction the equal protection of the laws.

SECTION 2

Representatives shall be apportioned among the several States according to their respective numbers, counting the whole number of persons in each State, excluding Indians not taxed. But when the right to vote at any election for the choice of electors for President and Vice-President of the United States, Representatives in Congress, the Executive and Judicial officers of a State, or the members of the Legislature thereof, is denied to any of the male inhabitants of such State, being twenty-one years of age,* and citizens of the United States, or in any way abridged, except for participation in rebellion, or other crime, the basis of representation therein shall be reduced in the proportion which the number of such male citizens shall bear to the whole number of male citizens twenty-one years of age in such State.

SECTION 3

No person shall be a Senator or Representative in Congress, or elector of President and Vice-President, or hold any office, civil or military, under the United States, or under any State, who, having previously taken an oath, as a member of Congress, or as an officer of the United States, or as a member of any State legislature, or as an executive or judicial officer of any State, to support the Constitution of the United States, shall have engaged in insurrection or rebellion against the same, or given aid or comfort to the enemies thereof. But Congress may by a vote of two-thirds of each House, remove such disability.

SECTION 4

The validity of the public debt of the United States, authorized by law, including debts incurred for payment of pensions and bounties for services in suppressing insurrection or rebellion, shall not be questioned. But neither the United States nor any State shall assume or pay any debt or obligation incurred in aid of insurrection or rebellion against the United States, or any claim for the loss or emancipation of any slave; but all such debts, obligations and claims shall be held illegal and void.

SECTION 5

The Congress shall have the power to enforce, by appropriate legislation, the provisions of this article.

*Changed by section 1 of the 26th amendment.

AMENDMENT XV

Passed by Congress February 26, 1869. Ratified February 3, 1870.

SECTION 1

The right of citizens of the United States to vote shall not be denied or abridged by the United States or by any State on account of race, color, or previous condition of servitude--

SECTION 2

The Congress shall have the power to enforce this article by appropriate legislation.

AMENDMENT XVI

Passed by Congress July 2, 1909. Ratified February 3, 1913.

(Note: Article I, section 9, of the Constitution was modified by amendment 16.)

The Congress shall have power to lay and collect taxes on incomes, from whatever source derived, without apportionment among the several States, and without regard to any census or enumeration.

Amendment XVII

Passed by Congress May 13, 1912. Ratified April 8, 1913.

(Note: Article I, section 3, of the Constitution was modified by the 17th amendment.)

The Senate of the United States shall be composed of two Senators from each State, elected by the people thereof, for six years; and each Senator shall have one vote. The electors in each State shall have the qualifications requisite for electors of the most numerous branch of the State legislatures.

When vacancies happen in the representation of any State in the Senate, the executive authority of such State shall issue writs of election to fill such vacancies: Provided, That the legislature of any State may empower the executive thereof to make temporary appointments until the people fill the vacancies by election as the legislature may direct.

This amendment shall not be so construed as to affect the election or term of any Senator chosen before it becomes valid as part of the Constitution.

Amendment XVIII

Passed by Congress December 18, 1917. Ratified January 16, 1919. Repealed by amendment 21.

Section 1

After one year from the ratification of this article the manufacture, sale, or transportation of intoxicating liquors within, the importation thereof into, or the exportation thereof from the United States and all territory subject to the jurisdiction thereof for beverage purposes is hereby prohibited.

SECTION 2

The Congress and the several States shall have concurrent power to enforce this article by appropriate legislation.

SECTION 3

This article shall be inoperative unless it shall have been ratified as an amendment to the Constitution by the legislatures of the several States, as provided in the Constitution, within seven years from the date of the submission hereof to the States by the Congress.

AMENDMENT XIX

Passed by Congress June 4, 1919. Ratified August 18, 1920.

The right of citizens of the United States to vote shall not be denied or abridged by the United States or by any State on account of sex.

Congress shall have power to enforce this article by appropriate legislation.

AMENDMENT XX

Passed by Congress March 2, 1932. Ratified January 23, 1933.

(Note: Article I, section 4, of the Constitution was modified by section 2 of this amendment. In addition, a portion of the 12th amendment was superseded by section 3.)

Section 1

The terms of the President and the Vice President shall end at noon on the 20th day of January, and the terms of Senators and Representatives at noon on the 3d day of January, of the years in which such terms would have ended if this article had not been ratified; and the terms of their successors shall then begin.

Section 2

The Congress shall assemble at least once in every year, and such meeting shall begin at noon on the 3d day of January, unless they shall by law appoint a different day.

Section 3

If, at the time fixed for the beginning of the term of the President, the President elect shall have died, the Vice President elect shall become President. If a President shall not have been chosen before the time fixed for the beginning of his term, or if the President elect shall have failed to qualify, then the Vice President elect shall act as President until a President shall have qualified; and the Congress may by law provide for the case wherein neither a President elect nor a Vice President elect shall have qualified, declaring who shall then act as President, or the manner in which one who is to act shall be selected, and such person shall act accordingly until a President or Vice President shall have qualified.

Section 4

The Congress may by law provide for the case of the death of any of the persons from whom the House of Representatives may choose a President whenever the right of choice shall have devolved upon them, and for the case of the death of any of the persons from whom the Senate may choose a Vice

President whenever the right of choice shall have devolved upon them.

SECTION 5

Sections 1 and 2 shall take effect on the 15th day of October following the ratification of this article.

SECTION 6

This article shall be inoperative unless it shall have been ratified as an amendment to the Constitution by the legislatures of three-fourths of the several States within seven years from the date of its submission.

AMENDMENT XXI

Passed by Congress February 20, 1933. Ratified December 5, 1933.

SECTION 1

The eighteenth article of amendment to the Constitution of the United States is hereby repealed.

SECTION 2

The transportation or importation into any State, Territory, or possession of the United States for delivery or use therein of intoxicating liquors, in violation of the laws thereof, is hereby prohibited.

SECTION 3

This article shall be inoperative unless it shall have been ratified as an amendment to the Constitution by conventions in the several States, as provided in the Constitution, within seven years from the date of the submission hereof to the States by the Congress.

Amendment XXII

Passed by Congress March 21, 1947. Ratified February 27, 1951.

Section 1

No person shall be elected to the office of the President more than twice, and no person who has held the office of President, or acted as President, for more than two years of a term to which some other person was elected President shall be elected to the office of the President more than once. But this Article shall not apply to any person holding the office of President when this Article was proposed by the Congress, and shall not prevent any person who may be holding the office of President, or acting as President, during the term within which this Article becomes operative from holding the office of President or acting as President during the remainder of such term.

Section 2

This article shall be inoperative unless it shall have been ratified as an amendment to the Constitution by the legislatures of three-fourths of the several States within seven years from the date of its submission to the States by the Congress.

Amendment XXIII

Passed by Congress June 16, 1960. Ratified March 29, 1961.

Section 1

The District constituting the seat of Government of the United States shall appoint in such manner as the Congress may direct:

A number of electors of President and Vice President equal to the whole number of Senators and Representatives in Congress to which the District would be entitled if it were a State, but in no event more than the least populous State; they shall be in addition to those appointed by the States, but they shall be considered, for the purposes of the election of President and Vice President, to be electors appointed by a State; and they shall meet in the District and perform such duties as provided by the twelfth article of amendment.

Section 2

The Congress shall have power to enforce this article by appropriate legislation.

Amendment XXIV

Passed by Congress August 27, 1962. Ratified January 23, 1964.

Section 1

The right of citizens of the United States to vote in any primary or other election for President or Vice President, for electors for President or Vice President, or for Senator or Representative in Congress, shall not be denied or abridged by the United States or any State by reason of failure to pay any poll tax or other tax.

Section 2

The Congress shall have power to enforce this article by appropriate legislation.

Amendment XXV

Passed by Congress July 6, 1965. Ratified February 10, 1967.

(Note: Article II, section 1, of the Constitution was affected by the 25th amendment.)

Section 1

In case of the removal of the President from office or of his death or resignation, the Vice President shall become President.

Section 2

Whenever there is a vacancy in the office of the Vice President, the President shall nominate a Vice President who shall take office upon confirmation by a majority vote of both Houses of Congress.

Section 3

Whenever the President transmits to the President pro tempore of the Senate and the Speaker of the House of Representatives his written declaration that he is unable to discharge the powers and duties of his office, and until he transmits to them a written declaration to the contrary, such powers and duties shall be discharged by the Vice President as Acting President.

SECTION 4

Whenever the Vice President and a majority of either the principal officers of the executive departments or of such other body as Congress may by law provide, transmit to the President pro tempore of the Senate and the Speaker of the House of Representatives their written declaration that the President is unable to discharge the powers and duties of his office, the Vice President shall immediately assume the powers and duties of the office as Acting President.

Thereafter, when the President transmits to the President pro tempore of the Senate and the Speaker of the House of Representatives his written declaration that no inability exists, he shall resume the powers and duties of his office unless the Vice President and a majority of either the principal officers of the executive department or of such other body as Congress may by law provide, transmit within four days to the President pro tempore of the Senate and the Speaker of the House of Representatives their written declaration that the President is unable to discharge the powers and duties of his office. Thereupon Congress shall decide the issue, assembling within forty-eight hours for that purpose if not in session. If the Congress, within twenty-one days after receipt of the latter written declaration, or, if Congress is not in session, within twenty-one days after Congress is required to assemble, determines by two-thirds vote of both Houses that the President is unable to discharge the powers and duties of his office, the Vice President shall continue to discharge the same as Acting President; otherwise, the President shall resume the powers and duties of his office.

AMENDMENT XXVI

Passed by Congress March 23, 1971. Ratified July 1, 1971.

(Note: Amendment 14, section 2, of the Constitution was modified by section 1 of the 26th amendment.)

SECTION 1

The right of citizens of the United States, who are eighteen years of age or older, to vote shall not be denied or abridged by the United States or by any State on account of age.

SECTION 2

The Congress shall have power to enforce this article by appropriate legislation.

AMENDMENT XXVII

Originally proposed Sept. 25, 1789. Ratified May 7, 1992.

No law, varying the compensation for the services of the Senators and Representatives, shall take effect, until an election of Representatives shall have intervened.

Signers of the United States Constitution

(Our Founding Fathers)

George Washington, Virginia

The eldest of six children from his father's second marriage, George Washington was born into the landed gentry in 1732 at Wakefield Plantation, VA. Until reaching 16 years of age, he lived there and at other plantations along the Potomac and Rappahannock Rivers, including the one that later became known as Mount Vernon. His education was rudimentary, probably being obtained from tutors but possibly also from private schools, and he learned surveying. After he lost his father when he was 11 years old, his half-brother Lawrence, who had served in the Royal Navy, acted as his mentor. As a result, the youth acquired an interest in pursuing a naval career, but his mother discouraged him from doing so.

At the age of 16, in 1748, Washington joined a surveying party sent out to the Shenandoah Valley by Lord Fairfax, a land baron. For the next few years, Washington conducted surveys in Virginia and present West Virginia and gained a lifetime interest in the West. In 1751-52 he also accompanied Lawrence on a visit he made to Barbados, West Indies, for health reasons just before his death.

The next year, Washington began his military career when the royal governor appointed him to an adjutantship in the militia, as a major. That same year, as a gubernatorial emissary, accompanied by a guide, he traveled to Fort Le Boeuf, PA, in the Ohio River Valley, and delivered to French authorities an ultimatum to cease fortification and settlement in English territory. During the trip, he tried to better British relations with various Indian tribes.

In 1754, winning the rank of lieutenant colonel and then colonel in the militia, Washington led a force that sought to challenge French control of the Ohio River Valley, but met defeat at Fort Necessity, PA - an event that helped trigger the French and Indian War (1754-63). Late in 1754, irked by the dilution of his rank because of the pending arrival of British regulars, he resigned his commission. That same year, he leased Mount Vernon, which he was to inherit in 1761.

In 1755 Washington reentered military service with the courtesy title of colonel, as an aide to Gen. Edward Braddock, and barely escaped death when the French defeated the general's forces in the Battle of the Monongahela, PA. As a reward for his bravery, Washington rewon his colonelcy and command of the Virginia militia forces, charged with defending the colony's frontier. Because of the shortage of men and equipment, he found the assignment challenging. Late in 1758 or early in 1759, disillusioned over governmental neglect of the militia and irritated at not rising in rank, he resigned and headed back to Mount Vernon.

Washington then wed Martha Dandridge Custis, a wealthy widow and mother of two children. The marriage produced no offspring, but Washington reared those of his wife as his own. During the period 1759-74, he managed his plantations and sat in the Virginia House of Burgesses. He supported the initial protests against British policies; took an active part in the nonimportation movement in Virginia; and, in time, particularly because of his military experience, became a Whig leader.

By the 1770s, relations of the colony with the mother country had become strained. Measured in his behavior but strongly sympathetic to the Whig position and resentful of British restrictions and commercial exploitation, Washington represented Virginia at the First and Second Continental Congresses. In 1775, after the bloodshed at Lexington and Concord, Congress appointed him as commander in chief of the Continental Army. Overcoming severe obstacles, especially in supply, he eventually fashioned a well-trained and disciplined fighting force.

The strategy Washington evolved consisted of continual harassment of British forces while avoiding general actions. Although his troops yielded much ground and lost a number of battles, they persevered even during the dark winters at Valley Forge, PA, and Morristown, NJ. Finally, with the aid of the French fleet and army, he won a climactic victory at the Battle of Yorktown, VA, in 1781.

During the next 2 years, while still commanding the agitated Continental Army, which was underpaid and poorly supplied, Washington denounced proposals that the military take over the government, including one that planned to appoint him as king, but supported army petitions to the Continental Congress for proper compensation. Once the Treaty of Paris (1783) was signed, he resigned his commission and returned once again to Mount Vernon. His wartime financial sacrifices and long absence, as well as generous loans to friends, had severely impaired his extensive fortune, which consisted mainly of his plantations, slaves, and landholdings in the West. At this point, however, he was to have little time to repair his finances, for his retirement was brief.

Dissatisfied with national progress under the Articles of Confederation, Washington advocated a stronger central government. He hosted the Mount Vernon Conference (1785) at his estate after its initial meetings in Alexandria, though he apparently did not directly participate in the discussions. Despite his sympathy with the goals of the Annapolis Convention (1786), he did not attend. But, the following year, encouraged by many of his friends, he presided over the

Constitutional Convention, whose success was immeasurably influenced by his presence and dignity. Following ratification of the new instrument of government in 1788, the electoral college unanimously chose him as the first President.

The next year, after a triumphal journey from Mount Vernon to New York City, Washington took the oath of office at Federal Hall. During his two precedent-setting terms, he governed with dignity as well as restraint. He also provided the stability and authority the emergent nation so sorely needed, gave substance to the Constitution, and reconciled competing factions and divergent policies within the government and his administration. Although not averse to exercising presidential power, he respected the role of Congress and did not infringe upon its prerogatives. He also tried to maintain harmony between his Secretary of State Thomas Jefferson and Secretary of the Treasury Alexander Hamilton, whose differences typified evolving party divisions from which Washington kept aloof.

Yet, usually leaning upon Hamilton for advice, Washington supported his plan for the assumption of state debts, concurred in the constitutionality of the bill establishing the Bank of the United States, and favored enactment of tariffs by Congress to provide federal revenue and protect domestic manufacturers.

Washington took various other steps to strengthen governmental authority, including suppression of the Whisky Rebellion (1794). To unify the country, he toured the Northeast in 1789 and the South in 1791. During his tenure, the government moved from New York to Philadelphia in 1790, he superintended planning for relocation to the District of Columbia, and he laid the cornerstone of the Capitol (1793).

In foreign affairs, despite opposition from the Senate, Washington exerted dominance. He fostered United States interests on the North American continent by treaties with Britain and Spain. Yet, until the nation was stronger, he insisted on the maintenance of neutrality. For example, when the French Revolution created war between France and Britain, he ignored the remonstrances of pro-French Jefferson and pro-English Hamilton.

Although many people encouraged Washington to seek a third term, he was weary of politics and refused to do so. In his "Farewell Address" (1796), he urged his countrymen to forswear party spirit and sectional differences and to avoid entanglement in the wars and domestic policies of other nations.

Washington enjoyed only a few years of retirement at Mount Vernon. Even then, demonstrating his continued willingness to make sacrifices for his country in 1798 when the nation was on the verge of war with France he agreed to command the army, though his services were not ultimately required. He died at the age of 67 in 1799. In his will, he emancipated his slaves.

GEORGE READ, DELAWARE

Read's mother was the daughter of a Welsh planter, and his Dublin-born father a landholder of means. Soon after George's birth in 1733 near the village of North East in Cecil County, MD, his family moved to New Castle, DE, where the youth, who was one of six sons, grew up. He attended school at Chester, PA, and Rev. Francis Alison's academy at New London, PA, and about the age of 15 he began reading with a Philadelphia lawyer.

In 1753 Read was admitted to the bar and began to practice. The next year, he journeyed back to New Castle, hung out his shingle, and before long enlisted a clientele that extended into Maryland. During this period he resided in New Castle but maintained Stonum a country retreat near the city. In

1763 he wed Gertrude Ross Till, the widowed sister of George Ross, like Read a future signer of the Declaration of Independence. She bore four sons and a daughter.

While crown attorney general (1763-74) for the Three Lower Counties (present Delaware), Read protested against the Stamp Act. In 1765 he began a career in the colonial legislature that lasted more than a decade. A moderate Whig, he supported nonimportation measures and dignified protests. His attendance at the Continental Congress (1774-77) was irregular. Like his friend John Dickinson, he was willing to protect colonial rights but was wary of extremism. He voted against independence on July 2, 1776, the only signer of the Declaration to do so, apparently either bowing to the strong Tory sentiment in Delaware, or believing reconciliation with Britain was still possible.

That same year, Read gave priority to state responsibilities. He presided over the Delaware constitutional convention, in which he chaired the drafting committee, and began a term as speaker of the legislative council, which in effect made him vice president of the state. When the British took Wilmington the next fall, they captured the president, a resident of the city. At first, because Read was away in Congress, Thomas McKean, speaker of the lower house, took over as acting president. But in November, after barely escaping from the British himself while he and his family were en route to Dover from Philadelphia, newly occupied by the redcoats, Read assumed the office and held it until the spring of 1778. Back in the legislative council, in 1779 he drafted the act directing Delaware congressional delegates to sign the Articles of Confederation.

During 1779, in poor health, Read resigned from the legislative council, refused reelection to Congress, and began a period of inactivity. During the years 1782-88, he again sat on the council and concurrently held the position of judge of the court of appeals in admiralty cases.

Meantime, in 1784, Read had served on a commission that adjusted New York-Massachusetts land claims. In 1786 he attended the Annapolis Convention. The next year, he participated in the Constitutional Convention, where he missed few if any sessions and championed the rights of the small states. Otherwise, he adopted a Hamiltonian stance, favoring a strong executive. He later led the ratification movement in Delaware, the first state to ratify.

In the U.S. Senate (1789-93), Read's attendance was again erratic, but when present he allied with the Federalists. He resigned to accept the post of chief justice of Delaware. He held it until his death at New Castle 5 years later, just 3 days after he celebrated his 65th birthday. His grave is there in the Immanuel Episcopal Churchyard.

GUNNING BEDFORD, JR., DELEWARE

Bedford was born in 1747 at Philadelphia and reared there. The fifth of seven children, he was descended from a distinguished family that originally settled in Jamestown, VA. He usually referred to himself as Gunning Bedford, Jr., to avoid confusion with his cousin and contemporary Delaware statesman and soldier, Col. Gunning Bedford.

In 1771 signer Bedford graduated with honors from the College of New Jersey (later Princeton), where he was a classmate of James Madison. Apparently while still in school, Bedford wed Jane B. Parker, who bore at least one daughter. After reading law with Joseph Read in Philadelphia, Bedford won admittance to the bar and set up a practice. Subsequently, he moved to Dover and then to Wilmington. He apparently served in the Continental Army, possibly as an aide to General Washington.

Following the war, Bedford figured prominently in the politics of his state and nation. He sat in the legislature, on the state council, and in the Continental Congress (1783-85).

In the latter year, he was chosen as a delegate to the Annapolis Convention but for some reason did not attend. From 1784 to 1789 he was attorney general of Delaware.

Bedford numbered among the more active members of the Constitutional Convention, and he missed few sessions. A large and forceful man, he spoke on several occasions and was a member of the committee that drafted the Great Compromise. An ardent small-state advocate, he attacked the pretensions of the large states over the small and warned that the latter might be forced to seek foreign alliances unless their interests were accommodated. He attended the Delaware ratifying convention.

For another 2 years, Bedford continued as Delaware's attorney general. In 1789 Washington designated him as a federal district judge for his state, an office he was to occupy for the rest of his life. His only other ventures into national politics came in 1789 and 1793, as a Federalist presidential elector. In the main, however, he spent his later years in judicial pursuits, in aiding Wilmington Academy, in fostering abolitionism, and in enjoying his Lombardy Hall farm.

Bedford died at the age of 65 in 1812 and was buried in the First Presbyterian Churchyard in Wilmington. Later, when the cemetery was abandoned, his body was transferred to the Masonic Home, on the Lancaster Turnpike in Christiana Hundred, DE.

JOHN DICKINSON, DELAWARE

Dickinson, "Penman of the Revolution," was born in 1732 at Crosiadore estate, near the village of Trappe in Talbot County, MD. He was the second son of Samuel Dickinson, the prosperous farmer, and his second wife, Mary (Cadwalader) Dickinson. In 1740 the family moved to Kent County near Dover, DE., where private tutors educated the youth. In 1750 he began to study law with John Moland in

Philadelphia. In 1753 Dickinson went to England to continue his studies at London's Middle Temple. Four years later, he returned to Philadelphia and became a prominent lawyer there. In 1770 he married Mary Norris, daughter of a wealthy merchant. The couple had at least one daughter.

By that time, Dickinson's superior education and talents had propelled him into politics. In 1760 he had served in the assembly of the Three Lower Counties (Delaware), where he held the speakership. Combining his Pennsylvania and Delaware careers in 1762, he won a seat as a Philadelphia member in the Pennsylvania assembly and sat there again in 1764. He became the leader of the conservative side in the colony's political battles. His defense of the proprietary governor against the faction led by Benjamin Franklin hurt his popularity but earned him respect for his integrity. Nevertheless, as an immediate consequence, he lost his legislative seat in 1764.

Meantime, the struggle between the colonies and the mother country had waxed strong and Dickinson had emerged in the forefront of Revolutionary thinkers. In the debates over the Stamp Act (1765), he played a key part. That year, he wrote The Late Regulations Respecting the British Colonies . . . Considered, an influential pamphlet that urged Americans to seek repeal of the act by pressuring British merchants. Accordingly, the Pennsylvania legislature appointed him as a delegate to the Stamp Act Congress, whose resolutions he drafted.

In 1767-68 Dickinson wrote a series of newspaper articles in the Pennsylvania Chronicle that came to be known collectively as Letters from a Farmer in Pennsylvania. They attacked British taxation policy and urged resistance to unjust laws, but also emphasized the possibility of a peaceful resolution. So popular were the Letters in the colonies that Dickinson received an honorary LL.D. from the College of New Jersey (later Princeton) and public thanks from a meeting in Boston. In 1768, responding to the Townshend Duties, he championed rigorous colonial resistance in the form of nonimportation and nonexportation agreements.

In 1771, Dickinson returned to the Pennsylvania legislature and drafted a petition to the king that was unanimously approved. Because of his continued opposition to the use of force, however, he lost much of his popularity by 1774. He particularly resented the tactics of New England leaders in that year and refused to support aid requested by Boston in the wake of the Intolerable Acts, though he sympathized with the city's plight. Reluctantly, Dickinson was drawn into the Revolutionary fray. In 1774 he chaired the Philadelphia committee of correspondence and briefly sat in the First Continental Congress as a representative from Pennsylvania.

Throughout 1775, Dickinson supported the Whig cause, but continued to work for peace. He drew up petitions asking the king for redress of grievances. At the same time, he chaired a Philadelphia committee of safety and defense and held a colonelcy in the first battalion recruited in Philadelphia to defend the city.

After Lexington and Concord, Dickinson continued to hope for a peaceful solution. In the Second Continental Congress (1775-76), still a representative of Pennsylvania, he drew up the Declaration of the Causes of Taking Up Arms. In the Pennsylvania assembly, he drafted an authorization to send delegates to Congress in 1776. It directed them to seek redress of grievances, but ordered them to oppose separation of the colonies from Britain.

By that time, Dickinson's moderate position had left him in the minority. In Congress he voted against the Declaration of Independence (1776) and refused to sign it. Nevertheless, he then became one of only two contemporary congressional members (with Thomas McKean) who entered the military. When he was not reelected he resigned his brigadier general's commission and withdrew to his estate in Delaware. Later in 1776, though reelected to Congress by his new constituency, he declined to serve and also resigned from the Pennsylvania Assembly. He may have taken part in the Battle of Brandywine, PA (September 11, 1777), as a private in a special Delaware force but otherwise saw no further military action.

Dickinson came out of retirement to take a seat in the Continental Congress (1779-80), where he signed the Articles of Confederation; earlier he had headed the committee that had drafted them. In 1781 he became president of Delaware's Supreme Executive Council. Shortly thereafter, he moved back to Philadelphia. There, he became president of Pennsylvania (1782-85). In 1786, representing Delaware, he attended and chaired the Annapolis Convention.

The next year, Delaware sent Dickinson to the Constitutional Convention. He missed a number of sessions and left early because of illness, but he made worthwhile contributions, including service on the Committee on Postponed Matters. Although he resented the forcefulness of Madison and the other nationalists, he helped engineer the Great Compromise and wrote public letters supporting constitutional ratification. Because of his premature departure from the convention, he did not actually sign the Constitution but authorized his friend and fellow-delegate George Read to do so for him.

Dickinson lived for two decades more but held no public offices. Instead, he devoted himself to writing on politics and in 1801 published two volumes of his collected works. He died at Wilmington in 1808 at the age of 75 and was entombed in the Friends Burial Ground.

Richard Bassett, Delaware

Bassett (Basset) was born in Cecil County, MD., in April 1745. After his tavern-keeper father deserted his mother, he was reared by a relative, Peter Lawson, from whom he later inherited Bohemia Manor (MD.) estate. He read for the law at Philadelphia and in 1770 received a license to practice in Dover, DE. He prospered as a lawyer and planter, and eventually came to own not only Bohemia Manor, but homes in Dover and Wilmington as well.

During the Revolution, Bassett captained a troop of Dover cavalry militia and served on the Delaware council of safety. Subsequently, he participated in Delaware's constitutional convention and sat in both the upper and lower houses of the legislature. In 1786 he represented his state in the Annapolis Convention.

At the U.S. Constitutional Convention the next year, Bassett attended diligently but made no speeches, served on no committees, and cast no critical votes. Like several other delegates of estimable reputation and talent, he allowed others to make the major steps.

Bassett subsequently went on to a bright career in the state and federal governments. In the Delaware ratifying convention, he joined in the 30-0 vote for the Constitution. Subsequently, in the years 1789-93, he served in the U.S. Senate. In that capacity, he voted in favor of the power of the President to remove governmental officers and against Hamilton's plan for the federal assumption of state debts.

From 1793 until 1799 Bassett held the chief justiceship of the court of common pleas. He espoused the Federalist cause in the 1790s, and served as a Presidential elector on behalf of John Adams in 1797. Two years later, Bassett was elected Governor of Delaware and continued in that post until 1801. That year, he became one of President Adams' "midnight" appointments as a judge of the U.S. Circuit Court. Subsequently, the Jeffersonian Republicans abolished his judgeship, and he spent the rest of his life in retirement.

Twice married, to Ann Ennals and a woman named Bruff, Bassett fathered several children. He was a devout Methodist, held religious meetings at Bohemia Manor, and supported the church financially. He died in 1815 at the age of 70 and is interred at the Wilmington and Brandywine Cemetery, Wilmington, DE.

JACOB BROOM, DELAWARE

Broom was born in 1752 at Wilmington, DE., the eldest son of a blacksmith who prospered in farming. The youth was educated at home and probably at the local Old Academy. Although he followed his father into farming and also studied surveying, he was to make his career primarily in mercantile pursuits, including shipping and the import trade, and in real estate. In 1773 he married Rachel Pierce, who bore eight children.

Broom was not a distinguished patriot. His only recorded service was the preparation of maps for George Washington before the Battle of Brandywine, PA. In 1776, at 24 years of age, Broom became assistant burgess of Wilmington. Over the next several decades, he held that office six times and that of chief burgess four times, as well as those of borough assessor, president of the city "street regulators," and justice of the peace for New Castle County.

Broom sat in the state legislature in the years 1784-86 and 1788, during which time he was chosen as a delegate to the Annapolis Convention, but he did not attend. At the Constitutional Convention, he never missed a session and spoke on several occasions, but his role was only a minor one.

After the convention, Broom returned to Wilmington, where in 1795 he erected a home near the Brandywine River on the outskirts of the city. He was its first postmaster (1790-92) and continued to hold various local offices and to participate in a variety of economic endeavors. For many years, he chaired the board of directors of Wilmington's Delaware Bank. He also operated a cotton mill, as well as a machine shop that produced and repaired mill machinery. He was involved, too, in an unsuccessful scheme to mine bog iron ore. A further interest was internal improvements: toll roads, canals, and bridges.

Broom also found time for philanthropic and religious activities. He served on the board of trustees of the College of Wilmington and as a lay leader at Old Swedes Church. He died at the age of 58 in 1810 while in Philadelphia on business and was buried there at Christ Church Burial Ground.

JAMES MCHENRY, MARYLAND

McHenry was born at Ballymena, County Antrim, Ireland, in 1753. He enjoyed a classical education at Dublin, and emigrated to Philadelphia in 1771. The following year, the rest of his family came to the colonies, and his brother and father established an import business at Baltimore. During that year, James continued schooling at Newark Academy in Delaware and then studied medicine for 2 years under the well-known Dr. Benjamin Rush in Philadelphia.

During the War for Independence, McHenry served as a military surgeon. Late in 1776, while he was on the staff of the 5th Pennsylvania Battalion, the British captured him at Fort Washington, NY. He was paroled early the next year and exchanged in March 1778. Returning immediately to duty, he was assigned to Valley Forge, PA, and in May became secretary to George Washington. About this time, McHenry apparently quit the practice of medicine to devote himself to politics and administration; he apparently never needed to return to it after the war because of his excellent financial circumstances.

McHenry stayed on Washington's staff until 1780, when he joined that of the Marquis de Lafayette, and he remained in that assignment until he entered the Maryland Senate (1781-86). During part of this period, he served concurrently in the Continental Congress (1783-86). In 1784 he married Margaret Allison Caldwell.

McHenry missed many of the proceedings at the Philadelphia convention, in part because of the illness of his brother, and played an insubstantial part in the debates when he was present. He did, however, maintain a private journal that has been useful to posterity. He campaigned strenuously for the Constitution in Maryland and attended the state ratifying convention.

From 1789 to 1791, McHenry sat in the state assembly and in the years 1791-96 again in the senate. A staunch Federalist, he then accepted Washington's offer of the post of Secretary of War and held it into the administration of John Adams. McHenry looked to Hamilton rather than to Adams for leadership. As time passed, the latter became increasingly dissatisfied with McHenry's performance and distrustful of his political motives and in 1800 forced him to resign. Subsequently, the Democratic-Republicans accused him of maladministration, but a congressional committee vindicated him.

McHenry returned to his estate near Baltimore and to semiretirement. He remained a loyal Federalist and opposed the War of 1812. He also held the office of president of a Bible society. He died in 1816 at the age of 62, survived by two of his three children. His grave is in Baltimore's Westminster Presbyterian Cemetery.

Daniel of St. Thomas Jenifer, Maryland

Jenifer was born in 1723 of Swedish and English descent at Coates Retirement (now Ellerslie) estate, near Port Tobacco in Charles County, Md. Little is known about his childhood or education, but as an adult he came into possession of a large estate near Annapolis, called Stepney, where he lived most of his life. He never married. The web of his far-reaching friendships included such illustrious personages as George Washington.

As a young man, Jenifer served as agent and receiver-general for the last two proprietors of Maryland. He also filled the post of justice of the peace in Charles County and later for the western circuit of Maryland. In 1760 he sat on a boundary commission that settled disputes between Pennsylvania and Delaware. Six years later, he became a member of the provincial court and from 1773 to 1776 sat on the Maryland royal governor's council.

Despite his association with conservative proprietary politics, Jenifer supported the Revolutionary movement, albeit at first reluctantly. He served as president of the Maryland council of safety (1775-77), then as president of the first state senate (1777-80). He sat in the Continental Congress (1778-82) and held the position of state revenue and financial manager (1782-85).

A conservative nationalist, Jenifer favored a strong and permanent union of the states and a Congress with taxation power. In 1785 he represented Maryland at the Mount Vernon Conference. Although he was one of 29 delegates who attended nearly every session of the Constitutional Convention, he did not speak often but backed Madison and the nationalist element.

Jenifer lived only 3 more years and never again held public office. He died at the age of 66 or 67 at Annapolis in 1790.

54

The exact location of his grave, possibly at Ellerslie estate, is unknown.

DANIEL CARROLL, MARYLAND

Daniel Carroll was member of a prominent Maryland family of Irish descent. A collateral branch was led by Charles Carroll of Carrollton, signer of the Declaration of Independence. Daniel's older brother was John Carroll, the first Roman Catholic bishop in the United States.

Daniel was born in 1730 at Upper Marlboro, MD. Befitting the son of a wealthy Roman Catholic family, he studied for 6 years (1742-48) under the Jesuits at St. Omer's in Flanders. Then, after a tour of Europe, he sailed home and soon married Eleanor Carroll, apparently a first cousin of Charles Carroll of Carrollton. Not much is known about the next two decades of his life except that he backed the War for Independence reluctantly and remained out of the public eye. No doubt he lived the life of a gentleman planter.

In 1781 Carroll entered the political arena. Elected to the Continental Congress that year, he carried to Philadelphia the news that Maryland was at last ready to accede to the Articles of Confederation, to which he soon penned his name. During the decade, he also began a tour in the Maryland senate that was to span his lifetime and helped George Washington promote the Patowmack Company, a scheme to canalize the Potomac River so as to provide a transportation link between the East and the trans-Appalachian West.

Carroll did not arrive at the Constitutional Convention until July 9, but thereafter he attended quite regularly. He spoke about 20 times during the debates and served on the Committee on Postponed Matters. Returning to Maryland after the convention, he campaigned for ratification of the Constitution but was not a delegate to the state convention.

In 1789 Carroll won a seat in the U.S. House of Representatives, where he voted for locating the Nation's Capital on the banks of the Potomac and for Hamilton's program for the federal assumption of state debts. In 1791 George Washington named his friend Carroll as one of three commissioners to survey and define the District of Columbia, where Carroll owned much land. Ill health caused him to resign this post 4 years later, and the next year at the age of 65 he died at his home near Rock Creek in Forest Glen, MD. He was buried there in St. John's Catholic Cemetery.

JOHN BLAIR, VIRGINIA

Scion of a prominent Virginia family, Blair was born at Williamsburg in 1732. He was the son of John Blair, a colonial official and nephew of James Blair, founder and first president of the College of William and Mary. Signer Blair graduated from that institution and studied law at London's Middle Temple. Thereafter, he practiced at Williamsburg. In the years 1766-70 he sat in the Virginia House of Burgesses as the representative of William and Mary. From 1770 to 1775 he held the position of clerk of the colony's council.

An active patriot, Blair signed the Virginia Association of June 22, 1770, which pledged to abandon importation of British goods until the Townshend Duties were repealed. He also underwrote the Association of May 27, 1774, calling for a meeting of the colonies in a Continental Congress and supporting the Bostonians. He took part in the Virginia constitutional convention (1776), at which he sat on the committee that framed a declaration of rights as well as the plan for a new government. He next served on the Privy Council (1776-78). In the latter year, the legislature elected him as a judge of the General Court, and he soon took over the chief justiceship. In 1780 he won election to Virginia's high chancery court, where his colleague was George Wythe.

Blair attended the Constitutional Convention religiously but never spoke or served on a committee. He usually sided with the position of the Virginia delegation. And, in the commonwealth ratifying convention, Blair helped win backing for the new framework of government.

In 1789 Washington named Blair as an associate justice of the U.S. Supreme Court, where he helped decide many important cases. Resigning that post in 1796, he spent his remaining years in Williamsburg. A widower, his wife (born Jean Balfour) having died in 1792, he lived quietly until he succumbed in 1800. He was 68 years old. His tomb is in the graveyard of Bruton Parish Church.

JAMES MADISON, VIRGINIA

The oldest of 10 children and a scion of the planter aristocracy, Madison was born in 1751 at Port Conway, King George County, VA, while his mother was visiting her parents. In a few weeks she journeyed back with her newborn son to Montpelier estate, in Orange County, which became his lifelong home. He received his early education from his mother, from tutors, and at a private school. An excellent scholar though frail and sickly in his youth, in 1771 he graduated from the College of New Jersey (later Princeton), where he demonstrated special interest in government and the law. But, considering the ministry for a career, he stayed on for a year of postgraduate study in theology.

Back at Montpelier, still undecided on a profession, Madison soon embraced the patriot cause, and state and local politics absorbed much of his time. In 1775 he served on the Orange County committee of safety; the next year at the Virginia convention, which, besides advocating various Revolutionary steps, framed the Virginia constitution; in 1776-77 in the House of Delegates; and in 1778-80 in the Council of State. His ill health precluded any military service.

In 1780 Madison was chosen to represent Virginia in the Continental Congress (1780-83 and 1786-88). Although originally the youngest delegate, he played a major role in the deliberations of that body. Meantime, in the years 1784-86, he had again sat in the Virginia House of Delegates. He was a guiding force behind the Mount Vernon Conference (1785), attended the Annapolis Convention (1786), and was otherwise highly instrumental in the convening of the Constitutional Convention in 1787. He had also written extensively about deficiencies in the Articles of Confederation.

Madison was clearly the preeminent figure at the convention. Some of the delegates favored an authoritarian central government; others, retention of state sovereignty; and most occupied positions in the middle of the two extremes. Madison, who was rarely absent and whose Virginia Plan was in large part the basis of the Constitution, tirelessly advocated a strong government, though many of his proposals were rejected. Despite his poor speaking capabilities, he took the floor more than 150 times, third only after Gouverneur Morris and James Wilson. Madison was also a member of numerous committees, the most important of which were those on postponed matters and style. His journal of the convention is the best single record of the event. He also played a key part in guiding the Constitution through the Continental Congress.

Playing a lead in the ratification process in Virginia, too, Madison defended the document against such powerful opponents as Patrick Henry, George Mason, and Richard Henry Lee. In New York, where Madison was serving in the Continental Congress, he collaborated with Alexander Hamilton and John Jay in a series of essays that in 1787-88 appeared in the newspapers and were soon published in book form as The Federalist (1788). This set of essays is a classic of political theory and a lucid exposition of the republican principles that dominated the framing of the Constitution.

In the U.S. House of Representatives (1789-97), Madison helped frame and ensure passage of the Bill of Rights. He also assisted in organizing the executive department and creating a system of federal taxation. As leaders of the opposition to Hamilton's policies, he and Jefferson founded the Democratic-Republican Party.

In 1794 Madison married a vivacious widow who was 16 years his junior, Dolley Payne Todd, who had a son; they were to raise no children of their own. Madison spent the period 1797-1801 in semiretirement, but in 1798 he wrote the Virginia Resolutions, which attacked the Alien and Sedition Acts. While he served as Secretary of State (1801-9), his wife often served as President Jefferson's hostess.

In 1809 Madison succeeded Jefferson. Like the first three Presidents, Madison was enmeshed in the ramifications of European wars. Diplomacy had failed to prevent the seizure of U.S. ships, goods, and men on the high seas, and a depression wracked the country. Madison continued to apply diplomatic techniques and economic sanctions, eventually effective to some degree against France. But continued British interference with shipping, as well as other grievances, led to the War of 1812.

The war, for which the young nation was ill prepared, ended in stalemate in December 1814 when the inconclusive Treaty of Ghent which nearly restored prewar conditions, was signed. But, thanks mainly to Andrew Jackson's spectacular victory at the Battle of New Orleans (Chalmette) in January 1815, most Americans believed they had won. Twice tested, independence had survived, and an ebullient nationalism marked Madison's last years in office, during which period the Democratic-Republicans held virtually uncontested sway.

In retirement after his second term, Madison managed Montpelier but continued to be active in public affairs. He devoted long hours to editing his journal of the Constitutional

Convention, which the government was to publish 4 years after his death. He served as co-chairman of the Virginia constitutional convention of 1829-30 and as rector of the University of Virginia during the period 1826-36. Writing newspaper articles defending the administration of Monroe, he also acted as his foreign policy adviser.

Madison spoke out, too, against the emerging sectional controversy that threatened the existence of the Union. Although a slaveholder all his life, he was active during his later years in the American Colonization Society, whose mission was the resettlement of slaves in Africa.

Madison died at the age of 85 in 1836, survived by his wife and stepson.

WILLIAM BLOUNT, NORTH CAROLINA

William Blount was the great-grandson of Thomas Blount, who came from England to Virginia soon after 1660 and settled on a North Carolina plantation. William, the eldest in a large family, was born in 1749 while his mother was visiting his grandfather's Rosefield estate, on the site of present Windsor near Pamlico Sound. The youth apparently received a good education.

Shortly after the War for Independence began, in 1776, Blount enlisted as a paymaster in the North Carolina forces. Two years later, he wed Mary Grainier (Granger); of their six children who reached adulthood, one son also became prominent in Tennessee politics.

Blount spent most of the remainder of his life in public office. He sat in the lower house of the North Carolina legislature (1780-84), including service as speaker, as well as in the upper (1788-90). In addition, he took part in national politics, serving in the Continental Congress in 1782-83 and 1786-87.

Appointed as a delegate to the Constitutional Convention at the age of 38, Blount was absent for more than a month because he chose to attend the Continental Congress on behalf of his state. He said almost nothing in the debates and signed the Constitution reluctantly--only, he said, to make it "the unanimous act of the States in Convention." Nonetheless, he favored his state's ratification of the completed document.

Blount hoped to be elected to the first U.S. Senate. When he failed to achieve that end, in 1790 he pushed westward beyond the Appalachians, where he held speculative land interests and had represented North Carolina in dealings with the Indians. He settled in what became Tennessee, to which he devoted the rest of his life. He resided first at Rocky Mount, a cabin near present Johnson City and in 1792 built a mansion in Knoxville.

Two years earlier, Washington had appointed Blount as Governor for the Territory South of the River Ohio (which included Tennessee) and also as Superintendent of Indian Affairs for the Southern Department, in which positions he increased his popularity with the frontiersmen. In 1796 he presided over the constitutional convention that transformed part of the territory into the State of Tennessee. He was elected as one of its first U.S. senators (1796-97).

During this period, Blount's affairs took a sharp turn for the worse. In 1797 his speculations in western lands led him into serious financial difficulties. That same year, he also apparently concocted a plan involving use of Indians, frontiersmen, and British naval forces to conquer for Britain the Spanish provinces of Florida and Louisiana. A letter he wrote alluding to the plan fell into the hands of President Adams, who turned it over to the Senate on July 3, 1797. Five days later, that body voted 25 to 1 to expel Blount. The House impeached him, but the Senate dropped the charges in

1799 on the grounds that no further action could be taken beyond his dismissal.

The episode did not hamper Blount's career in Tennessee. In 1798 he was elected to the senate and rose to the speakership. He died 2 years later at Knoxville in his early fifties. He is buried there in the cemetery of the First Presbyterian Church.

RICHARD DOBBS SPAIGHT, SR., NORTH CAROLINA

Spaight was born at New Bern, NC of distinguished English-Irish parentage in 1758. When he was orphaned at 8 years of age, his guardians sent him to Ireland, where he obtained an excellent education. He apparently graduated from Scotland's Glasgow University before he returned to North Carolina in 1778.

At that time, the War for Independence was in full swing, and Spaight's superior attainments soon gained him a commission. He became an aide to the state militia commander and in 1780 took part in the Battle of Camden, SC. The year before, he had been elected to the lower house of the legislature.

In 1781 Spaight left the military service to devote full time to his legislative duties. He represented New Bern and Craven County (1781-83 and 1785-87); in 1785 he became speaker. Between terms, he also served in the Continental Congress (1783-85).

In 1787, at the age of 29, Spaight joined the North Carolina delegation to the Philadelphia convention. He was not a leader but spoke on several occasions and numbered among those who attended every session. After the convention, he worked in his home state for acceptance of the Constitution.

Spaight met defeat in bids for the governorship in 1787 and the U.S. Senate 2 years later. From then until 1792, illness forced his retirement from public life, during which time he visited the West Indies, but he captured the governorship in the latter year (1792-95). In 1793 he served as presidential elector. Two years later, he wed Mary Leach, who bore three children.

In 1798 Spaight entered the U.S. House of Representatives as a Democratic-Republican and remained in office until 1801. During this time, he advocated repeal of the Alien and Sedition Acts and voted for Jefferson in the contested election of 1800. The next year, Spaight was voted into the lower house of the North Carolina legislature; the following year, to the upper.

Only 44 years old in 1802, Spaight was struck down in a duel at New Bern with a political rival, Federalist John Stanly. So ended the promising career of one of the state's foremost leaders. He was buried in the family sepulcher at Clermont estate, near New Bern.

HUGH WILLIAMSON, NORTH CAROLINA

The versatile Williamson was born of Scotch-Irish descent at West Nottingham, PA., in 1735. He was the eldest son in a large family, whose head was a clothier. Hoping he would become a Presbyterian minister, his parents oriented his education toward that calling. After attending preparatory schools at New London Cross Roads, DE, and Newark, DE, he entered the first class of the College of Philadelphia (later part of the University of Pennsylvania) and took his degree in 1757.

The next 2 years, at Shippensburg, PA, Williamson spent settling his father's estate. Then training in Connecticut for the ministry, he soon became a licensed Presbyterian preacher but was never ordained. Around this time, he also took a position as professor of mathematics at his alma mater.

In 1764 Williamson abandoned these pursuits and studied medicine at Edinburgh, London, and Utrecht, eventually obtaining a degree from the University of Utrecht. Returning to Philadelphia, he began to practice but found it to be emotionally exhausting. His pursuit of scientific interests continued, and in 1768 he became a member of the American Philosophical Society. The next year, he served on a commission that observed the transits of Venus and Mercury. In 1771 he wrote An Essay on Comets, in which he advanced several original ideas. As a result, the University of Leyden awarded him an LL.D. degree.

In 1773, to raise money for an academy in Newark, DE., Williamson made a trip to the West Indies and then to Europe. Sailing from Boston, he saw the Tea Party and carried news of it to London. When the British Privy Council called on him to testify as to what he had seen, he warned the councilors that the colonies would rebel if the British did not change their policies. While in England, he struck up a close friendship with fellow-scientist Benjamin Franklin, and they cooperated in electrical experiments. Moreover, Williamson furnished to Franklin the letters of Massachusetts Royal Governor Thomas Hutchinson to his lieutenant governor that created a sensation and tended to further alienate the mother country and colonies.

In 1775 a pamphlet Williamson had written while in England, called The Plea of the Colonies, was published. It solicited the support of the English Whigs for the American cause. When the United States proclaimed their independence the next year, Williamson was in the Netherlands. He soon sailed back to the United States, settling first in Charleston, SC, and then in Edenton, NC. There, he prospered in a mercantile business that traded with the French West Indies and once again took up the practice of medicine.

Williamson applied for a medical post with the patriot forces, but found all such positions filled. The governor of North Carolina, however, soon called on his specialized skills, and he became surgeon-general of state troops. After the Battle of Camden, SC, he frequently crossed British lines to tend to the wounded. He also prevented sickness among the troops by paying close attention to food, clothing, shelter, and hygiene.

After the war, Williamson began his political career. In 1782 he was elected to the lower house of the state legislature and to the Continental Congress. Three years later, he left Congress and returned to his legislative seat. In 1786 he was chosen to represent his state at the Annapolis Convention but arrived too late to take part. The next year, he again served in Congress (1787-89) and was chosen as a delegate to the Constitutional Convention. Attending faithfully and demonstrating keen debating skill, he served on five committees, notably on the Committee on Postponed Matters, and played a significant part in the proceedings, particularly the major compromise on representation.

After the convention, Williamson worked for ratification of the Constitution in North Carolina. In 1788 he was chosen to settle outstanding accounts between the state and the federal government. The next year, he was elected to the first U.S. House of Representatives, where he served two terms. In 1789 he married Maria Apthorpe, who bore at least two sons.

In 1793 Williamson moved to New York City to facilitate his literary and philanthropic pursuits. Over the years, he published many political, educational, economic, historical, and scientific works, but the last earned him the most praise. The University of Leyden awarded him an honorary degree. In addition, he was an original trustee of the University of North Carolina and later held trusteeships at the College of

Physicians and Surgeons and the University of the State of New York. He was also a founder of the Literary and Philosophical Society of New York and a prominent member of the New-York Historical Society.

In 1819, at the age of 83, Williamson died in New York City and was buried at Trinity Church.

JOHN RUTLEDGE, SOUTH CAROLINA

John Rutledge, elder brother of Edward Rutledge, signer of the Declaration of Independence, was born into a large family at or near Charleston, SC, in 1739. He received his early education from his father, an Irish immigrant and physician, and from an Anglican minister and a tutor. After studying law at London's Middle Temple in 1760, he was admitted to English practice. But, almost at once, he sailed back to Charleston to begin a fruitful legal career and to amass a fortune in plantations and slaves. Three years later, he married Elizabeth Grimke, who eventually bore him 10 children, and moved into a townhouse, where he resided most of the remainder of his life.

In 1761 Rutledge became politically active. That year, on behalf of Christ Church Parish, he was elected to the provincial assembly and held his seat until the War for Independence. For 10 months in 1764 he temporarily held the post of provincial attorney general. When the troubles with Great Britain intensified about the time of the Stamp Act in 1765, Rutledge, who hoped to ensure continued self-government for the colonies, sought to avoid severance from the British and maintained a restrained stance. He did, however, chair a committee of the Stamp Act Congress that drew up a petition to the House of Lords.

In 1774 Rutledge was sent to the First Continental Congress, where he pursued a moderate course. After spending the next year in the Second Continental Congress, he returned to

South Carolina and helped reorganize its government. In 1776 he served on the committee of safety and took part in the writing of the state constitution. That year, he also became president of the lower house of the legislature, a post he held until 1778. During this period, the new government met many stern tests.

In 1778 the conservative Rutledge, disapproving of democratic revisions in the state constitution, resigned his position. The next year, however, he was elected as governor. It was a difficult time. The British were invading South Carolina, and the military situation was desperate. Early in 1780, by which time the legislature had adjourned, Charleston was besieged. In May it fell, the American army was captured, and the British confiscated Rutledge's property. He ultimately escaped to North Carolina and set about attempting to rally forces to recover South Carolina. In 1781, aided by Gen. Nathanael Greene and a new Continental Army force, he reestablished the government. In January 1782 he resigned the governorship and took a seat in the lower house of the legislature. He never recouped the financial losses he suffered during the war.

In 1782-83 Rutledge was a delegate to the Continental Congress. He next sat on the state chancery court (1784) and again in the lower house of the legislature (1784-90). One of the most influential delegates at the Constitutional Convention, where he maintained a moderate nationalist stance and chaired the Committee of Detail, he attended all the sessions, spoke often and effectively, and served on five committees. Like his fellow South Carolina delegates, he vigorously advocated southern interests.

The new government under the Constitution soon lured Rutledge. He was a Presidential elector in 1789 and Washington then appointed him as Associate Justice of the U.S. Supreme Court, but for some reason he apparently served only a short time. In 1791 he became chief justice of the South Carolina supreme court. Four years later, Washington again appointed him to the U.S. Supreme Court, this time as Chief Justice to replace John Jay. But Rutledge's outspoken opposition to Jay's Treaty (1794), and the intermittent mental illness he had suffered from since the death of his wife in 1792, caused the Federalist-dominated Senate to reject his appointment and end his public career. Meantime, however, he had presided over one term of the Court.

Rutledge died in 1800 at the age of 60 and was interred at St. Michael's Episcopal Church in Charleston.

CHARLES COTESWORTH PINCKNEY, SOUTH CAROLINA

The eldest son of a politically prominent planter and a remarkable mother who introduced and promoted indigo culture in South Carolina, Charles Cotesworth Pinckney was born in 1746 at Charleston. Only 7 years later, he accompanied his father, who had been appointed colonial agent for South Carolina, to England. As a result, the youth enjoyed a European education.

Pinckney received tutoring in London, attended several preparatory schools, and went on to Christ Church College, Oxford, where he heard the lectures of the legal authority Sir William Blackstone and graduated in 1764. Pinckney next pursued legal training at London's Middle Temple and was accepted for admission into the English bar in 1769. He then spent part of a year touring Europe and studying chemistry, military science, and botany under leading authorities.

Late in 1769, Pinckney sailed home and the next year entered practice in South Carolina. His political career began in 1769, when he was elected to the provincial assembly. In 1773 he acted as attorney general for several towns in the colony. By

1775 he had identified with the patriot cause and that year sat in the provincial congress. Then, the next year, he was elected to the local committee of safety and made chairman of a committee that drew up a plan for the interim government of South Carolina.

When hostilities broke out, Pinckney, who had been a royal militia officer since 1769, pursued a full-time military calling. When South Carolina organized its forces in 1775, he joined the First South Carolina Regiment as a captain. He soon rose to the rank of colonel and fought in the South in defense of Charleston and in the North at the Battles of Brandywine, PA, and Germantown, PA. He commanded a regiment in the campaign against the British in the Floridas in 1778 and at the siege of Savannah. When Charleston fell in 1780, he was taken prisoner and held until 1782. The following year, he was discharged as a brevet brigadier general.

After the war, Pinckney resumed his legal practice and the management of estates in the Charleston area but found time to continue his public service, which during the war had included tours in the lower house of the state legislature (1778 and 1782) and the senate (1779).

Pinckney was one of the leaders at the Constitutional Convention. Present at all the sessions, he strongly advocated a powerful national government. His proposal that senators should serve without pay was not adopted, but he exerted influence in such matters as the power of the Senate to ratify treaties and the compromise that was reached concerning abolition of the international slave trade. After the convention, he defended the Constitution in South Carolina.

Under the new government, Pinckney became a devoted Federalist. Between 1789 and 1795 he declined presidential offers to command the U.S. Army and to serve on the Supreme Court and as Secretary of War and Secretary of

State. In 1796, however, he accepted the post of Minister to France, but the revolutionary regime there refused to receive him and he was forced to proceed to the Netherlands. The next year, though, he returned to France when he was appointed to a special mission to restore relations with that country. During the ensuing XYZ affair, refusing to pay a bribe suggested by a French agent to facilitate negotiations, he was said to have replied "No! No! Not a sixpence!"

When Pinckney arrived back in the United States in 1798, he found the country preparing for war with France. That year, he was appointed as a major general in command of American forces in the South and served in that capacity until 1800, when the threat of war ended. That year, he represented the Federalists as Vice-Presidential candidate, and in 1804 and 1808 as the Presidential nominee. But he met defeat on all three occasions.

For the rest of his life, Pinckney engaged in legal practice, served at times in the legislature, and engaged in philanthropic activities. He was a charter member of the board of trustees of South Carolina College (later the University of South Carolina), first president of the Charleston Bible Society, and chief executive of the Charleston Library Society. He also gained prominence in the Society of the Cincinnati, an organization of former officers of the War for Independence.

During the later period of his life, Pinckney enjoyed his Belmont estate and Charleston high society. He was twice married; first to Sarah Middleton in 1773 and after her death to Mary Stead in 1786. Survived by three daughters, he died in Charleston in 1825 at the age of 79. He was interred there in the cemetery at St. Michael's Episcopal Church.

CHARLES PINCKNEY, SOUTH CAROLINA

Charles Pinckney, the second cousin of fellow-signer Charles Cotesworth Pinckney, was born at Charleston, SC, in 1757. His father, Col. Charles Pinckney, was a rich lawyer and planter, who on his death in 1782 was to bequeath Snee Farm, a country estate outside the city, to his son Charles. The latter apparently received all his education in the city of his birth, and he started to practice law there in 1779.

About that time, well after the War for Independence had begun, young Pinckney enlisted in the militia, though his father demonstrated ambivalence about the Revolution. He became a lieutenant, and served at the siege of Savannah (September-October 1779). When Charleston fell to the British the next year, the youth was captured and remained a prisoner until June 1781.

Pinckney had also begun a political career, serving in the Continental Congress (1777-78 and 1784-87) and in the state legislature (1779-80, 1786-89, and 1792-96). A nationalist, he worked hard in Congress to ensure that the United States would receive navigation rights to the Mississippi and to strengthen congressional power.

Pinckney's role in the Constitutional Convention is controversial. Although one of the youngest delegates, he later claimed to have been the most influential one and contended he had submitted a draft that was the basis of the final Constitution. Most historians have rejected this assertion. They do, however, recognize that he ranked among the leaders. He attended full time, spoke often and effectively, and contributed immensely to the final draft and to the resolution of problems that arose during the debates. He also worked for ratification in South Carolina (1788). That same year, he married Mary Eleanor Laurens, daughter of a wealthy and politically powerful South Carolina merchant; she was to bear at least three children.

Subsequently, Pinckney's career blossomed. From 1789 to 1792 he held the governorship of South Carolina, and in 1790 chaired the state constitutional convention. During this period, he became associated with the Federalist Party, in which he and his cousin Charles Cotesworth Pinckney were leaders. But, with the passage of time, the former's views began to change. In 1795 he attacked the Federalist backed Jay's Treaty and increasingly began to cast his lot with Carolina back-country Democratic-Republicans against his own eastern aristocracy. In 1796 he became governor once again, and in 1798 his Democratic-Republican supporters helped him win a seat in the U.S. Senate. There, he bitterly opposed his former party, and in the presidential election of 1800 served as Thomas Jefferson's campaign manager in South Carolina.

The victorious Jefferson appointed Pinckney as Minister to Spain (1801-5), in which capacity he struggled valiantly but unsuccessfully to win cession of the Floridas to the United States and facilitated Spanish acquiescence in the transfer of Louisiana from France to the United States in 1803.

Upon completion of his diplomatic mission, his ideas moving ever closer to democracy, Pinckney headed back to Charleston and to leadership of the state Democratic-Republican Party. He sat in the legislature in 1805-6 and then was again elected as governor (1806-8). In this position, he favored legislative reapportionment, giving better representation to back-country districts, and advocated universal white manhood suffrage. He served again in the legislature from 1810 to 1814 and then temporarily withdrew from politics. In 1818 he won election to the U.S. House of Representatives, where he fought against the Missouri Compromise.

In 1821, Pinckney's health beginning to fail, he retired for the last time from politics. He died in 1824, just 3 days after his

67th birthday. He was laid to rest in Charleston at St. Philip's Episcopal Churchyard.

PIERCE BUTLER, SOUTH CAROLINA

One of the most aristocratic delegates at the convention, Butler was born in 1744 in County Carlow, Ireland. His father was Sir Richard Butler, member of Parliament and a baronet.

Like so many younger sons of the British aristocracy who could not inherit their fathers' estates because of primogeniture, Butler pursued a military career. He became a major in His Majesty's 29th Regiment and during the colonial unrest was posted to Boston in 1768 to quell disturbances there. In 1771 he married Mary Middleton, daughter of a wealthy South Carolinian, and before long resigned his commission to take up a planter's life in the Charleston area. The couple was to have at least one daughter.

When the Revolution broke out, Butler took up the Whig cause. He was elected to the assembly in 1778, and the next year he served as adjutant general in the South Carolina militia. While in the legislature through most of the 1780s, he took over leadership of the democratic upcountry faction in the state and refused to support his own planter group. The War for Independence cost him much of his property, and his finances were so precarious for a time that he was forced to travel to Amsterdam to seek a personal loan. In 1786 the assembly appointed him to a commission charged with settling a state boundary dispute.

The next year, Butler won election to both the Continental Congress (1787-88) and the Constitutional Convention. In the latter assembly, he was an outspoken nationalist who attended practically every session and was a key spokesman for the Madison-Wilson caucus. Butler also supported the interests of southern slaveholders. He served on the Committee on Postponed Matters.

On his return to South Carolina Butler defended the Constitution but did not participate in the ratifying convention. Service in the U.S. Senate (1789-96) followed. Although nominally a Federalist, he often crossed party lines. He supported Hamilton's fiscal program but opposed Jay's Treaty and Federalist judiciary and tariff measures.

Out of the Senate and back in South Carolina from 1797 to 1802, Butler was considered for but did not attain the governorship. He sat briefly in the Senate again in 1803-4 to fill out an unexpired term, and he once again demonstrated party independence. But, for the most part, his later career was spent as a wealthy planter. In his last years, he moved to Philadelphia, apparently to be near a daughter who had married a local physician. Butler died there in 1822 at the age of 77 and was buried in the yard of Christ Church.

WILLIAM FEW, GEORGIA

Few was born in 1748. His father's family had emigrated from England to Pennsylvania in the 1680s, but the father had subsequently moved to Maryland, where he married and settled on a farm near Baltimore. William was born there. He encountered much hardship and received minimal schooling. When he was 10 years of age, his father, seeking better opportunity, moved his family to North Carolina.

In 1771 Few, his father, and a brother associated themselves with the "Regulators," a group of frontiersmen who opposed the royal governor. As a result, the brother was hanged, the Few family farm was destroyed, and the father was forced to move once again, this time to Georgia. William remained behind, helping to settle his father's affairs, until 1776 when he joined his family near Wrightsboro, Ga. About this time,

74

he won admittance to the bar, based on earlier informal study, and set up practice in Augusta.

When the War for Independence began, Few enthusiastically aligned himself with the Whig cause. Although largely self-educated, he soon proved his capacity for leadership and won a lieutenant-colonelcy in the dragoons. In addition, he entered politics. He was elected to the Georgia provincial congress of 1776 and during the war twice served in the assembly, in 1777 and 1779. During the same period, he also sat on the state executive council besides holding the positions of surveyor-general and Indian commissioner. He also served in the Continental Congress (1780-88), during which time he was reelected to the Georgia Assembly (1783).

Four years later, Few was appointed as one of six state delegates to the Constitutional Convention, two of whom never attended and two others of whom did not stay for the duration. Few himself missed large segments of the proceedings, being absent during all of July and part of August because of congressional service, and never made a speech. Nonetheless, he contributed nationalist votes at critical times. Furthermore, as a delegate to the last sessions of the Continental Congress, he helped steer the Constitution past its first obstacle, approval by Congress. And he attended the state ratifying convention.

Few became one of his state's first U.S. senators (1789-93). When his term ended, he headed back home and served again in the assembly. In 1796 he received an appointment as a federal judge for the Georgia circuit. For reasons unknown, he resigned his judgeship in 1799 at the age of 52 and moved to New York City.

Few's career continued to blossom. He served 4 years in the legislature (1802-5) and then as inspector of prisons (1802-10), alderman (1813-14), and U.S. commissioner of loans (1804). From 1804 to 1814 he held a directorship at the

Manhattan Bank and later the presidency of City Bank. A devout Methodist, he also donated generously to philanthropic causes.

When Few died in 1828 at the age of 80 in Fishkill-on-the-Hudson (present Beacon), he was survived by his wife (born Catherine Nicholson) and three daughters. Originally buried in the yard of the local Reformed Dutch Church, his body was later reinterred at St. Paul's Church, Augusta, GA.

ABRAHAM BALDWIN, GEORGIA

Baldwin was born at Guilford, Conn., in 1754, the second son of a blacksmith who fathered 12 children by 2 wives. Besides Abraham, several of the family attained distinction. His sister Ruth married the poet and diplomat Joel Barlow, and his half-brother Henry attained the position of justice of the U.S. Supreme Court. Their ambitious father went heavily into debt to educate his children.

After attending a local village school, Abraham matriculated at Yale, in nearby New Haven. He graduated in 1772. Three years later, he became a minister and tutor at the college. He held that position until 1779, when he served as a chaplain in the Continental Army. Two years later, he declined an offer from his alma mater of a professorship of divinity. Instead of resuming his ministerial or educational duties after the war, he turned to the study of law and in 1783 gained admittance to the bar at Fairfield, CT.

Within a year, Baldwin moved to Georgia, won legislative approval to practice his profession, and obtained a grant of land in Wilkes County. In 1785 he sat in the assembly and the Continental Congress. Two years later, his father died and Baldwin undertook to pay off his debts and educate, out of his own pocket, his half-brothers and half-sisters.

That same year, Baldwin attended the Constitutional Convention, from which he was absent for a few weeks. Although usually inconspicuous, he sat on the Committee on Postponed Matters and helped resolve the large-small state representation crisis. At first, he favored representation in the Senate based upon property holdings, but possibly because of his close relationship with the Connecticut delegation he later came to fear alienation of the small states and changed his mind to representation by state.

After the convention, Baldwin returned to the Continental Congress (1787-89). He was then elected to the U.S. Congress, where he served for 18 years (House of Representatives, 1789-99; Senate, 1799-1807). During these years, he became a bitter opponent of Hamiltonian policies and, unlike most other native New Englanders, an ally of Madison and Jefferson and the Democratic-Republicans. In the Senate, he presided for a while as president pro tem.

By 1790 Baldwin had taken up residence in Augusta. Beginning in the preceding decade, he had begun efforts to advance the educational system in Georgia. Appointed with six others in 1784 to oversee the founding of a state college, he saw his dream come true in 1798 when Franklin College was founded. Modeled after Yale, it became the nucleus of the University of Georgia.

Baldwin, who never married, died after a short illness during his 53d year in 1807. Still serving in the Senate at the time, he was buried in Washington's Rock Creek Cemetery.

JOHN LANGDON, NEW HAMPSHIRE

Langdon was born in 1741 at or near Portsmouth, NH. His father, whose family had emigrated to America before 1660, was a prosperous farmer who sired a large family. The youth's education was intermittent. He attended a local grammar school, worked as an apprentice clerk, and spent some time at sea. Eventually he went into the mercantile business for himself and prospered.

Langdon, a vigorous supporter of the Revolution, sat on the New Hampshire committee of correspondence and a nonimportation committee. He also attended various patriot assemblies. In 1774 he participated in the seizure and confiscation of British munitions from the Portsmouth fort.

The next year, Langdon served as speaker of the New Hampshire assembly and also sat in the Continental Congress (1775-76). During the latter year, he accepted a colonelcy in the militia of his state and became its agent for British prizes on behalf of the Continental Congress, a post he held throughout the war. In addition, he built privateers for operations against the British--a lucrative occupation.

Langdon also actively took part in the land war. In 1777 he organized and paid for Gen. John Stark's expedition from New Hampshire against British Gen. John Burgoyne and was present in command of a militia unit at Saratoga, NY, when the latter surrendered. Langdon later led a detachment of troops during the Rhode Island campaign, but found his major outlet in politics. He was speaker of the New Hampshire legislature from 1777 to 1781. In 1777, meantime, he had married Elizabeth Sherburne, who was to give birth to one daughter.

In 1783 Langdon was elected to the Continental Congress; the next year, to the state senate; and the following year, as president, or chief executive, of New Hampshire. In 1784 he built a home at Portsmouth. In 1786-87 he was back again as speaker of the legislature and during the latter year for the third time in the Continental Congress.

Langdon was forced to pay his own expenses and those of Nicholas Gilman to the Constitutional Convention because New Hampshire was unable or unwilling to pay them. The pair did not arrive at Philadelphia until late July, by which time much business had already been consummated. Thereafter, Langdon made a significant mark. He spoke more than 20 times during the debates and was a member of the committee that struck a compromise on the issue of slavery. For the most part, his sympathies lay on the side of strengthening the national government. In 1788, once again as state president (1788-89), he took part in the ratifying convention.

From 1789 to 1801 Langdon sat in the U.S. Senate, including service as the first President pro tem for several sessions. During these years, his political affiliations changed. As a supporter of a strong central government, he had been a member of the Federalist Party, but by the time of Jay's Treaty (1794) he was opposing its policies. By 1801 he was firmly backing the Democratic-Republicans.

That year, Langdon declined Jefferson's offer of the Secretaryship of the Navy. Between then and 1812, he kept active in New Hampshire politics. He sat again in the legislature (1801-5), twice holding the position of speaker. After several unsuccessful attempts, in 1805 he was elected as governor and continued in that post until 1811 except for a year's hiatus in 1809. Meanwhile, in 1805, Dartmouth College had awarded him an honorary doctor of laws degree.

In 1812 Langdon refused the Democratic-Republican Vice-Presidential nomination on the grounds of age and health. He enjoyed retirement for another 7 years before he died at the age of 78. His grave is at Old North Cemetery in Portsmouth.

NICHOLAS GILMAN, NEW HAMPSHIRE

Member of a distinguished New Hampshire family and second son in a family of eight, Nicholas Gilman was born at Exeter in 1755. He received his education in local schools and worked at his father's general store. When the War for

Independence began, he enlisted in the New Hampshire element of the Continental Army, soon won a captaincy, and served throughout the war.

Gilman returned home, again helped his father in the store, and immersed himself in politics. In the period 1786-88 he sat in the Continental Congress, though his attendance record was poor. In 1787 he represented New Hampshire at the Constitutional Convention. He did not arrive at Philadelphia until July 21, by which time much major business had already occurred. Never much of a debater, he made no speeches and played only a minor part in the deliberations. He did, however, serve on the Committee on Postponed Matters. He was also active in obtaining New Hampshire's acceptance of the Constitution and in shepherding it through the Continental Congress.

Gilman later became a prominent Federalist politician. He served in the U.S. House of Representatives from 1789 until 1797; and in 1793 and 1797 was a presidential elector. He also sat in the New Hampshire legislature in 1795, 1802, and 1804, and in the years 1805-8 and 1811-14 he held the office of state treasurer.

Meantime, Gilman's political philosophy had begun to drift toward the Democratic-Republicans. In 1802, when he was defeated for the U.S. Senate, President Jefferson appointed him as a bankruptcy commissioner, and 2 years later as a Democratic-Republican he won election to the U.S. Senate. He was still serving there when he passed away at Philadelphia, while on his way home from Washington, DC, in 1814 at the age of 58. He is interred at the Winter Street Cemetery at Exeter.

NATHANIEL GORHAM, MASSACHUSETTS

Gorham, an eldest child, was born in 1738 at Charlestown, MA, into an old Bay Colony family of modest means. His father operated a packet boat. The youth's education was minimal. When he was about 15 years of age, he was apprenticed to a New London, CT, merchant. He quit in 1759, returned to his hometown and established a business which quickly succeeded. In 1763 he wed Rebecca Call, who was to bear nine children.

Gorham began his political career as a public notary but soon won election to the colonial legislature (1771-75). During the Revolution, he unswervingly backed the Whigs. He was a delegate to the provincial congress (1774-75), member of the Massachusetts Board of War (1778-81), delegate to the constitutional convention (1779-80), and representative in both the upper (1780) and lower (1781-87) houses of the legislature, including speaker of the latter in 1781, 1782, and 1785. In the last year, though he apparently lacked formal legal training, he began a judicial career as judge of the Middlesex County court of common pleas (1785-96). During this same period, he sat on the Governor's Council (1788-89).

During the war, British troops had ravaged much of Gorham's property, though by privateering and speculation he managed to recoup most of his fortune. Despite these pressing business concerns and his state political and judicial activities, he also served the nation. He was a member of the Continental Congress (1782-83 and 1785-87), and held the office of president from June 1786 until January 1787.

The next year, at age 49, Gorham attended the Constitutional Convention. A moderate nationalist, he attended all the sessions and played an influential role.. He spoke often, acted as chairman of the Committee of the Whole, and sat on the Committee of Detail. As a delegate to the Massachusetts ratifying convention, he stood behind the Constitution.

Some unhappy years followed. Gorham did not serve in the new government he had helped to create. In 1788 he and Oliver Phelps of Windsor, CT, and possibly others, contracted to purchase from the Commonwealth of Massachusetts 6 million acres of unimproved land in western New York. The price was $1 million in devalued Massachusetts scrip. Gorham and Phelps quickly succeeded in clearing Indian title to 2,600,000 acres in the eastern section of the grant and sold much of it to settlers. Problems soon arose, however. Massachusetts scrip rose dramatically in value, enormously swelling the purchase price of the vast tract. By 1790 the two men were unable to meet their payments. The result was a financial crisis that led to Gorham's insolvency--and a fall from the heights of Boston society and political esteem.

Gorham died in 1796 at the age of 58 and is buried at the Phipps Street Cemetery in Charlestown, MA.

RUFUS KING, MASSACHUSETTS

King was born at Scarboro (Scarborough), MA (present Maine), in 1755. He was the eldest son of a prosperous farmer-merchant. At age 12, after receiving an elementary education at local schools, he matriculated at Dummer Academy in South Byfield, MA, and in 1777 graduated from Harvard. He served briefly as a general's aide during the War for Independence. Choosing a legal career, he read for the law at Newburyport, MA, and entered practice there in 1780.

King's knowledge, bearing, and oratorical gifts soon launched him on a political career. From 1783 to 1785 he was a member of the Massachusetts legislature, after which that body sent him to the Continental Congress (1784-86). There, he gained a reputation as a brilliant speaker and an early opponent of slavery. Toward the end of his tour, in 1786, he married Mary Alsop, daughter of a rich New York City merchant. He performed his final duties for Massachusetts by representing her at the Constitutional Convention and by serving in the commonwealth's ratifying convention.

At age 32, King was not only one of the most youthful of the delegates at Philadelphia, but was also one of the most important. He numbered among the most capable orators. Furthermore, he attended every session. Although he came to the convention unconvinced that major changes should be made in the Articles of Confederation, his views underwent a startling transformation during the debates. With Madison, he became a leading figure in the nationalist caucus. He served with distinction on the Committee on Postponed Matters and the Committee of Style. He also took notes on the proceedings, which have been valuable to historians.

About 1788 King abandoned his law practice, moved from the Bay State to Gotham, and entered the New York political forum. He was elected to the legislature (1789-90), and in the former year was picked as one of the state's first U.S. senators. As political divisions grew in the new government, King expressed ardent sympathies for the Federalists. In Congress, he supported Hamilton's fiscal program and stood among the leading proponents of the unpopular Jay's Treaty (1794).

Meantime, in 1791, King had become one of the directors of the First Bank of the United States. Reelected to the U.S. Senate in 1795, he served only a year before he was appointed as Minister to Great Britain (1796-1803).

King's years in this post were difficult ones in Anglo-American relations. The wars of the French Revolution endangered U.S. commerce in the maritime clashes between the French and the British. The latter in particular violated American rights on the high seas, especially by the impressment of sailors. Although King was unable to bring about a change in this policy, he smoothed relations between the two nations.

In 1803 King sailed back to the United States and to a career in politics. In 1804 and 1808 fellow-signer Charles

Cotesworth Pinckney and he were the Federalist candidates for President and Vice President, respectively, but were decisively defeated. Otherwise, King largely contented himself with agricultural pursuits at King Manor, a Long Island estate he had purchased in 1805. During the War of 1812, he was again elected to the U.S. Senate (1813-25) and ranked as a leading critic of the war. Only after the British attacked Washington in 1814 did he come to believe that the United States was fighting a defensive action and to lend his support to the war effort.

In 1816 the Federalists chose King as their candidate for the presidency, but James Monroe beat him handily. Still in the Senate, that same year King led the opposition to the establishment of the Second Bank of the United States. Four years later, believing that the issue of slavery could not be compromised but must be settled once and for all by the immediate establishment of a system of compensated emancipation and colonization, he denounced the Missouri Compromise.

In 1825, suffering from ill health, King retired from the Senate. President John Quincy Adams, however, persuaded him to accept another assignment as Minister to Great Britain. He arrived in England that same year, but soon fell ill and was forced to return home the following year. Within a year, at the age of 72, in 1827, he died. Surviving him were several offspring, some of whom also gained distinction. He was laid to rest near King Manor in the cemetery of Grace Episcopal Church, Jamaica, Long Island, NY.

WILLIAM SAMUEL JOHNSON, CONNECTICUT

William Samuel Johnson was the son of Samuel Johnson, the first president of King's College (later Columbia College and University). William was born at Stratford, CT, in 1727. His father, who was a well-known Anglican clergyman-philosopher, prepared him for college and he graduated from

Yale in 1744. About 3 years later he won a master of arts degree from the same institution and an honorary master's from Harvard.

Resisting his father's wish that he become a minister, Johnson embraced law instead--largely by educating himself and without benefit of formal training. After admittance to the bar, he launched a practice in Stratford, representing clients from nearby New York State as well as Connecticut, and before long he established business connections with various mercantile houses in New York City. In 1749, adding to his already substantial wealth, he married Anne Beach, daughter of a local businessman. The couple was to have five daughters and six sons, but many of them died at an early age.

Johnson did not shirk the civic responsibilities of one of his station. In the 1750s he began his public career as a Connecticut militia officer. In 1761 and 1765 he served in the lower house of the colonial assembly. In 1766 and 1771 he was elected to the upper house. At the time of the Revolution, Johnson was disturbed by conflicting loyalties. Although he attended the Stamp Act Congress in 1765, moderately opposed the Townshend Duties of 1767, and believed that most British policies were unwise, he retained strong transatlantic ties and found it difficult to choose sides. Many of his friends resided in Britain; in 1765 and 1766 Oxford University conferred honorary master's and doctor's degrees upon him; he had a strong association with the Anglican Church; he acted as Connecticut's agent in Britain during the years 1767-71; and he was friendly with men such as Jared Ingersoll, Sr., who were affiliated with the British administration.

Johnson finally decided to work for peace between Britain and the colonies and to oppose the extremist Whig faction. On that basis, he refused to participate in the First Continental Congress, to which he was elected in 1774, following service as a judge of the Connecticut colonial supreme court (1772-74). When hostilities broke out, he confined his activities to peacemaking efforts. In April 1775 Connecticut sent him and another emissary to speak to British Gen. Thomas Gage about ending the bloodshed. But the time was not ripe for negotiations and they failed. Johnson fell out of favor with radical patriot elements who gained the ascendancy in Connecticut government and they no longer called upon his service. Although he was arrested in 1779 on charges of communicating with the enemy, he cleared himself and was released.

Once the passions of war had ebbed, Johnson resumed his political career. In the Continental Congress (1785-87), he was one of the most influential and popular delegates. Playing a major role in the Constitutional Convention, he missed no sessions after arriving on June 2; espoused the Connecticut Compromise; and chaired the Committee of Style, which shaped the final document. He also worked for ratification in Connecticut.

Johnson took part in the new government, in the U.S. Senate where he contributed to passage of the Judiciary Act of 1789. In 1791, the year after the government moved from New York to Philadelphia, he resigned mainly because he preferred to devote all his energies to the presidency of Columbia College (1787-1800), in New York City. During these years, he established the school on a firm basis and recruited a fine faculty.

Johnson retired from the college in 1800, a few years after his wife died, and in the same year wed Mary Brewster Beach, a relative of his first bride. They resided at his birthplace, Stratford. He died there in 1819 at the age of 92 and was buried at Old Episcopal Cemetery.

Roger Sherman, Connecticut

In 1723, when Sherman was 2 years of age, his family relocated from his Newton, MA, birthplace to Dorchester (present Stoughton). As a boy, he was spurred by a desire to learn and read widely in his spare time to supplement his minimal education at a common school. But he spent most of his waking hours helping his father with farming chores and learning the cobbler's trade from him. In 1743, 2 years after his father's death, Sherman joined an elder brother who had settled in New Milford, CT.

Purchasing a store, becoming a county surveyor, and winning a variety of town offices, Sherman prospered and assumed leadership in the community. In 1749 he married Elizabeth Hartwell, by whom he had seven children. Without benefit of a formal legal education, he was admitted to the bar in 1754 and embarked upon a distinguished judicial and political career. In the period 1755-61, except for a brief interval, he served as a representative in the colonial legislature and held the offices of justice of the peace and county judge. Somehow he also eked out time to publish an essay on monetary theory and a series of almanacs incorporating his own astronomical observations and verse.

In 1761, Sherman abandoned his law practice, and moved to New Haven, CT. There, he managed two stores, one that catered to Yale students, and another in nearby Wallingford. He also became a friend and benefactor of Yale College, and served for many years as its treasurer. In 1763, or 3 years after the death of his first wife, he wed Rebecca Prescott, who bore eight children.

Meanwhile, Sherman's political career had blossomed. He rose from justice of the peace and county judge to an associate judge of the Connecticut Superior Court and to representative in both houses of the colonial assembly. Although opposed to extremism, he promptly joined the fight against Britain. He supported nonimportation measures and headed the New Haven committee of correspondence.

Sherman was a longtime and influential member of the Continental Congress (1774-81 and 1783-84). He won membership on the committees that drafted the Declaration of Independence and the Articles of Confederation, as well as those concerned with Indian affairs, national finances, and military matters. To solve economic problems, at both national and state levels, he advocated high taxes rather than excessive borrowing or the issuance of paper currency.

While in Congress, Sherman remained active in state and local politics, continuing to hold the office of judge of the Connecticut Superior Court, as well as membership on the council of safety (1777-79). In 1783 he helped codify Connecticut's statutory laws. The next year, he was elected mayor of New Haven (1784-86).

Although on the edge of insolvency, mainly because of wartime losses, Sherman could not resist the lure of national service. In 1787 he represented his state at the Constitutional Convention, and attended practically every session. Not only did he sit on the Committee on Postponed Matters, but he also probably helped draft the New Jersey Plan and was a prime mover behind the Connecticut, or Great, Compromise, which broke the deadlock between the large and small states over representation. He was, in addition, instrumental in Connecticut's ratification of the Constitution.

Sherman concluded his career by serving in the U.S. House of Representatives (1789-91) and Senate (1791-93), where he espoused the Federalist cause. He died at New Haven in 1793 at the age of 72 and is buried in the Grove Street Cemetery.

ALEXANDER HAMILTON, NEW YORK

Hamilton was born in 1757 on the island of Nevis, in the Leeward group, British West Indies. He was the illegitimate son of a common-law marriage between a poor itinerant Scottish merchant of aristocratic descent and an English-French Huguenot mother who was a planter's daughter. In 1766, after the father had moved his family elsewhere in the Leewards to St. Croix in the Danish (now United States) Virgin Islands, he returned to St. Kitts while his wife and two sons remained on St. Croix.

The mother, who opened a small store to make ends meet, and a Presbyterian clergyman provided Hamilton with a basic education, and he learned to speak fluent French. About the time of his mother's death in 1768, he became an apprentice clerk at Christiansted in a mercantile establishment, whose proprietor became one of his benefactors. Recognizing his ambition and superior intelligence, they raised a fund for his education.

In 1772, bearing letters of introduction, Hamilton traveled to New York City. Patrons he met there arranged for him to attend Barber's Academy at Elizabethtown (present Elizabeth), NJ. During this time, he met and stayed for a while at the home of William Livingston, who would one day be a fellow signer of the Constitution. Late the next year, 1773, Hamilton entered King's College (later Columbia College and University) in New York City, but the Revolution interrupted his studies.

Although not yet 20 years of age, in 1774-75 Hamilton wrote several widely read pro-Whig pamphlets. Right after the war broke out, he accepted an artillery captaincy and fought in the principal campaigns of 1776-77. In the latter year, winning the rank of lieutenant colonel, he joined the staff of General Washington as secretary and aide-de-camp and soon became his close confidant as well.

In 1780 Hamilton wed New Yorker Elizabeth Schuyler, whose family was rich and politically powerful; they were to have eight children. In 1781, after some disagreements with Washington, he took a command position under Lafayette in the Yorktown, VA, campaign (1781). He resigned his commission that November.

Hamilton then read law at Albany and quickly entered practice, but public service soon attracted him. He was elected to the Continental Congress in 1782-83. In the latter year, he established a law office in New York City. Because of his interest in strengthening the central government, he represented his state at the Annapolis Convention in 1786, where he urged the calling of the Constitutional Convention.

In 1787 Hamilton served in the legislature, which appointed him as a delegate to the convention. He played a surprisingly small part in the debates, apparently because he was frequently absent on legal business, his extreme nationalism put him at odds with most of the delegates, and he was frustrated by the conservative views of his two fellow delegates from New York. He did, however, sit on the Committee of Style, and he was the only one of the three delegates from his state who signed the finished document. Hamilton's part in New York's ratification the next year was substantial, though he felt the Constitution was deficient in many respects. Against determined opposition, he waged a strenuous and successful campaign, including collaboration with John Jay and James Madison in writing The Federalist. In 1787 Hamilton was again elected to the Continental Congress.

When the new government got under way in 1789, Hamilton won the position of Secretary of the Treasury. He began at once to place the nation's disorganized finances on a sound footing. In a series of reports (1790-91), he presented a program not only to stabilize national finances but also to shape the future of the country as a powerful, industrial nation. He proposed establishment of a national bank, funding of the national debt, assumption of state war debts, and the encouragement of manufacturing.

Hamilton's policies soon brought him into conflict with Jefferson and Madison. Their disputes with him over his pro-business economic program, sympathies for Great Britain, disdain for the common man, and opposition to the principles and excesses of the French revolution contributed to the formation of the first U.S. party system. It pitted Hamilton and the Federalists against Jefferson and Madison and the Democratic-Republicans.

During most of the Washington administration, Hamilton's views usually prevailed with the President, especially after 1793 when Jefferson left the government. In 1795 family and financial needs forced Hamilton to resign from the Treasury Department and resume his law practice in New York City. Except for a stint as inspector-general of the Army (1798-1800) during the undeclared war with France, he never again held public office.

While gaining stature in the law, Hamilton continued to exert a powerful impact on New York and national politics. Always an opponent of fellow-Federalist John Adams, he sought to prevent his election to the presidency in 1796. When that failed, he continued to use his influence secretly within Adams' cabinet. The bitterness between the two men became public knowledge in 1800 when Hamilton denounced Adams in a letter that was published through the efforts of the Democratic-Republicans.

In 1802 Hamilton and his family moved into The Grange, a country home he had built in a rural part of Manhattan not far north of New York City. But the expenses involved and investments in northern land speculations seriously strained his finances.

Meanwhile, when Jefferson and Aaron Burr tied in Presidential electoral votes in 1800, Hamilton threw valuable support to Jefferson. In 1804, when Burr sought the governorship of New York, Hamilton again managed to defeat him. That same year, Burr, taking offense at remarks he believed to have originated with Hamilton, challenged him to a duel, which took place at present Weehawken, NJ, on July 11. Mortally wounded, Hamilton died the next day. He was in his late forties at death. He was buried in Trinity Churchyard in New York City.

WILLIAM LIVINGSTON, NEW JERSEY

Livingston was born in 1723 at Albany, NY. His maternal grandmother reared him until he was 14, and he then spent a year with a missionary among the Mohawk Indians. He attended Yale and graduated in 1741.

Rejecting his family's hope that he would enter the fur trade at Albany or mercantile pursuits in New York City, young Livingston chose to pursue a career in law at the latter place. Before he completed his legal studies, in 1745 he married Susanna French, daughter of a well-to-do New Jersey landowner. She was to bear 13 children.

Three years later, Livingston was admitted to the bar and quickly gained a reputation as the supporter of popular causes against the more conservative factions in the city. Associated with the Calvinists in religion, he opposed the dominant Anglican leaders in the colony and wielded a sharply satirical pen in verses and broadsides. Livingston attacked the Anglican attempt to charter and control King's College (later Columbia College and University) and the dominant De Lancey party for its Anglican sympathies, and by 1758 rose to the leadership of his faction. For a decade, it controlled the colonial assembly and fought against parliamentary interference in the colony's affairs. During this time, 1759-61, Livingston sat in the assembly.

In 1769 Livingston's supporters, split by the growing debate as to how to respond to British taxation of the colonies, lost control of the assembly. Not long thereafter, Livingston, who had also grown tired of legal practice, moved to the Elizabethtown (present Elizabeth), NJ, area, where he had purchased land in 1760. There, in 1772-73, he built the estate, Liberty Hall, continued to write verse, and planned to live the life of a gentleman farmer.

The Revolutionary upsurge, however, brought Livingston out of retirement. He soon became a member of the Essex County, NJ, committee of correspondence; in 1774 a representative in the First Continental Congress; and in 1775-76 a delegate to the Second Continental Congress. In June 1776 he left Congress to command the New Jersey militia as a brigadier general and held this post until he was elected later in the year as the first governor of the state.

Livingston held the position throughout and beyond the war-- in fact, for 14 consecutive years until his death in 1790. During his administration, the government was organized, the war won, and New Jersey launched on her path as a sovereign state. Although the pressure of affairs often prevented it, he enjoyed his estate whenever possible, conducted agricultural experiments, and became a member of the Philadelphia Society for Promoting Agriculture. He was also active in the antislavery movement.

In 1787 Livingston was selected as a delegate to the Constitutional Convention, though his gubernatorial duties prevented him from attending every session. He did not arrive until June 5 and missed several weeks in July, but he performed vital committee work, particularly as chairman of the one that reached a compromise on the issue of slavery. He also supported the New Jersey Plan. In addition, he spurred New Jersey's rapid ratification of the Constitution (1787). The next year, Yale awarded him an honorary doctor of laws degree.

Livingston died at Liberty Hall in his 67th year in 1790. He was originally buried at the local Presbyterian Churchyard, but a year later his remains were moved to a vault his son owned at Trinity Churchyard in Manhattan and in 1844 were again relocated, to Brooklyn's Greenwood Cemetery.

DAVID BREARLY, NEW JERSEY

Brearly (Brearley) was descended from a Yorkshire, England, family, one of whose members migrated to New Jersey around 1680. Signer Brearly was born in 1745 at Spring Grove near Trenton, was reared in the area, and attended but did not graduate from the nearby College of New Jersey (later Princeton). He chose law as a career and originally practiced at Allentown, NJ. About 1767 he married Elizabeth Mullen.

Brearly avidly backed the Revolutionary cause. The British arrested him for high treason, but a group of patriots freed him. In 1776 he took part in the convention that drew up the state constitution. During the War for Independence, he rose from a captain to a colonel in the militia.

In 1779 Brearly was elected as chief justice of the New Jersey supreme court, a position he held until 1789. He presided over the precedent-setting case of Holmes v. Walton. His decision, rendered in 1780, represented an early expression of the principle of judicial review. The next year, the College of New Jersey bestowed an honorary M.A. degree on him.

Brearly was 42 years of age when he participated in the Constitutional Convention. Although he did not rank among the leaders, he attended the sessions regularly. A follower of Paterson, who introduced the New Jersey Plan, Brearly opposed proportional representation of the states and favored one vote for each of them in Congress. He also chaired the Committee on Postponed Matters.

94

Brearly's subsequent career was short, for he had only 3 years to live. He presided at the New Jersey convention that ratified the Constitution in 1788, and served as a presidential elector in 1789. That same year, President Washington appointed him as a federal district judge, and he served in that capacity until his death.

When free from his judicial duties, Brearly devoted much energy to lodge and church affairs. He was one of the leading members of the Masonic Order in New Jersey, as well as state vice president of the Society of the Cincinnati, an organization of former officers of the Revolutionary War. In addition, he served as a delegate to the Episcopal General Conference (1786) and helped write the church's prayer book. In 1783, following the death of his first wife, he had married Elizabeth Higbee.

Brearly died in Trenton at the age of 45 in 1790. He was buried there at St. Michael's Episcopal Church.

WILLIAM PATERSON, NEW JERSEY

William Paterson (Patterson) was born in County Antrim, Ireland, in 1745. When he was almost 2 years of age, his family emigrated to America, disembarking at New Castle, DE. While the father traveled about the country, apparently selling tinware, the family lived in New London, other places in Connecticut, and in Trenton, NJ. In 1750 he settled in Princeton, NJ. There, he became a merchant and manufacturer of tin goods. His prosperity enabled William to attend local private schools and the College of New Jersey (later Princeton). He took a B.A. in 1763 and an M.A. 3 years later.

Meantime, Paterson had studied law in the city of Princeton under Richard Stockton, who later was to sign the Declaration of Independence, and near the end of the decade began practicing at New Bromley, in Hunterdon County.

Before long, he moved to South Branch, in Somerset County, and then in 1779 relocated near New Brunswick at Raritan estate.

When the War for Independence broke out, Paterson joined the vanguard of the New Jersey patriots. He served in the provincial congress (1775-76), the constitutional convention (1776), legislative council (1776-77), and council of safety (1777). During the last year, he also held a militia commission. From 1776 to 1783 he was attorney general of New Jersey, a task that occupied so much of his time that it prevented him from accepting election to the Continental Congress in 1780. Meantime, the year before, he had married Cornelia Bell, by whom he had three children before her death in 1783. Two years later, he took a new bride, Euphemia White, but it is not known whether or not they had children.

From 1783, when he moved into the city of New Brunswick, until 1787, Paterson devoted his energies to the law and stayed out of the public limelight. Then he was chosen to represent New Jersey at the Constitutional Convention, which he attended only until late July. Until then, he took notes of the proceedings. More importantly, he figured prominently because of his advocacy and coauthorship of the New Jersey, or Paterson, Plan, which asserted the rights of the small states against the large. He apparently returned to the convention only to sign the final document. After supporting its ratification in New Jersey, he began a career in the new government.

In 1789 Paterson was elected to the U.S. Senate (1789-90), where he played a pivotal role in drafting the Judiciary Act of 1789. His next position was governor of his state (1790-93). During this time, he began work on the volume later published as Laws of the State of New Jersey (1800) and began to revise the rules and practices of the chancery and common law courts.

During the years 1793-1806, Paterson served as an associate justice of the U.S. Supreme Court. Riding the grueling circuit to which federal judges were subjected in those days and sitting with the full Court, he presided over a number of major trials.

In September 1806, his health failing, the 60-year-old Paterson embarked on a journey to Ballston Spa, NY, for a cure but died en route at Albany in the home of his daughter, who had married Stephen Van Rensselaer. Paterson was at first laid to rest in the nearby Van Rensselaer manor house family vault, but later his body was apparently moved to the Albany Rural Cemetery, Menands, NY

JONATHAN DAYTON, NEW JERSEY

Dayton was born at Elizabethtown (present Elizabeth), NJ, in 1760. His father was a storekeeper who was also active in local and state politics. The youth obtained a good education, graduating from the College of New Jersey (later Princeton) in 1776. He immediately entered the Continental Army and saw extensive action. Achieving the rank of captain by the age of 19 and serving under his father, Gen. Elias Dayton, and the Marquis de Lafayette, he was a prisoner of the British for a time and participated in the Battle of Yorktown, VA.

After the war, Dayton returned home, studied law, and established a practice. During the 1780s he divided his time between land speculation, legal practice, and politics. He sat in the assembly in 1786-87. In the latter year, he was chosen as a delegate to the Constitutional Convention after the leaders of his political faction, his father and his patron, Abraham Clark, declined to attend. Dayton did not arrive at Philadelphia until June 21 but thereafter faithfully took part in the proceedings. He spoke with moderate frequency during the debates and, though objecting to some provisions of the Constitution, signed it.

After sitting in the Continental Congress in 1788, Dayton became a foremost Federalist legislator in the new government. Although elected as a representative, he did not serve in the First Congress in 1789, preferring instead to become a member of the New Jersey council and speaker of the state assembly. In 1791, however, he entered the U.S. House of Representatives (1791-99), becoming Speaker in the Fourth and Fifth Congresses. During this period, he backed Hamilton's fiscal program, suppression of the Whisky Rebellion, Jay's Treaty, and a host of other Federalist measures.

In personal matters Dayton purchased Boxwood Hall in 1795 as his home in Elizabethtown and resided there until his death. He was elevated to the U.S. Senate (1799-1805). He supported the Louisiana Purchase (1803) and, in conformance with his Federalist views, opposed the repeal of the Judiciary Act of 1801.

In 1806 illness prevented Dayton from accompanying Aaron Burr's abortive expedition to the Southwest, where the latter apparently intended to conquer Spanish lands and create an empire. Subsequently indicted for treason, Dayton was not prosecuted but could not salvage his national political career. He remained popular in New Jersey, however, continuing to hold local offices and sitting in the assembly (1814-15).

In 1824 the 63-year-old Dayton played host to Lafayette during his triumphal tour of the United States, and his death at Elizabeth later that year may have been hastened by the exertion and excitement. He was laid to rest at St. John's Episcopal Church in his hometown. Because he owned 250,000 acres of Ohio land between the Big and Little Miami Rivers, the city of Dayton, was named after him--his major monument. He had married Susan Williamson, but the date of their wedding is unknown. They had two daughters.

Benjamin Franklin, Pennsylvania

Franklin was born in 1706 at Boston. He was the tenth son of a soap and candlemaker. He received some formal education but was principally self-taught. After serving an apprenticeship to his father between the ages of 10 and 12, he went to work for his half-brother James, a printer. In 1721 the latter founded the New England Courant, the fourth newspaper in the colonies. Benjamin secretly contributed 14 essays to it, his first published writings.

In 1723, because of dissension with his half-brother, Franklin moved to Philadelphia, where he obtained employment as a printer. He spent only a year there and then sailed to London for 2 more years. Back in Philadelphia, he rose rapidly in the printing industry. He published The Pennsylvania Gazette (1730-48), which had been founded by another man in 1728, but his most successful literary venture was the annual Poor Richard 's Almanac (1733-58). It won a popularity in the colonies second only to the Bible, and its fame eventually spread to Europe.

Meantime, in 1730 Franklin had taken a common-law wife, Deborah Read, who was to bear him a son and daughter, and he also apparently had children with another nameless woman out of wedlock. By 1748 he had achieved financial independence and gained recognition for his philanthropy and the stimulus he provided to such civic causes as libraries, educational institutions, and hospitals. Energetic and tireless, he also found time to pursue his interest in science, as well as to enter politics.

Franklin served as clerk (1736-51) and member (1751-64) of the colonial legislature and as deputy postmaster of Philadelphia (1737-53) and deputy postmaster general of the colonies (1753-74). In addition, he represented Pennsylvania at the Albany Congress (1754), called to unite the colonies during the French and Indian War. The congress adopted his

"Plan of Union," but the colonial assemblies rejected it because it encroached on their powers.

During the years 1757-62 and 1764-75, Franklin resided in England, originally in the capacity of agent for Pennsylvania and later for Georgia, New Jersey, and Massachusetts. During the latter period, which coincided with the growth of colonial unrest, he underwent a political metamorphosis. Until then a contented Englishman in outlook, primarily concerned with Pennsylvania provincial politics, he distrusted popular movements and saw little purpose to be served in carrying principle to extremes. Until the issue of parliamentary taxation undermined the old alliances, he led the Quaker party attack on the Anglican proprietary party and its Presbyterian frontier allies. His purpose throughout the years at London in fact had been displacement of the Penn family administration by royal authority-the conversion of the province from a proprietary to a royal colony.

It was during the Stamp Act crisis that Franklin evolved from leader of a shattered provincial party's faction to celebrated spokesman at London for American rights. Although as agent for Pennsylvania he opposed by every conceivable means the enactment of the bill in 1765, he did not at first realize the depth of colonial hostility. He regarded passage as unavoidable and preferred to submit to it while actually working for its repeal.

Franklin's nomination of a friend and political ally as stamp distributor for Pennsylvania, coupled with his apparent acceptance of the legislation, armed his proprietary opponents with explosive issues. Their energetic exploitation of them endangered his reputation at home until reliable information was published demonstrating his unabated opposition to the act. For a time, mob resentment threatened his family and new home in Philadelphia until his tradesmen supporters rallied. Subsequently, Franklin's defense of the American position in the House of Commons during the debates over the Stamp Act's repeal restored his prestige at home.

Franklin returned to Philadelphia in May 1775 and immediately became a distinguished member of the Continental Congress. Thirteen months later, he served on the committee that drafted the Declaration of Independence. He subsequently contributed to the government in other important ways, including service as postmaster general, and took over the duties of president of the Pennsylvania constitutional convention.

But, within less than a year and a half after his return, the aged statesman set sail once again for Europe, beginning a career as diplomat that would occupy him for most of the rest of his life. In the years 1776-79, as one of three commissioners, he directed the negotiations that led to treaties of commerce and alliance with France, where the people adulated him, but he and the other commissioners squabbled constantly. While he was sole commissioner to France (1779-85), he and John Jay and John Adams negotiated the Treaty of Paris (1783), which ended the War for Independence.

Back in the United States, in 1785 Franklin became president of the Supreme Executive Council of Pennsylvania. At the Constitutional Convention, though he did not approve of many aspects of the finished document and was hampered by his age and ill-health, he missed few if any sessions, lent his prestige, soothed passions, and compromised disputes.

In his twilight years, working on his Autobiography, Franklin could look back on a fruitful life as the toast of two continents. Energetic nearly to the last, in 1787 he was elected as first president of the Pennsylvania Society for Promoting the Abolition of Slavery-a cause to which he had committed himself as early as the 1730s. His final public act was signing a memorial to Congress recommending dissolution of the slavery system. Shortly thereafter, in 1790 at the age of 84, Franklin passed away in Philadelphia and was laid to rest in Christ Church Burial Ground.

THOMAS MIFFLIN, PENNSYLVANIA

A member of the fourth generation of a Pennsylvania Quaker family who had emigrated from England, Mifflin was born at Philadelphia in 1744, the son of a rich merchant and local politician. He studied at a Quaker school and then at the College of Philadelphia (later part of the University of Pennsylvania), from which he won a diploma at the age of 16 and whose interests he advanced for the rest of his life.

Mifflin then worked for 4 years in a Philadelphia countinghouse. In 1764 he visited Europe, and the next year entered the mercantile business in Philadelphia with his brother. In 1767 he wed Sarah Morris. Although he prospered in business, politics enticed him.

In the Pennsylvania legislature (1772-76), Mifflin championed the colonial position against the crown. In 1774 he attended the Continental Congress (1774-76). Meanwhile, he had helped to raise troops and in May 1775 won appointment as a major in the Continental Army, which caused him to be expelled from his Quaker faith. In the summer of 1775 he first became an aide-de-camp to Washington and then Quartermaster General of the Continental Army. Late in 1775 he became a colonel and in May 1776 a brigadier general. Preferring action to administration, after a time he began to perform his quartermaster duties perfunctorily. Nevertheless, he participated directly in the war effort. He took part in the Battles of Long Island, NY, Trenton, NJ, and Princeton, NJ. Furthermore, through his persuasive oratory, he apparently convinced many men not to leave the military service.

In 1777 Mifflin attained the rank of major general but, restive at criticism of his quartermaster activities, he resigned. About the same time, though he later became a friend of Washington, he became involved in the cabal that advanced Gen. Horatio Gates to replace him in command of the Continental Army. In 1777-78 Mifflin sat on the Congressional Board of War. In the latter year, he briefly reentered the military, but continuing attacks on his earlier conduct of the quartermastership soon led him to resign once more.

Mifflin returned immediately to politics. He sat in the state assembly (1778-79) and again in the Continental Congress (1782-84), from December 1783 to the following June as its president. In 1787 he was chosen to take part in the Constitutional Convention. He attended regularly, but made no speeches and did not play a substantial role.

Mifflin continued in the legislature (1785-88 and 1799-1800); succeeded Franklin as president of the Supreme Executive Council (1788-90); chaired the constitutional convention (1789-90); and held the governorship (1790-99), during which time he affiliated himself with the emerging Democratic-Republican Party.

Although wealthy most of his life, Mifflin was a lavish spender. Pressure from his creditors forced him to leave Philadelphia in 1799, and he died at Lancaster the next year, aged 56. The Commonwealth of Pennsylvania paid his burial expenses at the local Trinity Lutheran Church.

ROBERT MORRIS, PENNSYLVANIA

Robert Morris was born at or near Liverpool, England, in 1734. When he reached 13 years of age, he emigrated to Maryland to join his father, a tobacco exporter at Oxford, Md. After brief schooling at Philadelphia, the youth obtained employment with Thomas and Charles Willing's well-known shipping-banking firm. In 1754 he became a partner and for almost four decades was one of the company's directors as well as an influential Philadelphia citizen. Wedding Mary White at the age of 35, he fathered five sons and two daughters.

During the Stamp Act turmoil in 1765, Morris joined other merchants in protest, but not until the outbreak of hostilities a decade later did he fully commit himself to the Revolution. In 1775 the Continental Congress contracted with his firm to import arms and ammunition, and he was elected to the Pennsylvania council of safety (1775-76), the committee of correspondence, the provincial assembly (1775-76), the legislature (1776-78), and the Continental Congress (1775-78). In the last body, on July 1, 1776, he voted against independence, which he personally considered premature, but the next day he purposely absented himself to facilitate an affirmative ballot by his delegation.

Morris, a key congressman, specialized in financial affairs and military procurement. Although he and his firm profited handsomely, had it not been for his assiduous labors the Continental Army would probably have been forced to demobilize. He worked closely with General Washington, wheedled money and supplies from the states, borrowed money in the face of overwhelming difficulties, and on occasion even obtained personal loans to further the war cause.

Immediately following his congressional service, Morris sat for two more terms in the Pennsylvania legislature (1778-81). During this time, Thomas Paine and others attacked him for profiteering in Congress, which investigated his accounts and vindicated him. Nevertheless, his reputation suffered.

Morris embarked on the most dramatic phase of his career by accepting the office of Superintendent of Finance (1781-84) under the Articles of Confederation. Congress, recognizing

104

the perilous state of the nation's finances and its impotence to provide remedies, granted him dictatorial powers and acquiesced to his condition that he be allowed to continue his private commercial enterprises. He slashed all governmental and military expenditures, personally purchased army and navy supplies, tightened accounting procedures, prodded the states to fulfill quotas of money and supplies, and when necessary strained his personal credit by issuing notes over his own signature or borrowing from friends.

To finance Washington's Yorktown campaign in 1781, in addition to the above techniques, Morris obtained a sizable loan from France. He used part of it, along with some of his own fortune, to organize the Bank of North America, chartered that December. The first government-incorporated bank in the United States, it aided war financing.

Although Morris was reelected to the Pennsylvania legislature for 1785-86, his private ventures consumed most of his time. In the latter year, he attended the Annapolis Convention, and the following year the Constitutional Convention, where he sympathized with the Federalists but was, for a man of his eminence, strangely silent. Although in attendance at practically every meeting, he spoke only twice in debates and did not serve on any committees. In 1789, declining Washington's offer of appointment as the first Secretary of the Treasury, he took instead a U.S. Senate seat (1789-95).

During the later years of his public life, Morris speculated wildly, often on overextended credit, in lands in the West and at the site of Washington, DC. To compound his difficulties, in 1794 he began constructing on Philadelphia's Chestnut Street a mansion designed by Maj. Pierre Charles L'Enfant. Not long thereafter, Morris attempted to escape creditors by retreating to The Hills, the country estate along the Schuylkill River on the edge of Philadelphia that he had acquired in 1770.

Arrested at the behest of creditors in 1798 and forced to abandon completion of the mansion, thereafter known in its unfinished state as "Morris' Folly," Morris was thrown into the Philadelphia debtor's prison, where he was nevertheless well treated. By the time he was released in 1801, under a federal bankruptcy law, however, his property and fortune had vanished, his health had deteriorated, and his spirit had been broken. He lingered on in poverty and obscurity, living in a simple Philadelphia home on an annuity obtained for his wife by fellow-signer Gouverneur Morris.

Robert Morris died in 1806 in his 73d year and was buried in the yard of Christ Church.

GEORGE CLYMER, PENNSYLVANIA

Clymer was orphaned in 1740, only a year after his birth in Philadelphia. A wealthy uncle reared and informally educated him and advanced him from clerk to full-fledged partner in his mercantile firm, which on his death he bequeathed to his ward. Later Clymer merged operations with the Merediths, a prominent business family, and cemented the relationship by marrying his senior partner's daughter, Elizabeth, in 1765.

Motivated at least partly by the impact of British economic restrictions on his business, Clymer early adopted the Revolutionary cause and was one of the first to recommend independence. He attended patriotic meetings, served on the Pennsylvania council of safety, and in 1773 headed a committee that forced the resignation of Philadelphia tea consignees appointed by Britain under the Tea Act. Inevitably, in light of his economic background, he channeled his energies into financial matters. In 1775-76 he acted as one of the first two Continental treasurers, even personally underwriting the war by exchanging all his own specie for Continental currency.

In the Continental Congress (1776-77 and 1780-82) the quiet and unassuming Clymer rarely spoke in debate but made his mark in committee efforts, especially those pertaining to commerce, finance, and military affairs. During the War for Independence, he also served on a series of commissions that conducted important field investigations. In December 1776, when Congress fled from Philadelphia to Baltimore, he and George Walton and Robert Morris remained behind to carry on congressional business. Within a year, after their victory at the Battle of Brandywine, Pa. (September 11, 1777), British troops advancing on Philadelphia detoured for the purpose of vandalizing Clymer's home in Chester County about 25 miles outside the city. His wife and children hid nearby in the woods.

After a brief retirement following his last term in the Continental Congress, Clymer was reelected for the years 1784-88 to the Pennsylvania legislature, where he had also served part time in 1780-82 while still in Congress. As a state legislator, he advocated a bicameral legislature and reform of the penal code and opposed capital punishment. At the Constitutional Convention, where he rarely missed a meeting, he spoke seldom but effectively and played a modest role in shaping the final document.

The next phase of Clymer's career consisted of service in the U.S. House of Representatives in the First Congress (1789-91), followed by appointment as collector of excise taxes on alcoholic beverages in Pennsylvania (1791-94). In 1795-96 he sat on a Presidential commission that negotiated a treaty with the Cherokee and Creek Indians in Georgia. During his retirement, Clymer advanced various community projects, including the Philadelphia Society for Promoting Agriculture and the Pennsylvania Academy of the Fine Arts, and served as the first president of the Philadelphia Bank. At the age of 73, in 1813, he died at Summerseat, an estate a few miles outside Philadelphia at Morrisville that he had purchased and moved to in 1806. His grave is in the Friends Meeting House Cemetery at Trenton, NJ.

THOMAS FITZSIMONS, PENNSYLVANIA

Fitzsimons (FitzSimons; Fitzsimmons) was born in Ireland in 1741. Coming to America about 1760, he pursued a mercantile career in Philadelphia. The next year, he married Catherine Meade, the daughter of a prominent local merchant, Robert Meade, and not long afterward went into business with one of his brothers-in-law. The firm of George Meade and Company soon became one of the leading commercial houses in the city and specialized in the West India trade.

When the Revolution erupted, Fitzsimons enthusiastically endorsed the Whig position. During the war, he commanded a company of militia (1776-77). He also sat on the Philadelphia committee of correspondence, council of safety, and navy board. His firm provided supplies and "fire" ships to the military forces and, toward the end of the war, donated £: 5,000 to the Continental Army.

In 1782-83 Fitzsimons entered politics as a delegate to the Continental Congress. In the latter year, he became a member of the Pennsylvania council of censors and served as a legislator (1786-89). His attendance at the Constitutional Convention was regular, but he did not make any outstanding contributions to the proceedings. He was, however, a strong nationalist.

After the convention, Fitzsimons continued to demonstrate his nationalistic proclivities as a three-term U.S. representative (1789-95). He allied himself closely with the program of Hamilton and the emerging Federalist Party. Once again demonstrating his commercial orientation, he advocated a protective tariff and retirement of the national debt.

Fitzsimons spent most of the remainder of his life in private business, though he retained an interest in public affairs. His views remained essentially Federalist. During the maritime difficulties in the late 1790s, he urged retaliation against British and French interference with American shipping. In the first decade of the 19th century, he vigorously opposed Jefferson's embargo of 1807-9. In 1810, again clashing with the Jeffersonians, he championed the recharter of the First United States Bank.

But Fitzsimons's prominence stemmed from his business leadership. In 1781 he had been one of the founders of the Bank of North America. He also helped organize and held a directorship in the Insurance Company of North America and several times acted as president of the Philadelphia Chamber of Commerce. His financial affairs, like those somewhat earlier of his associate and fellow-signer Robert Morris, took a disastrous turn in 1805. He later regained some of his affluence, but his reputation suffered.

Despite these troubles, Fitzsimons never ceased his philanthropy. He was an outstanding supporter of Philadelphia's St. Augustine's Roman Catholic Church. He also strived to improve public education in the commonwealth and served as trustee of the University of Pennsylvania.

Fitzsimons died at Philadelphia in 1811 after seven decades of life. His tomb is there in the graveyard at St. Mary's Roman Catholic Church, which is in present Independence National Historical Park.

JARED INGERSOLL, PENNSYLVANIA

The son of Jared Ingersoll, Sr., a British colonial official and later prominent Loyalist, Ingersoll was born at New Haven, CT, in 1749. He received an excellent education and graduated from Yale in 1766. He then oversaw the financial affairs of his father, who had relocated from New Haven to Philadelphia. Later, the youth joined him, took up the study of law, and won admittance to the Pennsylvania bar.

In the midst of the Revolutionary fervor, which neither father nor son shared, in 1773, on the advice of the elder Ingersoll, Jared, Jr., sailed to London and studied law at the Middle Temple. Completing his work in 1776, he made a 2-year tour of the Continent, during which time for some reason he shed his Loyalist sympathies.

Returning to Philadelphia and entering the legal profession, Ingersoll attended to the clients of one of the city's leading lawyers and a family friend, Joseph Reed, who was then occupied with the affairs of the Supreme Executive Council of Pennsylvania. In 1781 Ingersoll married Elizabeth Pettit (Petit). The year before, he had entered politics by winning election to the Continental Congress (1780-81).

Although Ingersoll missed no sessions at the Constitutional Convention, had long favored revision of the Articles of Confederation, and as a lawyer was used to debate, he seldom spoke during the proceedings.

Subsequently, Ingersoll held a variety of public positions: member of the Philadelphia common council (1789); attorney general of Pennsylvania (1790-99 and 1811-17); Philadelphia city solicitor (1798-1801); U.S. District Attorney for Pennsylvania (1800-01); and presiding judge of the Philadelphia District Court (1821-22). Meantime, in 1812, he had been the Federalist Vice-Presidential candidate, but failed to win election.

While pursuing his public activities, Ingersoll attained distinction in his legal practice. For many years, he handled the affairs of Stephen Girard, one of the nation's leading businessmen. In 1791 Ingersoll began to practice before the U.S. Supreme Court and took part in some memorable cases.

Although in both Chisholm v. Georgia (1792) and Hylton v. United States (1796) he represented the losing side, his arguments helped to clarify difficult constitutional issues. He also represented fellow-signer William Blount, a senator, when he was threatened with impeachment in the late 1790s.

Ingersoll's long career ended in 1822, when he died less than a week after his 73d birthday. Survived by three children, he was buried in the cemetery of Philadelphia's First Presbyterian Church.

JAMES WILSON, PENNSYLVANIA

Wilson was born in 1741 or 1742 at Carskerdo, near St. Andrews, Scotland, and educated at the universities of St. Andrews, Glasgow, and Edinburgh. He then emigrated to America, arriving in the midst of the Stamp Act agitations in 1765. Early the next year, he accepted a position as Latin tutor at the College of Philadelphia (later part of the University of Pennsylvania) but almost immediately abandoned it to study law under John Dickinson.

In 1768, the year after his admission to the Philadelphia bar, Wilson set up practice at Reading, Pa. Two years later, he moved westward to the Scotch-Irish settlement of Carlisle, and the following year he took a bride, Rachel Bird. He specialized in land law and built up a broad clientele. On borrowed capital, he also began to speculate in land. In some way he managed, too, to lecture on English literature at the College of Philadelphia, which had awarded him an honorary master of arts degree in 1766.

Wilson became involved in Revolutionary politics. In 1774 he took over chairmanship of the Carlisle committee of correspondence, attended the first provincial assembly, and completed preparation of Considerations on the Nature and Extent of the Legislative Authority of the British Parliament.

This tract circulated widely in England and America and established him as a Whig leader.

The next year, Wilson was elected to both the provincial assembly and the Continental Congress, where he sat mainly on military and Indian affairs committees. In 1776, reflecting the wishes of his constituents, he joined the moderates in Congress voting for a 3-week delay in considering Richard Henry Lee's resolution of June 7 for independence. On the July 1 and 2 ballots on the issue, however, he voted in the affirmative and signed the Declaration of Independence on August 2.

Wilson's strenuous opposition to the republican Pennsylvania constitution of 1776, besides indicating a switch to conservatism on his part, led to his removal from Congress the following year. To avoid the clamor among his frontier constituents, he repaired to Annapolis during the winter of 1777-78 and then took up residence in Philadelphia.

Wilson affirmed his newly assumed political stance by closely identifying with the aristocratic and conservative republican groups, multiplying his business interests, and accelerating his land speculation. He also took a position as Advocate General for France in America (1779-83), dealing with commercial and maritime matters, and legally defended Loyalists and their sympathizers.

In the fall of 1779, during a period of inflation and food shortages, a mob which included many militiamen and was led by radical constitutionalists, set out to attack the republican leadership. Wilson was a prime target. He and some 35 of his colleagues barricaded themselves in his home at Third and Walnut Streets, thereafter known as "Fort Wilson." During a brief skirmish, several people on both sides were killed or wounded. The shock cooled sentiments and pardons were issued all around, though major political battles over the commonwealth constitution still lay ahead.

During 1781 Congress appointed Wilson as one of the directors of the Bank of North America, newly founded by his close associate and legal client Robert Morris. In 1782, by which time the conservatives had regained some of their power, the former was reelected to Congress, and he also served in the period 1785-87.

Wilson reached the apex of his career in the Constitutional Convention (1787), where his influence was probably second only to that of Madison. Rarely missing a session, he sat on the Committee of Detail and in many other ways applied his excellent knowledge of political theory to convention problems. Only Gouverneur Morris delivered more speeches.

That same year, overcoming powerful opposition, Wilson led the drive for ratification in Pennsylvania, the second state to endorse the instrument. The new commonwealth constitution, drafted in 1789-90 along the lines of the U.S. Constitution, was primarily Wilson's work and represented the climax of his 14-year fight against the constitution of 1776.

For his services in the formation of the federal government, though Wilson expected to be appointed Chief Justice of the Supreme Court, in 1789 President Washington named him as an associate justice. He was chosen that same year as the first law professor at the College of Philadelphia. Two years later he began an official digest of the laws of Pennsylvania, a project he never completed, though he carried on for a while after funds ran out.

Wilson, who wrote only a few opinions, did not achieve the success on the Supreme Court that his capabilities and experience promised. Indeed, during those years he was the object of much criticism and barely escaped impeachment. For one thing, he tried to influence the enactment of legislation in Pennsylvania favorable to land speculators. Between 1792 and 1795 he also made huge but unwise land investments in western New York and Pennsylvania, as well as in Georgia. This did not stop him from conceiving a grandiose but ill-fated scheme, involving vast sums of European capital, for the recruitment of European colonists and their settlement in the West. Meantime, in 1793, as a widower with six children, he remarried to Hannah Gray; their one son died in infancy.

Four years later, to avoid arrest for debt, the distraught Wilson moved from Philadelphia to Burlington, NJ. The next year, apparently while on federal circuit court business, he arrived at Edenton, NC, in a state of acute mental stress and was taken into the home of James Iredell, a fellow Supreme Court justice. He died there within a few months. Although first buried at Hayes Plantation near Edenton, his remains were later reinterred in the yard of Christ Church at Philadelphia.

GOUVERNEUR MORRIS, PENNSYLVANIA

Gouverneur Morris was born at Morrisania estate, in Westchester (present Bronx) County, NY, in 1752. His family was wealthy and enjoyed a long record of public service. His elder half-brother, Lewis, signed the Declaration of Independence.

Gouverneur was educated by private tutors and at a Huguenot school in New Rochelle. In early life, he lost a leg in a carriage accident. He attended King's College (later Columbia College and University) in New York City, graduating in 1768 at the age of 16. Three years later, after reading law in the city, he gained admission to the bar.

When the Revolution loomed on the horizon, Morris became interested in political affairs. Because of his conservatism, however, he at first feared the movement, which he believed would bring mob rule. Furthermore, some of his family and many of his friends were Loyalists. But, beginning in 1775, for some reason he sided with the Whigs. That same year, representing Westchester County, he took a seat in New York's Revolutionary provincial congress (1775-77). In 1776, when he also served in the militia, along with John Jay and Robert R. Livingston he drafted the first constitution of the state. Subsequently he joined its council of safety (1777).

In 1777-78 Morris sat in the legislature and in 1778-79 in the Continental Congress, where he numbered among the youngest and most brilliant members. During this period, he signed the Articles of Confederation and drafted instructions for Benjamin Franklin, in Paris, as well as those that provided a partial basis for the treaty ending the War for Independence. Morris was also a close friend of Washington and one of his strongest congressional supporters.

Defeated in his bid for reelection to Congress in 1779 because of the opposition of Gov. George Clinton's faction, Morris relocated to Philadelphia and resumed the practice of law. This temporarily removed him from the political scene, but in 1781 he resumed his public career when he became the principal assistant to Robert Morris, Superintendent of Finance for the United States, to whom he was unrelated. Gouverneur held this position for 4 years.

Morris emerged as one of the leading figures at the Constitutional Convention. IIis speeches, more frequent than those by anyone else, numbered 173. Although sometimes presented in a light vein, they were usually substantive. A strong advocate of nationalism and aristocratic rule, he served on many committees, including those on postponed matters and style, and stood in the thick of the decision-making process. Above all, it was apparently he who actually drafted the Constitution. Morris subsequently left public life for a time to devote his attention to business. Having purchased the family home from his half-brother, Lewis, he moved back to New York. Afterward, in 1789, Gouverneur joined in a business venture with Robert Morris, and traveled to France, where he witnessed the beginnings of the French Revolution.

Morris was to remain in Europe for about a decade. In 1790-91 he undertook a diplomatic mission to London to try to negotiate some of the outstanding problems between the United States and Great Britain. The mission failed, but in 1792 Washington appointed him as Minister to France, to replace Thomas Jefferson. Morris was recalled 2 years later but did not come home. Instead, he traveled extensively in Europe for more than 4 years, during which time he handled his complicated business affairs and contemplated the complex political situation.

Morris returned to the United States in 1799. The next year, he was elected to finish an unexpired term in the U.S. Senate. An ardent Federalist, he was defeated in his bid for reelection in 1802 and left office the following year.

Morris retired to a glittering life at Morrisania, where he had built a new residence. In 1809 he married Anne Cary (Carey) Randolph of Virginia, and they had one son. During his last years, he continued to speak out against the Democratic-Republicans and violently opposed the War of 1812. In the years 1810-13 he served as chairman of the Erie Canal Commission.

Morris died at Morrisania in 1816 at the age of 64 and was buried at St. Anne's Episcopal Churchyard, in the Bronx, New York City.

The Three Branches of the United States Government

The Executive Branch

The power of the Executive Branch is vested in the President of the United States, who also acts as head of state and Commander-in-Chief of the armed forces. The President is responsible for implementing and enforcing the laws written by Congress and, to that end, appoints the heads of the federal agencies, including the Cabinet. The Vice President is also part of the Executive Branch, ready to assume the Presidency should the need arise.

The Cabinet and independent federal agencies are responsible for the day-to-day enforcement and administration of federal laws. These departments and agencies have missions and responsibilities as widely divergent as those of the Department of Defense and the Environmental Protection Agency, the Social Security Administration and the Securities and Exchange Commission.

Including members of the armed forces, the Executive Branch employs more than 4 million Americans.

THE PRESIDENT

The President is both the head of state and head of government of the United States of America, and Commander-in-Chief of the armed forces.

Under Article II of the Constitution, the President is responsible for the execution and enforcement of the laws created by Congress. Fifteen executive departments — each led by an appointed member of the President's Cabinet — carry out the day-to-day administration of the federal government. They are joined in this by other executive agencies such as the CIA and Environmental Protection Agency, the heads of which are not part of the Cabinet, but who are under the full authority of the President. The President also appoints the heads of more than 50 independent federal commissions, such as the Federal Reserve Board or the Securities and Exchange Commission, as well as federal judges, ambassadors, and other federal offices. The Executive Office of the President (EOP) consists of the immediate staff to the President, along with entities such as the Office of Management and Budget and the Office of the United States Trade Representative.

The President has the power either to sign legislation into law or to veto bills enacted by Congress, although Congress may override a veto with a two-thirds vote of both houses. The Executive Branch conducts diplomacy with other nations, and the President has the power to negotiate and sign treaties, which also must be ratified by two-thirds of the Senate. The President can issue executive orders, which direct executive officers or clarify and further existing laws. The President also has unlimited power to extend pardons and clemencies for federal crimes, except in cases of impeachment.

With these powers come several responsibilities, among them a constitutional requirement to "from time to time give to the Congress Information of the State of the Union, and recommend to their Consideration such Measures as he shall judge necessary and expedient." Although the President may fulfill this requirement in any way he or she chooses, Presidents have traditionally given a State of the Union address to a joint session of Congress each January (except in inaugural years) outlining their agenda for the coming year.

The Constitution lists only three qualifications for the Presidency — the President must be 35 years of age, be a natural born citizen, and must have lived in the United States for at least 14 years. And though millions of Americans vote in a presidential election every four years, the President is not, in fact, directly elected by the people. Instead, on the first Tuesday in November of every fourth year, the people elect the members of the Electoral College. Apportioned by population to the 50 states — one for each member of their congressional delegation (with the District of Columbia receiving 3 votes) — these Electors then cast the votes for President. There are currently 538 electors in the Electoral College.

President Barack Obama is the 44th President of the United States. He is, however, only the 43rd person ever to serve as President; President Grover Cleveland served two nonconsecutive terms, and thus is recognized as both the 22nd and the 24th President. Today, the President is limited to two four-year terms, but until the 22nd Amendment to the Constitution, ratified in 1951, a President could serve an unlimited number of terms. Franklin Delano Roosevelt was elected President four times, serving from 1932 until his death in 1945; he is the only President ever to have served more than two terms.

By tradition, the President and the First Family live in the White House in Washington, D.C., also the location of the President's Oval Office and the offices of the his senior staff. When the President travels by plane, his aircraft is designated Air Force One; he may also use a Marine Corps helicopter, known as Marine One while the President is on board. For ground travel, the President uses an armored Presidential limousine.

THE VICE PRESIDENT

The primary responsibility of the Vice President of the United States is to be ready at a moment's notice to assume the Presidency if the President is unable to perform his duties. This can be because of the President's death, resignation, or temporary incapacitation, or if the Vice President and a majority of the Cabinet judge that the President is no longer able to discharge the duties of the presidency.

The Vice President is elected along with the President by the Electoral College — each elector casts one vote for President and another for Vice President. Before the ratification of the 12th Amendment in 1804, electors only voted for President, and the person who received the second greatest number of votes became Vice President.

The Vice President also serves as the President of the United States Senate, where he or she casts the deciding vote in the case of a tie. Except in the case of tiebreaking votes, the Vice President rarely actually presides over the Senate. Instead, the Senate selects one of their own members, usually junior members of the majority party, to preside over the Senate each day.

Joseph R. Biden is the 47th Vice President of the United States. Of the 45 previous Vice Presidents, nine have succeeded to the Presidency, and four have been elected to the Presidency in their own right. The duties of the Vice President, outside of those enumerated in the Constitution, are at the discretion of the current President. Each Vice President approaches the role differently — some take on a specific policy portfolio, others serve simply as a top adviser to the President.

The Vice President has an office in the West Wing of the White House, as well as in the nearby Eisenhower Executive Office Building. Like the President, he also maintains an official residence, at the United States Naval Observatory in Northwest Washington, D.C. This peaceful mansion, has been the official home of the Vice President since 1974 — previously, Vice Presidents had lived in their own private residences. The Vice President also has his own limousine, operated by the United States Secret Service, and flies on the same aircraft the President uses — but when the Vice President is aboard, the craft are referred to as Air Force Two and Marine Two.

EXECUTIVE OFFICE OF THE PRESIDENT

Every day, the President of the United States is faced with scores of decisions, each with important consequences for America's future. To provide the President with the support the he or she needs to govern effectively, the Executive Office of the President (EOP) was created in 1939 by President Franklin D. Roosevelt. The EOP has responsibility for tasks ranging from communicating the President's message to the American people to promoting our trade interests abroad.

The EOP, overseen by the White House Chief of Staff, has traditionally been home to many of the President's closest advisers. While Senate confirmation is required for some advisers, such as the Director of the Office of Management and Budget, most are appointed with full Presidential discretion. The individual offices that these advisors oversee have grown in size and number since the EOP was created. Some were formed by Congress, others as the President has needed them — they are constantly shifting as each President identifies his needs and priorities, with the current EOP employing over 1,800 people.

Perhaps the most visible parts of the EOP are the White House Communications Office and Press Secretary's Office. The Press Secretary provides daily briefings for the media on the President's activities and agenda. Less visible to most Americans is the National Security Council, which advises the President on foreign policy, intelligence, and national security.

There are also a number of offices responsible for the practicalities of maintaining the White House and providing logistical support for the President. These include the White House Military Office, which is responsible for services ranging from Air Force One to the dining facilities, and the Office of Presidential Advance, which prepares sites remote from the White House for the President's arrival.

Many senior advisors in the EOP work near the President in the West Wing of the White House. However, the majority of the staff is housed in the Eisenhower Executive Office Building, just a few steps away and part of the White House compound.

THE CABINET

The Cabinet is an advisory body made up of the heads of the 15 executive departments. Appointed by the President and confirmed by the Senate, the members of the Cabinet are often the President's closest confidants. In addition to running major federal agencies, they play an important role in the Presidential line of succession — after the Vice President, Speaker of the House, and Senate President pro tempore, the line of succession continues with the Cabinet offices in the order in which the departments were created. All the members of the Cabinet take the title Secretary, excepting the head of the Justice Department, who is styled Attorney General.

Department of Agriculture

The U.S. Department of Agriculture (USDA) develops and executes policy on farming, agriculture, and food. Its aims include meeting the needs of farmers and ranchers, promoting agricultural trade and production, assuring food safety, protecting natural resources, fostering rural communities, and ending hunger in America and abroad.

The USDA employs more than 100,000 employees and has an annual budget of approximately $95 billion. It consists of 17 agencies, including the Animal and Plant Health Inspection Service, the Food and Nutrition Service, and the Forest Service. The bulk of the department's budget goes towards mandatory programs that provide services required by law, such as programs designed to provide nutrition assistance, promote agricultural exports, and conserve our environment. The USDA also plays an important role in overseas aid programs by providing surplus foods to developing countries.

The United States Secretary of Agriculture administers the USDA.

Department of Commerce

The Department of Commerce is the government agency tasked with improving living standards for all Americans by promoting economic development and technological innovation.

The department supports U.S. business and industry through a number of services, including gathering economic and demographic data, issuing patents and trademarks, improving understanding of the environment and oceanic life, and ensuring the effective use of scientific and technical resources. The agency also formulates telecommunications and technology policy, and promotes U.S. exports by assisting and enforcing international trade agreements.

The Secretary of Commerce oversees a $6.5 billion budget and approximately 38,000 employees.

Department of Defense

The mission of the Department of Defense (DOD) is to provide the military forces needed to deter war and to protect the security of our country. The department's headquarters is at the Pentagon.

The DOD consists of the Departments of the Army, Navy, and Air Force, as well as many agencies, offices, and commands, including the Joint Chiefs of Staff, the Pentagon Force Protection Agency, the National Security Agency, and the Defense Intelligence Agency. The DOD occupies the vast majority of the Pentagon building in Arlington, VA.

The Department of Defense is the largest government agency, with more than 1.3 million men and women on active duty, nearly 700,000 civilian personnel, and 1.1 million citizens who serve in the National Guard and Reserve forces. Together, the military and civilian arms of DOD protect national interests through war-fighting, providing humanitarian aid, and performing peacekeeping and disaster relief services.

Department of Education

The mission of the Department of Education is to promote student achievement and preparation for competition in a global economy by fostering educational excellence and ensuring equal access to educational opportunity.

The Department administers federal financial aid for education, collects data on America's schools to guide improvements in education quality, and works to complement the efforts of state and local governments, parents, and students.

The U.S. Secretary of Education oversees the Department's 4,200 employees and $68.6 billion budget.

Department of Energy

The mission of the Department of Energy (DOE) is to advance the national, economic, and energy security of the United States.

The DOE promotes America's energy security by encouraging the development of reliable, clean, and affordable energy. It administers federal funding for scientific research to further the goal of discovery and innovation — ensuring American economic competitiveness and improving the quality of life for Americans.

The DOE is also tasked with ensuring America's nuclear security, and with protecting the environment by providing a responsible resolution to the legacy of nuclear weapons production.

The United States Secretary of Energy oversees a budget of approximately $23 billion and more than 100,000 federal and contract employees.

Department of Health and Human Services

The Department of Health and Human Services (HHS) is the United States government's principal agency for protecting the health of all Americans and providing essential human services, especially for those who are least able to help themselves. Agencies of HHS conduct health and social science research, work to prevent disease outbreaks, assure food and drug safety, and provide health insurance.

In addition to administering Medicare and Medicaid, which together provide health insurance to one in four Americans, HHS also oversees the National Institutes of Health, the Food and Drug Administration, and the Centers for Disease Control.

The Secretary of Health and Human Services oversees a budget of approximately $700 billion and approximately 65,000 employees. The Department's programs are administered by 11 operating divisions, including 8 agencies in the U.S. Public Health Service and 3 human services agencies.

Department of Homeland Security

The missions of the Department of Homeland Security are to prevent and disrupt terrorist attacks; protect the American people, our critical infrastructure, and key resources; and respond to and recover from incidents that do occur. The third largest Cabinet department, DHS was established by the Homeland Security Act of 2002, largely in response to the terrorist attacks on September 11, 2001. The new department consolidated 22 executive branch agencies, including the U.S. Customs Service, the U.S. Coast Guard, the U.S. Secret Service, the Transportation Security Administration, and the Federal Emergency Management Agency.

DHS employs 216,000 people in its mission to patrol borders, protect travelers and our transportation infrastructure, enforce immigration laws, and respond to disasters and emergencies. The agency also promotes preparedness and emergency prevention among citizens. Policy is coordinated by the Homeland Security Council at the White House, in cooperation with other defense and intelligence agencies, and led by the Assistant to the President for Homeland Security.

Department of Housing and Urban Development

The Department of Housing and Urban Development (HUD) is the federal agency responsible for national policies and programs that address America's housing needs, that improve and develop the nation's communities, and that enforce fair housing laws. The Department plays a major role in supporting homeownership for lower- and moderate-income families through its mortgage insurance and rent subsidy programs.

Offices within HUD include the Federal Housing Administration, which provides mortgage and loan insurance; the Office of Fair Housing and Equal Opportunity, which ensures all Americans equal access to the housing of their choice; and the Community Development Block Grant Program, which helps communities with economic development, job opportunities, and housing rehabilitation. HUD also administers public housing and homeless assistance.

The Secretary of Housing and Urban Development oversees approximately 9,000 employees on a budget of approximately $40 billion.

Department of the Interior

The Department of the Interior (DOI) is the nation's principal conservation agency. Its mission is to protect America's natural resources, offer recreation opportunities, conduct scientific research, conserve and protect fish and wildlife, and honor our trust responsibilities to American Indians, Alaskan Natives, and our responsibilities to island communities.

DOI manages 500 million acres of surface land, or about one-fifth of the land in the United States, and manages hundreds of dams and reservoirs. Agencies within the DOI include the

Bureau of Indian Affairs, the Minerals Management Service, and the U.S. Geological Survey. The DOI manages the national parks and is tasked with protecting endangered species.

The Secretary of the Interior oversees about 70,000 employees and 200,000 volunteers on a budget of approximately $16 billion. Every year it raises billions in revenue from energy, mineral, grazing, and timber leases, as well as recreational permits and land sales.

Department of Justice

The mission of the Department of Justice (DOJ) is to enforce the law and defend the interests of the United States according to the law; to ensure public safety against threats foreign and domestic; to provide federal leadership in preventing and controlling crime; to seek just punishment for those guilty of unlawful behavior; and to ensure fair and impartial administration of justice for all Americans.

The DOJ is comprised of 40 component organizations, including the Drug Enforcement Administration, the Federal Bureau of Investigation, the U.S. Marshals, and the Federal Bureau of Prisons. The Attorney General is the head of the DOJ and chief law enforcement officer of the federal government. The Attorney General represents the United States in legal matters, advises the President and the heads of the executive departments of the government, and occasionally appears in person before the Supreme Court.

With a budget of approximately $25 billion, the DOJ is the world's largest law office and the central agency for the enforcement of federal laws.

Department of Labor

The Department of Labor oversees federal programs for ensuring a strong American workforce. These programs address job training, safe working conditions, minimum hourly wage and overtime pay, employment discrimination, and unemployment insurance.

The Department of Labor's mission is to foster and promote the welfare of the job seekers, wage earners, and retirees of the United States by improving their working conditions, advancing their opportunities for profitable employment, protecting their retirement and health care benefits, helping employers find workers, strengthening free collective bargaining, and tracking changes in employment, prices, and other national economic measurements.

Offices within the Department of Labor include the Bureau of Labor Statistics, the federal government's principal statistics agency for labor economics, and the Occupational Safety & Health Administration, which promotes the safety and health of America's working men and women.

The Secretary of Labor oversees 15,000 employees on a budget of approximately $50 billion.

Department of State

The Department of State plays the lead role in developing and implementing the President's foreign policy. Major responsibilities include United States representation abroad, foreign assistance, foreign military training programs, countering international crime, and a wide assortment of services to U.S. citizens and foreign nationals seeking entrance to the U.S.

The U.S. maintains diplomatic relations with approximately 180 countries — each posted by civilian U.S. Foreign Service

129

employees — as well as with international organizations. At home, more than 5,000 civil employees carry out the mission of the Department.

The Secretary of State serves as the President's top foreign policy adviser, and oversees 30,000 employees and a budget of approximately $35 billion.

Department of Transportation

The mission of the Department of Transportation (DOT) is to ensure a fast, safe, efficient, accessible and convenient transportation system that meets our vital national interests and enhances the quality of life of the American people.

Organizations within the DOT include the Federal Highway Administration, the Federal Aviation Administration, the National Highway Traffic Safety Administration, the Federal Transit Administration, the Federal Railroad Administration and the Maritime Administration.

The U.S. Secretary of Transportation oversees approximately 55,000 employees and a budget of approximately $70 billion.

Department of the Treasury

The Department of the Treasury is responsible for promoting economic prosperity and ensuring the soundness and security of the U.S. and international financial systems.

The Department operates and maintains systems that are critical to the nation's financial infrastructure, such as the production of coin and currency, the disbursement of payments to the American public, the collection of taxes, and the borrowing of funds necessary to run the federal government. The Department works with other federal agencies, foreign governments, and international financial institutions to encourage global economic growth, raise standards of living, and, to the extent possible, predict and prevent economic and financial crises. The Treasury Department also performs a critical and far-reaching role in enhancing national security by improving the safeguards of our financial systems, implementing economic sanctions against foreign threats to the U.S., and identifying and targeting the financial support networks of national security threats.

The Secretary of the Treasury oversees a budget of approximately $13 billion and a staff of more than 100,000 employees.

Department of Veterans Affairs

The Department of Veterans Affairs is responsible for administering benefit programs for veterans, their families, and their survivors. These benefits include pension, education, disability compensation, home loans, life insurance, vocational rehabilitation, survivor support, medical care, and burial benefits. Veterans Affairs became a cabinet-level department in 1989.

Of the 25 million veterans currently alive, nearly three of every four served during a war or an official period of hostility. About a quarter of the nation's population — approximately 70 million people — are potentially eligible for V.A. benefits and services because they are veterans, family members, or survivors of veterans.

The Secretary of Veterans Affairs oversees a budget of approximately $90 billion and a staff of approximately 235,000 employees.

THE LEGISLATIVE BRANCH

Established by Article I of the Constitution, the Legislative Branch consists of the House of Representatives and the Senate, which together form the United States Congress. The Constitution grants Congress the sole authority to enact legislation and declare war, the right to confirm or reject many Presidential appointments, and substantial investigative powers.

The House of Representatives is made up of 435 elected members, divided among the 50 states in proportion to their total population. In addition, there are 6 non-voting members, representing the District of Columbia, the Commonwealth of Puerto Rico, and four other territories of the United States. The presiding officer of the chamber is the Speaker of the House, elected by the Representatives. He or she is third in the line of succession to the Presidency.

Members of the House are elected every two years and must be 25 years of age, a U.S. citizen for at least seven years, and a resident of the state (but not necessarily the district) they represent.

The House has several powers assigned exclusively to it, including the power to initiate revenue bills, impeach federal officials, and elect the President in the case of an electoral college tie.

The Senate is composed of 100 Senators, 2 for each state. Until the ratification of the 17th Amendment in 1913, Senators were chosen by state legislatures, not by popular vote. Since then, they have been elected to six-year terms by the people of each state. Senator's terms are staggered so that about one-third of the Senate is up for reelection every two years. Senators must be 30 years of age, U.S. citizens for at least nine years, and residents of the state they represent.

The Vice President of the United States serves as President of the Senate and may cast the decisive vote in the event of a tie in the Senate.

The Senate has the sole power to confirm those of the President's appointments that require consent, and to ratify treaties. There are, however, two exceptions to this rule: the House must also approve appointments to the Vice Presidency and any treaty that involves foreign trade. The Senate also tries impeachment cases for federal officials referred to it by the House.

In order to pass legislation and send it to the President for his signature, both the House and the Senate must pass the same bill by majority vote. If the President vetoes a bill, they may override his veto by passing the bill again in each chamber with at least two-thirds of each body voting in favor.

THE LEGISLATIVE PROCESS

The first step in the legislative process is the introduction of a bill to Congress. Anyone can write it, but only members of Congress can introduce legislation. Some important bills are traditionally introduced at the request of the President, such as the annual federal budget. During the legislative process, however, the initial bill can undergo drastic changes.

After being introduced, a bill is referred to the appropriate committee for review. There are 17 Senate committees, with 70 subcommittees, and 23 House committees, with 104 subcommittees. The committees are not set in stone, but change in number and form with each new Congress as required for the efficient consideration of legislation. Each committee oversees a specific policy area, and the subcommittees take on more specialized policy areas. For example, the House Committee on Ways and Means includes subcommittees on Social Security and Trade.

A bill is first considered in a subcommittee, where it may be accepted, amended, or rejected entirely. If the members of the subcommittee agree to move a bill forward, it is reported to the full committee, where the process is repeated again. Throughout this stage of the process, the committees and subcommittees call hearings to investigate the merits and flaws of the bill. They invite experts, advocates, and opponents to appear before the committee and provide testimony, and can compel people to appear using subpoena power if necessary.

If the full committee votes to approve the bill, it is reported to the floor of the House or Senate, and the majority party leadership decides when to place the bill on the calendar for consideration. If a bill is particularly pressing, it may be considered right away. Others may wait for months or never be scheduled at all.

When the bill comes up for consideration, the House has a very structured debate process. Each member who wishes to speak only has a few minutes, and the number and kind of amendments are usually limited. In the Senate, debate on most bills is unlimited — Senators may speak to issues other than the bill under consideration during their speeches, and any amendment can be introduced. Senators can use this to filibuster bills under consideration, a procedure by which a Senator delays a vote on a bill — and by extension its passage — by refusing to stand down. A supermajority of 60 Senators can break a filibuster by invoking cloture, or the cession of debate on the bill, and forcing a vote. Once debate is over, the votes of a simple majority passes the bill.

A bill must pass both houses of Congress before it goes to the President for consideration. Though the Constitution requires that the two bills have the exact same wording, this rarely happens in practice. To bring the bills into alignment, a Conference Committee is convened, consisting of members from both chambers. The members of the committee produce a conference report, intended as the final version of the bill. Each chamber then votes again to approve the conference report. Depending on where the bill originated, the final text is then enrolled by either the Clerk of the House or the Secretary of the Senate, and presented to the Speaker of the House and the President of the Senate for their signatures. The bill is then sent to the President.

When receiving a bill from Congress, the President has several options. If the President agrees substantially with the bill, he or she may sign it into law, and the bill is then printed in the Statutes at Large. If the President believes the law to be bad policy, he may veto it and send it back to Congress. Congress may override the veto with a two-thirds vote of each chamber, at which point the bill becomes law and is printed.

There are two other options that the President may exercise. If Congress is in session and the President takes no action within 10 days, the bill becomes law. If Congress adjourns before 10 days are up and the President takes no action, then the bill dies and Congress may not vote to override. This is called a pocket veto, and if Congress still wants to pass the legislation, they must begin the entire process anew.

POWERS OF CONGRESS

Congress, as one of the three coequal branches of government, is ascribed significant powers by the Constitution. All legislative power in the government is vested in Congress, meaning that it is the only part of the government that can make new laws or change existing laws. Executive Branch agencies issue regulations with the full force of law, but these are only under the authority of laws enacted by Congress. The President may veto bills Congress passes, but Congress may also override a veto by a two-thirds vote in both the Senate and the House of Representatives.

Article I of the Constitution enumerates the powers of Congress and the specific areas in which it may legislate. Congress is also empowered to enact laws deemed "necessary and proper" for the execution of the powers given to any part of the government under the Constitution.

Part of Congress's exercise of legislative authority is the establishment of an annual budget for the government. To this end, Congress levies taxes and tariffs to provide funding for essential government services. If enough money cannot be raised to fund the government, then Congress may also authorize borrowing to make up the difference. Congress can also mandate spending on specific items: legislatively directed spending, commonly known as "earmarks," specifies funds for a particular project, rather than for a government agency.

Both chambers of Congress have extensive investigative powers, and may compel the production of evidence or testimony toward whatever end they deem necessary. Members of Congress spend much of their time holding hearings and investigations in committee. Refusal to cooperate with a Congressional subpoena can result in charges of contempt of Congress, which could result in a prison term.

The Senate maintains several powers to itself: It ratifies treaties by a two-thirds supermajority vote and confirms the appointments of the President by a majority vote. The consent of the House of Representatives is also necessary for the ratification of trade agreements and the confirmation of the Vice President.

Congress also holds the sole power to declare war.

GOVERNMENT OVERSIGHT

Oversight of the executive branch is an important Congressional check on the President's power and a balance against his discretion in implementing laws and making regulations.

A major way that Congress conducts oversight is through hearings. The House Committee on Oversight and Government Reform and the Senate Committee on Homeland Security and Government Affairs are both devoted to overseeing and reforming government operations, and each committee conducts oversight in its policy area.

Congress also maintains an investigative organization, the Government Accountability Office (GAO). Founded in 1921 as the General Accounting Office, its original mission was to audit the budgets and financial statements sent to Congress by the Secretary of the Treasury and the Director of the Office of Management and Budget. Today, the GAO audits and generates reports on every aspect of the government, ensuring that taxpayer dollars are spent with the effectiveness and efficiency that the American people deserve.

The executive branch also polices itself: Sixty-four Inspectors General, each responsible for a different agency, regularly audit and report on the agencies to which they are attached.

THE JUDICIAL BRANCH

Where the Executive and Legislative branches are elected by the people, members of the Judicial Branch are appointed by the President and confirmed by the Senate.

Article III of the Constitution, which establishes the Judicial Branch, leaves Congress significant discretion to determine the shape and structure of the federal judiciary. Even the number of Supreme Court Justices is left to Congress — at times there have been as few as six, while the current number (nine, with one Chief Justice and eight Associate Justices) has only been in place since 1869. The Constitution also grants Congress the power to establish courts inferior to the Supreme Court, and to that end Congress has established the United States district courts, which try most federal cases, and 13 United States courts of appeals, which review appealed district court cases.

Federal judges can only be removed through impeachment by the House of Representatives and conviction in the Senate. Judges and justices serve no fixed term — they serve until their death, retirement, or conviction by the Senate. By design, this insulates them from the temporary passions of the public, and allows them to apply the law with only justice in mind, and not electoral or political concerns.

Generally, Congress determines the jurisdiction of the federal courts. In some cases, however — such as in the example of a dispute between two or more U.S. states — the Constitution grants the Supreme Court original jurisdiction, an authority that cannot be stripped by Congress.

The courts only try actual cases and controversies — a party must show that it has been harmed in order to bring suit in court. This means that the courts do not issue advisory opinions on the constitutionality of laws or the legality of actions if the ruling would have no practical effect. Cases brought before the judiciary typically proceed from district court to appellate court and may even end at the Supreme Court, although the Supreme Court hears comparatively few cases each year.

Federal courts enjoy the sole power to interpret the law, determine the constitutionality of the law, and apply it to individual cases. The courts, like Congress, can compel the production of evidence and testimony through the use of a subpoena. The inferior courts are constrained by the decisions of the Supreme Court — once the Supreme Court interprets a law, inferior courts must apply the Supreme Court's interpretation to the facts of a particular case.

THE SUPREME COURT OF THE UNITED STATES

The Supreme Court of the United States is the highest court in the land and the only part of the federal judiciary specifically required by the Constitution.

The Constitution does not stipulate the number of Supreme Court Justices; the number is set instead by Congress. There have been as few as six, but since 1869 there have been nine Justices, including one Chief Justice. All Justices are nominated by the President, confirmed by the Senate, and hold their offices under life tenure. Since Justices do not have to run or campaign for re-election, they are thought to be insulated from political pressure when deciding cases. Justices may remain in office until they resign, pass away, or are impeached and convicted by Congress.

The Court's caseload is almost entirely appellate in nature, and the Court's decisions cannot be appealed to any authority, as it is the final judicial arbiter in the United States on matters of federal law. However, the Court may consider appeals from the highest state courts or from federal appellate courts. The Court also has original jurisdiction in cases involving ambassadors and other diplomats, and in cases between states.

Although the Supreme Court may hear an appeal on any question of law provided it has jurisdiction, it usually does not hold trials. Instead, the Court's task is to interpret the meaning of a law, to decide whether a law is relevant to a particular set of facts, or to rule on how a law should be applied. Lower courts are obligated to follow the precedent set by the Supreme Court when rendering decisions.

In almost all instances, the Supreme Court does not hear appeals as a matter of right; instead, parties must petition the Court for a writ of certiorari. It is the Court's custom and practice to "grant cert" if four of the nine Justices decide that they should hear the case. Of the approximately 7,500 requests for certiorari filed each year, the Court usually grants cert to fewer than 150. These are typically cases that the Court considers sufficiently important to require their review; a common example is the occasion when two or more of the federal courts of appeals have ruled differently on the same question of federal law.

If the Court grants certiorari, Justices accept legal briefs from the parties to the case, as well as from amicus curiae, or "friends of the court." These can include industry trade groups, academics, or even the U.S. government itself. Before issuing a ruling, the Supreme Court usually hears oral arguments, where the various parties to the suit present their arguments and the Justices ask them questions. If the case involves the federal government, the Solicitor General of the United States presents arguments on behalf of the United States. The Justices then hold private conferences, make their decision, and (often after a period of several months) issue the Court's opinion, along with any dissenting arguments that may have been written.

THE JUDICIAL PROCESS

Article III of the Constitution of the United States guarantees that every person accused of wrongdoing has the right to a fair trial before a competent judge and a jury of one's peers.

The Fourth, Fifth, and Sixth Amendments to the Constitution provide additional protections for those accused of a crime. These include:

- A guarantee that no person shall be deprived of life, liberty, or property without the due process of law
- Protection against being tried for the same crime twice ("double jeopardy")
- The right to a speedy trial by an impartial jury
- The right to cross-examine witnesses, and to call witnesses to support their case
- The right to legal representation
- The right to avoid self-incrimination
- Protection from excessive bail, excessive fines, and cruel and unusual punishments

Criminal proceedings can be conducted under either state or federal law, depending on the nature and extent of the crime. A criminal legal procedure typically begins with an arrest by a law enforcement officer. If a grand jury chooses to deliver an indictment, the accused will appear before a judge and be formally charged with a crime, at which time he or she may enter a plea.

The defendant is given time to review all the evidence in the case and to build a legal argument. Then, the case is brought to trial and decided by a jury. If the defendant is determined to be not guilty of the crime, the charges are dismissed. Otherwise, the judge determines the sentence, which can include prison time, a fine, or even execution.

Civil cases are similar to criminal ones, but instead of arbitrating between the state and a person or organization, they deal with disputes between individuals or organizations. If a party believes that it has been wronged, it can file suit in civil court to attempt to have that wrong remedied through an order to cease and desist, alter behavior, or award monetary damages. After the suit is filed and evidence is gathered and presented by both sides, a trial proceeds as in a criminal case. If the parties involved waive their right to a jury trial, the case can be decided by a judge; otherwise, the case is decided and damages awarded by a jury.

After a criminal or civil case is tried, it may be appealed to a higher court — a federal court of appeals or state appellate court. A litigant who files an appeal, known as an "appellant," must show that the trial court or administrative agency made a legal error that affected the outcome of the case. An appellate court makes its decision based on the record of the case established by the trial court or agency — it does not receive additional evidence or hear witnesses. It may also review the factual findings of the trial court or agency, but typically may only overturn a trial outcome on factual grounds if the findings were "clearly erroneous." If a defendant is found not guilty in a criminal proceeding, he or she cannot be retried on the same set of facts.

Federal appeals are decided by panels of three judges. The appellant presents legal arguments to the panel, in a written document called a "brief." In the brief, the appellant tries to persuade the judges that the trial court made an error, and that the lower decision should be reversed. On the other hand, the party defending against the appeal, known as the "appellee" or "respondent," tries in its brief to show why the trial court decision was correct, or why any errors made by the trial court are not significant enough to affect the outcome of the case.

The court of appeals usually has the final word in the case, unless it sends the case back to the trial court for additional proceedings. In some cases the decision may be reviewed en banc — that is, by a larger group of judges of the court of appeals for the circuit.

A litigant who loses in a federal court of appeals, or in the highest court of a state, may file a petition for a "writ of certiorari," which is a document asking the Supreme Court to review the case. The Supreme Court, however, is not obligated to grant review. The Court typically will agree to hear a case only when it involves a new and important legal principle, or when two or more federal appellate courts have interpreted a law differently. (There are also special circumstances in which the Supreme Court is required by law to hear an appeal.) When the Supreme Court hears a case, the parties are required to file written briefs and the Court may hear oral argument.

PRESIDENTS OF THE UNITED STATES OF AMERICA

1. GEORGE WASHINGTON (1789-1797)
2. JOHN ADAMS (1797-1801)
3. THOMAS JEFFERSON (1801-1809)
4. JAMES MADISON (1809-1817)
5. JAMES MONROE (1817-1825)
6. JOHN QUINCY ADAMS (1825-1829)
7. ANDREW JACKSON (1829-1837)
8. MARTIN VAN BUREN (1837-1841)
9. WILLIAM HENRY HARRISON (1841)
10. JOHN TYLER (1841-1845)
11. JAMES K. POLK (1845-1849)
12. ZACHARY TAYLOR (1849-1850)
13. MILLARD FILLMORE (1850-1853)
14. FRANKLIN PIERCE (1853-1857)
15. JAMES BUCHANAN (1857-1861)
16. ABRAHAM LINCOLN (1861-1865)
17. ANDREW JOHNSON (1865-1869)
18. ULYSSES S. GRANT (1869 – 1877)
19. RUTHERFORD B. HAYES (1877-1881)
20. JAMES A. GARFIELD (1881)
21. CHESTER A. ARTHUR (1881-1885)
22. GROVER CLEVELAND (1885-1889)
23. BENJAMIN HARRISON (1889-1893)

24. GROVER CLEVELAND (1893-1897)

25. WILLIAM MCKINLEY (1897-1901)

26. THEODORE ROOSEVELT (1901-1909)

27. WILLIAM HOWARD TAFT (1909-1913)

28. WOODROW WILSON (1913-1921)

29. WARREN G. HARDING (1921-1923)

30. CALVIN COOLIDGE (1923-1929)

31. HERBERT HOOVER (1929-1933)

32. FRANKLIN D. ROOSEVELT (1933-1945)

33. HARRY S. TRUMAN (1945-1953)

34. DWIGHT D. EISENHOWER (1953-1961)

35. JOHN F. KENNEDY (1961-1963)

36. LYNDON B. JOHNSON (1963-1969).

37. RICHARD M. NIXON (1969-1974)

38. GERALD R. FORD (1974-1977)

39. JIMMY CARTER (1977-1981)

40. RONALD REAGAN (1981-1989)

41. GEORGE H.W. BUSH (1989-1993)

42. BILL CLINTON (1993-2001)

43. GEORGE W. BUSH (2001-2009)

44. BARACK OBAMA (2009-2017)

45. DONALD J. TRUMP (2017-)

1. George Washington (1789-1797)

George Washington 1789-1797

Born: February 22, 1732, Pope's Creek, Virginia
Nickname: "Father of His Country"
Education: The equivalent of an elementary school education
Religion: Episcopalian
Marriage: January 6, 1759, to Martha Dandridge Custis (1731–1802)
Children: None
Career: Soldier, Planter
Political Party: Federalist
Died: December 14, 1799, Mount Vernon, Virginia

George Washington was born into a mildly prosperous Virginia farming family in 1732. After his father died when George was eleven, George's mother, Mary, a tough and driven woman, struggled to hold their home together with the help of her two sons from a previous marriage. Although he never received more than an elementary school education, young George displayed a gift for mathematics. This knack for numbers combined with his quiet confidence and ambition caught the attention of Lord Fairfax, head of one of the most powerful families in Virginia. While working for Lord Fairfax as a surveyor at the age of sixteen, the young Washington traveled deep into the American wilderness for weeks at a time.

British Army Service

Tragedy struck the young man with the death of his half brother Lawrence, who had guided and mentored George after his father's death. George inherited Mount Vernon from his brother, living there for the rest of his life. At the time, England and France were enemies in America, vying for control of the Ohio River Valley. Holding a commission in the British army, Washington led a poorly trained and equipped force of 150 men to build a fort on the banks of the Ohio River. On the way, he encountered and attacked a small French force, killing a French minister in the process. The incident touched off open fighting between the British and the French, and in one fateful engagement, the British were routed by the superior tactics of the French.

Although hailed as a hero in the colonies when word spread of his heroic valor and leadership against the French, the Royal government in England blamed the colonials for the defeat. Angry at the lack of respect and appreciation shown to him, Washington resigned from the army and returned to farming in Virginia. In 1759, he married Martha Custis, a wealthy widow, and thereafter devoted his time to running the family plantation. By 1770, Washington had emerged as an experienced leader—a justice of the peace in Fairfax County, a member of the Virginia House of Burgesses, and a respected vestryman (a lay leader in his church). He also was among the first prominent Americans to openly support resistance to England's new policies of taxation and strict regulation of the colonial economy (the Navigation Acts) beginning in the early 1770s.

A Modest Military Leader

Washington was elected by the Virginia legislature to both the First and the Second Continental Congress, held in 1774 and 1775. In 1775, after local militia units from Massachusetts had engaged British troops near Lexington and Concord, the Second Continental Congress appointed Washington commander of all the colonial forces. Showing the modesty that was central to his character, and would later serve the young Republic so well, Washington proclaimed, "I do not think myself equal to the command I am honored with."

After routing the British from Boston in the spring of 1776, Washington fought a series of humiliating battles in a losing effort to defend New York. But on Christmas Day that same year, he led his army through a ferocious blizzard, crossed the Delaware into New Jersey, and defeated the Hessian forces at Trenton. In May 1778, the French agreed to an alliance with the Americans, marking the turning point of the Revolution. Washington knew that one great victory by his army would collapse the British Parliament's support for its war against the colonies. In October 1781, Washington's troops, assisted by the French Navy, defeated Cornwallis at Yorktown. By the following spring the British government was ready to end hostilities.

King Washington?

Following the war, Washington quelled a potentially disastrous bid by some of his officers to declare him king. He then returned to Mount Vernon and the genteel life of a tobacco planter, only to be called out of retirement to preside at the Constitutional Convention in 1787. His great stature gave credibility to the call for a new government and insured his election as the first President of the United States. Keenly aware that his conduct as President would set precedents for the future of the office, he carefully weighed every step he took. He appointed Thomas Jefferson and Alexander Hamilton to his cabinet. Almost immediately, these two men began to quarrel over a wide array of issues, but Washington valued them for the balance they lent his cabinet. Literally the "Father of the Nation," Washington almost single-handedly created a new government—shaping its institutions, offices, and political practices.

Although he badly wanted to retire after the first term, Washington was unanimously supported by the Electoral College for a second term in 1792. Throughout both his terms, Washington struggled to prevent the emergence of political parties, viewing them as factions harmful to the public good. Nevertheless, in his first term, the ideological division between Jefferson and Hamilton deepened, forming the outlines of the nation's first party system. This system was composed of Federalists, who supported expansive federal power and Alexander Hamilton, and the Democratic-Republicans, followers of Thomas Jefferson's philosophy of states' rights and limited federal power. Washington generally backed Hamilton on key issues, such as the funding of the national debt, the assumption of state debts, and the establishment of a national bank.

Throughout his two terms, Washington insisted on his power to act independent of Congress in foreign conflicts, especially when war broke out between France and England in 1793 and he issued a Declaration of Neutrality on his own authority. He also acted decisively in putting down a rebellion by farmers in western Pennsylvania who protested a federal whiskey tax (the Whiskey Rebellion of 1794). After he left office, exhausted and discouraged over the rise of political factions, Washington returned to Mount Vernon, where he died almost three years later.

Historians agree that no one other than George Washington could have held the disparate colonies and, later, the struggling young Republic together. To the Revolution's last day, Washington's troops were ragged, starving, and their pay was months in arrears. In guiding this force during year after year of humiliating defeat to final victory, more than once paying his men out of his own pocket to keep them from going home, Washington earned the unlimited confidence of those early citizens of the United States. Perhaps most importantly, Washington's balanced and devoted service as President persuaded the American people that their prosperity and best hope for the future lay in a union under a strong but cautious central authority. His refusal to accept a proffered crown and his willingness to relinquish the office after two terms established the precedents for limits on the power of the presidency. Washington's profound achievements built the foundations of a powerful national government that has survived for more than two centuries.

2. JOHN ADAMS (1797-1801)

2.
John Adams 1797-1801

Born: October 30, 1735, North Precinct of Braintree (now Quincy), Massachusetts
Nickname: "Atlas of Independence"
Education: Harvard College (graduated 1755)
Religion: Unitarian
Career: Lawyer
Marriage: October 25, 1764, to Abigail Smith (1744–1818)
Children: Abigail Amelia (1765–1813), John Quincy (1767–1848), Susanna (1768–1770), Charles (1770–1800), Thomas Boylston (1772–1832)
Political Party: Federalist
Died: July 4, 1826, in Quincy, Massachusetts

Before becoming President in 1797, John Adams built his reputation as a blunt-speaking man of independent mind. A fervent patriot and brilliant intellectual, Adams served as a delegate from Massachusetts to the Continental Congress between 1774 and 1777, as a diplomat in Europe from 1778 to 1788, and as vice president during the Washington administration.

Federalists versus Democratic-Republicans

The Federalists, led by Alexander Hamilton, supported a strong central government that favored industry, landowners, banking interests, merchants, and close ties with England. Opposed to them were the Democratic-Republicans, led by Thomas Jefferson, who advocated limited powers for the federal government. Adams's Federalist leanings and high visibility as vice president positioned him as the leading contender for President in 1796.

In the early days of the American electoral process, the candidate receiving the second-largest vote in the Electoral College became vice president. This is how Thomas Jefferson, who opposed Adams in the election, came to serve as Adams's vice president in 1797. Adams won the election principally because he identified himself with Washington's administration and because he was able to win two electoral ballots from normally secure Jeffersonian states. In 1800, Adams faced a much tougher battle for reelection, as the differences between the Federalists and the Republicans intensified—by that time, the terms "Democratic-Republican" and "Republican" were used interchangeably.

The Adams presidency was characterized by continuing crises in foreign policy, which dramatically affected affairs at home. Suspicious of the French Revolution and its potential for terror and anarchy, Adams opposed close ties with France. Relations between America and France deteriorated to the brink of war, allowing Adams to justify his signing of the extremely controversial Alien and Sedition Acts. Drafted by Federalist lawmakers, these four laws were largely aimed at immigrants, who tended to become Republicans. Furious over Adams's foreign policy and his signing of the Alien and Sedition Acts, Republicans responded with the Kentucky and Virginia Resolutions, which challenged the legitimacy of federal authority over the states.

Republicans were equally incensed by the heavy taxation necessary for Adams's military buildup; farmers in Pennsylvania staged Fries's Rebellion in protest. At the same time, Adams faced disunity in his own party due to conflict with Hamilton over the undeclared naval war with France. This rivalry with Hamilton and the Federalist Party cost Adams the 1800 election. He lost to Thomas Jefferson, who was backed by the united and far more organized Republicans.

A Personal Life Filled with Politics

John Adams sacrificed his family life for his political one, spending much of his time separated from his wife, Abigail Adams, and their children. John Quincy Adams, Adams's son, grew up to become the sixth President of the United States. Interestingly, he joined the opposition party, the Democratic-Republicans.

Often lonely and miserable, Abigail viewed her suffering as a patriotic sacrifice but was distraught that her husband was away during the birth of their children and the loss of their unborn baby in 1777. After his term as President, John Adams lived a quiet life with Abigail on the family farm in Quincy, Massachusetts. There, Adams wrote prolifically for the next twenty-six years, including a fascinating correspondence with his political adversary and friend, Thomas Jefferson. Interestingly, both men died on Independence Day in 1826.

Although Abigail Adams saw herself as first and foremost her husband's wife and helpmate, she was a gifted intellectual in her own right, leaving behind nearly 2,000 letters containing some of the most profoundly compelling commentary on the society and politics of her time. A firm advocate of patriotic motherhood, Abigail believed that women best served the Republic in their roles as educated and independently thinking wives and mothers. Although she did not openly advocate voting rights for women, she did fight for their legal right to divorce and to own property.

The American Political Landscape

Indeed, property was a requirement for political participation during Adams's time, and he fought to keep it that way, feeling that the "rich, the well-born, and the able" should represent the nation. But the western migration into frontier America—Kentucky and Tennessee were admitted to the Union in 1792 and 1796, respectively—weakened the property requirement for voting in the West. Everywhere except on the frontier, however, wealthy merchants and slave owners dominated office holding, and financial and kinship ties were crucial to political advancement.

Historians have difficulty assessing Adams's presidency. Adams was able to avoid war with France, arguing against Hamilton that war should be a last resort to diplomacy. In this argument, the President won the nation the respect of its most powerful adversaries. Although Adams was fiercely criticized for signing the Alien and Sedition Acts, he never advocated their passage nor personally implemented them, and he pardoned the instigators of Fries's Rebellion. Seen in this light, Adams's legacy is one of reason, virtuous leadership, compassion, and a cautious but vigorous foreign policy. At the same time, Adams's stubborn independence left him politically isolated. He alienated his own cabinet, and his elite republicanism stood in stark contrast to the more egalitarian Jeffersonian democracy that was poised to assume power in the new century.

3. THOMAS JEFFERSON (1801-1809)

3.
Thomas Jefferson 1801-1809

Born: April 13, 1743, Shadwell plantation, Goochland County, Virginia
Nickname: "Man of the People," "Sage of Monticello"
Education: College of William and Mary (graduated 1762)
Religion: No formal affiliation
Marriage: January 1, 1772, to Martha Wayles Skelton (1748–1782)
Children: Martha (1772–1836), Jane Randolph (1774–1775), infant son (1777), Mary (1778–1804), Lucy Elizabeth (1780–1781), Lucy Elizabeth (1782–1785)
Career: Lawyer, Planter
Political Party: Democratic-Republican
Died: July 4, 1826, Monticello, near Charlottesville, Virginia

Thomas Jefferson, the author of the Declaration of Independence, spent his childhood roaming the woods and studying his books on a remote plantation in the Virginia Piedmont. Thanks to the prosperity of his father, Jefferson had an excellent education. After years in boarding school, where he excelled in classical languages, Jefferson enrolled in William and Mary College in his home state of Virginia, taking classes in science, mathematics, rhetoric, philosophy, and literature. He also studied law, and by the time he was admitted to the Virginia bar in April 1767, many considered him to have one of the nation's best legal minds.

Shaping America's Political Philosophy

Jefferson was shy in person, but his pen proved to be a mighty weapon. His pamphlet entitled "A Summary View of the Rights of British America," written in 1774, articulated the colonial position for independence and foreshadowed many of the ideas in the Declaration of Independence, the work for which he is most famous. By 1774, Jefferson was actively involved in organizing opposition to British rule, and in 1776, he was appointed to the Second Continental Congress. As a powerful prose stylist and an influential Virginia representative, Jefferson was chosen to write the Declaration of Independence. This document is a brilliant assertion of fundamental human rights and also serves as America's most succinct statement of its philosophy of government.

Before becoming the nation's third President, Jefferson served as delegate to the Virginia House of Delegates, where he drafted legislation that abolished primogeniture, the law that made the eldest son the sole inheritor of his father's property. He also promoted religious freedom, helping to establish the country's separation between church and state, and he advocated free public education, an idea considered radical by his contemporaries.

During the Revolution, Jefferson served two years as governor of Virginia, during which time he barely escaped capture by British forces by fleeing from Monticello, his home. He was later charged with being a coward for not confronting the enemy. After the war, Jefferson served as America's minister to France, where he witnessed firsthand the dramatic events leading up to the French Revolution.

While abroad, Jefferson corresponded with members of the Constitutional Convention, particularly his close associate from Virginia, James Madison. He agreed to support the Constitution and the strong federal government it created. Jefferson's support, however, hinged upon the condition that Madison add a Bill of Rights to the document in the form of ten amendments. The rights that Jefferson insisted upon—among them were freedom of speech, assembly, and practice of religion—have become fundamental to and synonymous with American life ever since.

Presidential Politics

Jefferson served as secretary of state under Washington, but quarrels with Secretary of Treasury Alexander Hamilton over his vision of a centralized national bank caused Jefferson to resign his post in 1793. In the election of 1796, Jefferson was the favorite of Democratic-Republican opponents of the Washington administration. He came in second to Federalist John Adams in Electoral College votes and became Adams's vice president.

In 1800, however, the political tide had turned against the Federalist Party of Adams and Hamilton. After a bitterly contested election, a tie vote in the Electoral College, and a protracted deadlock in the House of Representatives, Jefferson finally emerged as the winner—thanks, in part, to the three-fifths clause of the Constitution, which gave states with large slave populations additional votes. In his inaugural address, Jefferson pled for national unity in an attempt to heal the wounds of a vicious campaign and to gain support from the Federalist-controlled Congress. Due to a relatively placid first term, prosperity, lower taxes, and a reduction of the national debt, Jefferson won a landslide victory in 1804.

Defining the Powers of the Government

Jefferson believed in a "wise and frugal Government, which shall restrain men from injuring one another" but which otherwise left them free to regulate their own affairs. In an effort to minimize the influence of the central government, he reduced the number of government employees, slashed Army enlistments, and cut the national debt. Similar to his predecessor, John Adams, Jefferson had to deal with the political war waged between his Republican Party and the Federalists. The battles were focused on the nation's judiciary branch. The landmark ruling in Marbury v. Madison, which established the independent power of the Supreme Court, was handed down during Jefferson's presidency.

Foreign affairs dominated his day-to-day attentions while President, often pushing him toward Federalist policies that contrasted with his political philosophy. To ensure the safety of American ships on the high seas, Jefferson attempted to put an end to the bribes that the United States had been paying to the Barbary states for many years. This resulted in a war with Tripoli, in which Jefferson was forced to use his navy and to rethink his policy of reducing the U.S. military. While the United States at first enjoyed an economic boom due to the war between England and France, the British navy's practice of forcing American sailors into British service led to Jefferson's disastrous suspension of trade with both France and England. This trade war devastated the economy, alienated the hard-hit mercantile Northeast, and propelled America into war with England.

His brilliant negotiation and ties to France led to the Louisiana Purchase for $15 million, doubling the size of the nation. Nonetheless, the deal troubled Jefferson, who did not wish to overstep the central government's powers as outlined by the Constitution, which made no mention of the power to acquire new territory. It was Jefferson who authorized the famous Lewis and Clark Expedition (1804-1806), led by
158

Meriwether Lewis, a military officer who was Jefferson's clerk at the White House.

A Private Portrait of Contradictions

Jefferson preferred to live a simple lifestyle during his time in office, often greeting his dinner guests in old homespun clothes and a pair of worn bedroom slippers. Having lost his beloved wife, Martha Wayles Skelton, in 1782 to childbirth, Jefferson relied on his two married daughters and the wife of his secretary of state, Dolley Madison, as his official hostesses. Although he disliked pomp and circumstance, Jefferson knew how to live well; his wine bill upon leaving the presidency exceeded $10,000. In 1809, Jefferson retired to his Virginia plantation home, Monticello, where he continued pursuing his widely diverse interests in science, natural history, philosophy, and the classics. Jefferson also devoted himself to founding the University of Virginia.

Contemporary debates continue to rage—as they did during Jefferson's own lifetime—concerning his relationship with Sally Hemings, one of Jefferson's slaves, after Martha's death. Recent DNA evidence presents a convincing case that Jefferson was indeed the biological father of Heming's children, and most historians now believe that Jefferson and Hemings had a long-term sexual relationship. Jefferson was ambivalent about slavery throughout his career. As a young politician, he argued for the prohibition of slavery in new American territories, yet he never freed his own slaves. How could a man responsible for writing the sacred words "We hold these truths to be self evident, that all men are created equal" have been a slave owner? He never resolved his internal conflict on this issue.

After carrying on a long and fascinating correspondence with John Adams while both men were in the twilight of their lives, Jefferson died on July 4, 1826—exactly fifty years to the day from the signing of the Declaration of Independence.

4. JAMES MADISON (1809-1817)

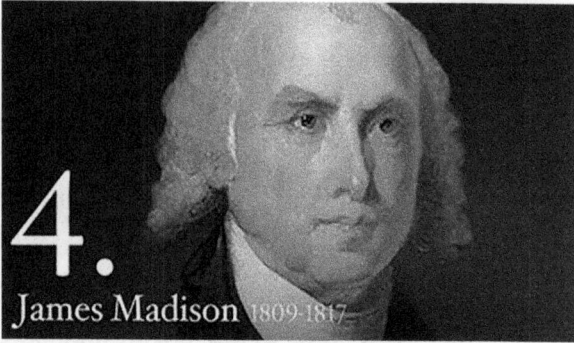

Born: March 16, 1751, Port Conway, Virginia
Nickname: "Father of the Constitution"
Education: College of New Jersey (now Princeton University, graduated 1771)
Religion: Episcopalian
Marriage: September 15, 1794, to Dolley Payne Todd (1768–1849)
Children: None
Career: Politician, Planter
Political Party: Democratic-Republican
Died: June 28, 1836, Montpelier, Orange County, Virginia

Like his close friend Thomas Jefferson, James Madison came from a prosperous family of Virginia planters, received an excellent education, and quickly found himself drawn into the debates over independence. In 1776, he became a delegate to the revolutionary Virginia Convention, where he worked closely with Thomas Jefferson to push through religious freedom statutes, among other liberal measures. The youngest member of the Continental Congress, Madison was small in stature. His soft spoken, shy demeanor was a foil for his brilliant persistence in advocating his political agenda. Madison emerged as a respected leader of the congress, known for his hard work and careful preparation.

Leader of Political Battles

Believing that the Articles of Confederation rendered the new republic subject to foreign attack and domestic turmoil, James Madison helped set the wheels in motion for a national convention to draft the young nation's Constitution. Madison led the Virginia delegation to the Philadelphia meeting, which began on May 14, 1787, and supported the cry for General Washington to chair the meeting. Madison's "Virginia Plan" became the blueprint for the constitution that finally emerged, eventually earning him the revered title, "Father of the Constitution." Having fathered the document, Madison worked hard to ensure its ratification. Along with Alexander Hamilton and John Jay, he published the Federalist Papers, a series of articles arguing for a strong central government subject to an extensive system of checks and balances.

Elected to the House of Representatives in 1789, Madison served as Washington's chief supporter. In this capacity, he fulfilled a promise to Thomas Jefferson, introducing the Bill of Rights, a constitutional guarantee of civil liberties. As Washington continued to move closer to Secretary of Treasury Alexander Hamilton's Federalist vision of a strong central government that promoted commercial and financial interests over agrarian interests, Madison broke with Washington, joining Jefferson to form the opposition party of Democratic-Republicans. During John Adams's presidency, Madison led the Republican fight against the Alien and Sedition Acts, which attempted to quell Republican opposition to Federalist foreign policy toward France. Madison authored the Virginia Resolutions, which declared the laws unconstitutional. Under Thomas Jefferson, Madison served as secretary of state, supporting the Louisiana Purchase and the embargo against Britain and France. Indeed, Madison shaped foreign policy during Jefferson's administration, emerging from behind the scenes in 1808 to succeed him as the fourth President of the United States.

It was not at all clear that Madison would carry the day. Jefferson's embargo of all trade with Britain and France had devastated the nation. New England states spoke of open secession from the Union. The Federalists, convinced they would ride national outrage to victory, re-nominated their 1804 contender, Charles C. Pinckney of South Carolina. Meanwhile, George Clinton, who had agreed to run as Madison's vice president, also consented to run for President! Madison swamped the opposition, winning 122 votes to Pinckney's 44. His reelection was also dramatic. Madison's nomination for a second term came just fifteen days prior to his war message to Congress, listing American grievances against Britain. Congress voted the United States into the War of 1812, largely guaranteeing Madison's reelection.

Second War of Independence

The War of 1812 amounted to a second war of independence for the new republic, and quickly helped Madison's popularity. Much of the War of 1812 centered on bloody battles against the Native American tribes that were aided by the British, such as the Creek tribe led by the notorious Tecumseh, who was finally defeated by General William Henry Harrison. In 1814 the British took the nation's new capital, torching the White House and other federal buildings. They were finally defeated at the epic battle of New Orleans by General Andrew Jackson's ragtag army, many of whom were volunteers, including free blacks and slaves, and nearly 1,000 French pirates! The victories against Tecumseh and at New Orleans revitalized the nation and earned him the esteem of his constituents. Madison's critics, who organized the Hartford Convention to protest his policies, looked like traitors to the victorious nation; their anti-war criticism further weakened the Federalist Party.

Life of Surprises

Everyone was shocked when the shy and reticent James Madison announced his marriage to the vivacious Dolley Payne Todd, who became one of the most popular and vibrant First Ladies to ever grace the White House. Dolley Madison was already familiar with her role in Washington, since she had occassionally served as Jefferson's hostess during his administration. A beautiful woman who enjoyed a party, Dolley Madison quickly earned a reputation among conservatives and political enemies, who criticized her for gambling, wearing make-up, and using tobacco. Dolley was hurt by her critics, but was gratified to keep her popularity and public acclaim long after her husband had left office.

Despite Madison's popularity and his outstanding achievements, he has traditionally been misjudged in the past as a less-than-spectacular President. Recently, however, historians have begun to pay more attention to Madison, seeing his handling of the war as similar to Lincoln's war-time management. Madison's government marshaled resources, faced down secessionist threats from New England and proved to the British the folly of fighting wars with the Americans. He established respect for American rights on the high seas, and emerged from the war with more popular support than when he was first inaugurated in 1808. Additionally, when considering the fact that he ended up on the winning side of every important issue that faced the young nation from 1776 to 1816, Madison was the most successful—and possibly the most influential—of all the founding fathers.

5. JAMES MONROE (1817-1825)

James Monroe 1817-1825

Born: April 28, 1758, Westmoreland County, Virginia
Nickname: "The Last Cocked Hat," "Era-of-Good-Feelings President"
Education: College of William and Mary (graduated 1776)
Religion: Episcopalian
Marriage: February 16, 1786, to Elizabeth Kortright (1768–1830)
Children: Eliza Kortright (1786–1835), James Spence (1799–1800), Maria Hester (1803–1850)
Career: Lawyer
Political Party: Democratic-Republican
Died: July 4, 1831, New York City, New York

James Monroe was the last American President of the "Virginia Dynasty"—of the first five men who held that position, four hailed from Virginia. Monroe also had a long and distinguished public career as a soldier, diplomat, governor, senator, and cabinet official. His presidency, which began in 1817 and lasted until 1825, encompassed what came to be called the "Era of Good Feelings." One of his lasting achievements was the Monroe Doctrine, which became a major tenet of U.S. foreign policy in the Western Hemisphere.

Early Revolutionary

James Monroe was born in 1758 to prosperous Virginia planters. His parents died when he was a teenager, leaving him part of the family farm. He enrolled at the College of William and Mary in Williamsburg in 1774, and almost immediately began participating in revolutionary activities. With a group of classmates, he raided the arsenal at the British Governor's Palace, escaping with 200 muskets and 300 swords, which the students presented to the Virginia militia. He became an officer in the Continental Army in early 1776 and, shortly thereafter, joined General George Washington's army at New York. He was severely wounded at the Battle of Trenton.

Monroe was promoted to captain and then major, and was assigned to the staff of General William Alexander, where he served for more than a year. After resigning his commission in the Continental Army in 1779, he was appointed colonel in the Virginia service. In 1780, Governor Thomas Jefferson sent Monroe to North Carolina to report on the advance of the British.

After the war, Monroe studied law with Jefferson and was elected to the Continental Congress in 1783. While a delegate to the Congress, then meeting in New York, he met Elizabeth Kortright, the daughter of a New York City merchant. A year later they were married; he was twenty-seven and she was seventeen. The newlyweds moved to Fredericksburg, Virginia, where Monroe practiced law.

High Political Office

In 1787, Monroe began serving in the Virginia assembly and was chosen the following year as a delegate to the Virginia convention considering ratification of the new U.S. Constitution. He voted against ratification, holding out for the direct election of presidents and senators, and for the inclusion of a bill of rights. Partly due to politicians, such as Monroe, who brought attention to the omission of such constitutional guarantees, the Bill of Rights became the first ten amendments of the Constitution upon ratification in 1791.

Although Monroe narrowly lost a congressional election to James Madison in 1790, the Virginia state legislature appointed him to the U.S. Senate. As a member of that body, he allied himself with Madison and Thomas Jefferson, his close personal friends, against the Federalist faction led by Vice President John Adams and Secretary of the Treasury Alexander Hamilton.

In 1794, President Washington sent Monroe to Paris as U.S. minister to France. Monroe's actions as minister angered the Federalists, however, and Washington recalled him in 1797. In 1799, he was elected governor of Virginia, where he served three one-year terms. In 1803, President Thomas Jefferson sent him back to France to help negotiate the Louisiana Purchase. Monroe continued to serve his government in Europe, representing the United States as U.S. minister to Britain from 1803 to 1807, with a brief stint as special envoy to Spain in 1805.

After he returned home, dissident Republicans nominated him to oppose James Madison for the Democratic-Republican presidential nomination in 1808. Monroe, however, never considered the challenge serious, and Madison won the election easily. Monroe was once again elected governor of Virginia in January 1811, but headed back to Washington, D.C., that April, when President Madison named him secretary of state. Monroe served in that capacity, and also for a time as secretary of war, until 1817.

Easy Race to the White House

When President Madison announced his decision to continue the custom of serving only two terms, Monroe became the

166

logical candidate for the Democratic-Republicans. After some maneuvering within the party, Monroe prevailed to win the nomination. He had little opposition during the general election campaign. The Federalists were so out of favor with the public that a majority had abandoned the party name altogether. They ultimately nominated New York's Rufus King, but the result was a foregone conclusion. In the Electoral College, Monroe carried sixteen states to King's three.

Monroe began his presidency by embarking on a presidential tour, a practice initiated by George Washington. His trip through the northern states took fifteen weeks, by which time more Americans had seen him than they had any other sitting President. A newspaper in Boston described Monroe's reception there as the beginning of a new "Era of Good Feelings" for the nation. The President later made two similar tours, one of the Chesapeake Bay area in 1818 and one of the South and West in 1819.

Era of Good Feelings

At the beginning of Monroe's presidency, the nation had much to feel good about. It had declared victory in the War of 1812 and its economy was booming, allowing the administration to turn its attention toward domestic issues. The economy was booming. The organized opposition, in the form of the Federalists, had faded largely from sight, although the government had adopted many Federalist programs, including protective tariffs and a national bank. The President, moreover, was personable, extremely popular, and interested in reaching out to all the regions of the country.

Monroe faced his first crisis as President with the Panic of 1819, which resulted in high unemployment as well as increased foreclosures and bankruptcies. Some critics derided Monroe for not responding more forcefully to the depression.

Although he believed that such troubles were natural for a maturing economy and that the situation would soon turn around, he could do little to alleviate their short-term effects.

Monroe's second crisis came the same year, when the entrance of Missouri to the Union as a slave state threatened to disrupt the legislative balance between North and South. Congress preserved that equilibrium, negotiating a compromise in which Massachusetts allowed its northernmost counties to apply for admission to the Union as the new free state of Maine. The Missouri Compromise also called for the prohibition of slavery in the western territories of the Louisiana Purchase above the 36/30' north latitude line. Monroe worked in support of the compromise and, after ascertaining that the provisions were constitutional, signed the bill.

In trying to sustain the "Era of Good Feelings," Monroe had hoped to preside over the decline of political parties. However, his administration offered only a brief respite from divisive partisan politics. The rancor surrounding the 1824 presidential election was a reminder that strong feelings still animated American political life even without the existence of two distinct parties. In fact, the Monroe presidency stood at the forefront of a transition from the first party system of the Democratic-Republicans and the Federalists to the second party system of the Democrats and the Whigs.

Spanish Florida and the Monroe Doctrine

In 1818, President Monroe sent General Andrew Jackson to Spanish Florida to subdue the Seminole Indians, who were raiding American settlements. Liberally interpreting his vague instructions, Jackson led his troops deep into areas of Florida under the control of Spain and captured two Spanish forts. In addition to securing greater protection for American settlements, the mission pointed out the vulnerability of Spanish rule in Florida. Monroe and his secretary of state,

John Quincy Adams, used that vulnerability to pressure Spain into selling Florida to the United States.

As Spain's dominion in the America's continued to disintegrate, revolutions throughout its colonies brought independence to Argentina, Peru, Chile, Colombia, and Mexico. When European powers threatened to form an alliance to help Spain regain its lost domains, Monroe, with the prodding of Secretary of State Adams, declared that America would resist European intervention in the Western Hemisphere. Announced in the President's message to Congress on December 2, 1823, the Monroe Doctrine thus became a cornerstone of American foreign policy.

Leaving Washington after a lifetime of public service, Monroe and his wife retired to their estate in Loudoun County, Virginia. Monroe returned to private life deeply in debt and spent many of his later years trying to resolve his financial problems. He petitioned the government to repay him for past services, with the government eventually providing a portion of the amount he sought. After his wife died in 1830, Monroe moved to New York City to live with his daughter. He died there on July 4, 1831.

6. JOHN QUINCY ADAMS (1825-1829)

Born: July 11, 1767, Braintree (now Quincy), Massachusetts

Nickname: "Old Man Eloquent"
Education: Harvard College (graduated 1787)
Religion: Unitarian
Marriage: July 26, 1797, to Louisa Catherine Johnson (1775–1852)
Children: George Washington (1801–1829), John (1803–1834), Charles Francis (1807–1886), Louisa Catherine (1811–1812)
Career: Lawyer, Senator, Diplomat
Political Party: Federalist, Democratic-Republican, Whig
Died: February 23, 1848, Washington, D.C.

Reared for public service, John Quincy Adams became one of the nation's preeminent secretaries of state but proved the wrong man for the presidency. Aloof, stubborn, and ferociously independent, he failed to develop the support he needed in Washington, even among his own party. Faced throughout his term with organized opposition from the Democrats—who were committed to limiting Adams to a single term and replacing him with Andrew Jackson—Adams refused to forge the political alliances necessary to push his ideas into policy. His father, President John Adams, had also ignored the political side of the office and served only one term. History repeated itself with his son: John Quincy Adams lost his reelection bid to Jackson in 1828.

Worldly Upbringing

John Quincy Adams was born on July 11, 1767, the son of a father who would serve in the Continental Congress and helped draft the Declaration of Independence. When John Quincy was ten, his father was posted to Europe as a special envoy of the revolutionary American government, and John Quincy accompanied him. For the boy, it was an incredible introduction to the courts of Europe and the practice of diplomacy. For seven years, except for a few months back in Massachusetts, John Quincy lived in Paris, Amsterdam, and St. Petersburg. He was a student at the University of Leiden for about a year when, because of his excellence in French, he was asked to serve as secretary and translator for Francis Dana, posted as emissary to St. Petersburg from 1781 to 1783. John Quincy returned to Paris in 1783 to serve as secretary to his father through the negotiation of peace ending the American Revolutionary War and, in 1785, returned home to complete his education at Harvard College. He graduated two years later. During this period, John Quincy began keeping a diary, and he maintained it from 1779 until 1848, shortly before he died.

Admitted to the bar in 1790, Adams practiced law in Boston. In 1794, President George Washington appointed him minister to the Netherlands, where he served with distinction until 1797. He also reencountered the woman he would marry, Louisa Catherine Johnson, the daughter of an American merchant living abroad. Adams had first met Louisa in France when he was twelve. For months while in London on diplomatic assignment, Adams visited her family nightly, always leaving when the daughters sat down at the piano to play and sing—he disliked the sound of the female voice in song. Despite his taste in music and some reservations from his parents who did not think his son should have a foreign-born wife, the two were married in 1797.

Political Trials and Tribulations

After an assignment as the minister to Prussia from 1797 to 1801, Adams returned home and won election to the Massachusetts legislature. In 1803, the legislature appointed him to the United States Senate (senators were not chosen by popular vote until 1913). As a senator, he supported Thomas Jefferson in the Louisiana Purchase, one of only two Federalists to do so, and also endorsed other Democratic-Republican projects, including the Embargo Act of 1807. These actions led the Federalist-dominated Massachusetts legislature to decline to return him to the Senate, and Adams immediately resigned his post. He then switched his allegiance to the Democratic-Republican Party.

In 1809, President James Madison named him the first U.S. minister to Russia and later also assigned him to head the five-person delegation empowered to negotiate a peace agreement ending the War of 1812. The treaty, universally seen as a victory for the young American nation, was signed on December 24, 1814, and Adams was subsequently posted to the English court for two years.

With the election of James Monroe to the presidency, Adams came home to become secretary of state, arguably his period of greatest accomplishment. He played a major role in formulating the Monroe Doctrine, which warned European nations not to meddle in the affairs of the Western Hemisphere. He also negotiated the Adams-Onís Treaty with Spain, which extended U.S. boundaries to the Pacific Ocean and ceded Florida to the United States. During his eight years as secretary of state, he built a powerful and efficient American diplomatic service.

Bitter Fight for the White House

In the presidential election of 1824, four men campaigned: former Secretary of War William H. Crawford of Georgia, House Speaker Henry Clay of Kentucky, General Andrew Jackson of Tennessee, and John Quincy Adams. All were nominally Democratic-Republicans, and Crawford won the party's congressional caucus nomination, but at a time when the caucus system was being called into question as undemocratic.

The 1824 presidential election was a landmark one, the first in which popular vote actually mattered. Eighteen states had moved to choose presidential electors by popular vote while six still left the choice up to the state legislature. After a fierce campaign, Jackson took a plurality in the popular vote, followed, in order, by Adams, Clay, and Crawford. In the Electoral College, however, Jackson had thirty-two votes fewer than he needed to prevail. Acting under the Twelfth Amendment, the House of Representatives met to select the President. Speaker of the House Clay threw his support behind Adams and gave him the election by a single vote. Soon thereafter, Adams named Clay secretary of state. It was a bad beginning for the Adams presidency. Jackson resigned from the Senate and vowed to unseat Adams in 1828.

Adams believed strongly that it was constitutional and appropriate for the federal government to sponsor broad programs to improve American society and prosperity. He backed Henry Clay's proposed "American System," envisioning a national marketplace in which North and South, town and country, were tied together by trade and exchange. To realize this vision, Adams proposed to Congress an ambitious program involving the construction of roads, canals, educational institutions, and other initiatives. Lacking congressional allies, however, Adams was unable to maneuver most of these programs into law. Congress also blocked many of his foreign initiatives. His support of the so-called Tariff of Abominations of 1828, which protected American interests but caused higher prices, cost him popularity among the voters.

By 1828, Andrew Jackson had been campaigning for three years. He characterized Adams's election as a "corrupt bargain" typical of the elitist eastern "gamesters." Following a campaign marred by vicious personal attacks—Jackson's wife was called an adulteress, Adams was accused of procuring prostitutes for the Russian czar—Jackson won in a landslide.

Post-White House Career

John Quincy Adams had one of the most politically active post-presidencies of any U.S. President. Two years after his defeat, Adams ran for Congress from his home district in Massachusetts. He accepted the nomination on two conditions: that he would never solicit their votes and that he would follow his conscience at all times. He served nine consecutive terms in the House of Representatives, earning the nickname "Old Man Eloquent" because of his extraordinary speeches in opposition to slavery. He was instrumental in ending the "gag rule" that prohibited debate on slavery in the House of Representatives and also continued to champion internal improvements for the country. Historically, Adams has won more acclaim for this long congressional career than for his presidency. He suffered a stroke on the floor of the House on February 21, 1848, and died two days later.

7. ANDREW JACKSON (1829-1837)

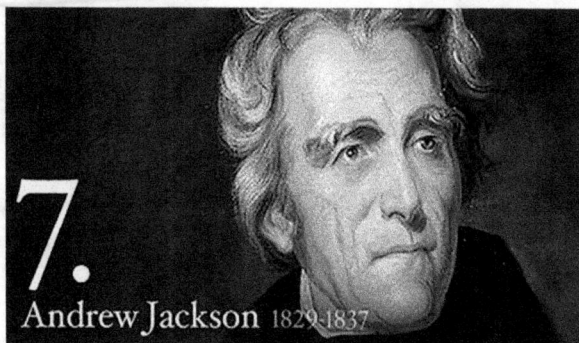

Andrew Jackson 1829-1837

Born: March 15, 1767, Waxhaw area, on North Carolina-South Carolina border
Nickname: "Old Hickory"
Religion: Presbyterian
Marriage: August 1791 (2nd ceremony, January 17, 1794), to Rachel Donelson Robards (1767–1828)
Children: Andrew Jackson, Jr. (adopted nephew, 1808-1865)
Career: Lawyer, Soldier
Political Party: Democrat

Died: June 8, 1845, Nashville, Tennessee

Andrew Jackson, seventh President of the United States, was the dominant actor in American politics between Thomas Jefferson and Abraham Lincoln. Born to obscure parents and orphaned in youth, he was the first "self-made man" and the first westerner to reach the White House. He became a democratic symbol and founder of the Democratic Party, the country's most venerable political organization. During his two-term presidency, he expanded executive powers and transformed the President's role from chief administrator to popular tribune.

Jackson was born in 1767 in Waxhaw, South Carolina, to Scotch-Irish immigrants. He fought as a boy in the Revolutionary War, studied law, and in 1788 moved west to Nashville. In 1791, he began living with Rachel Donelson Robards, whose husband had abandoned her. They were formally married after her divorce in 1794. Charges of adultery arising from the episode dogged Jackson's later political career. After serving as Tennessee prosecutor, judge, congressman, and senator, he won fame as a major general in the War of 1812 with smashing victories against the Creek Indians in 1814 and the British at New Orleans in January 1815.

Jackson's triumph at New Orleans quickly became the stuff of legend and made him America's greatest military hero since George Washington. In 1818, he led an army in pursuit of Seminole Indians into Spanish Florida, touching off an international furor. After Spain ceded Florida, Jackson served briefly as territorial governor and then as a senator, representing Tennessee, from 1823 to 1825. In a confused, four-candidate presidential race in 1824, Jackson led the popular and electoral vote but lost in the House of Representatives, through the influence of Speaker Henry Clay, to John Quincy Adams. Jackson challenged Adams again in 1828 and defeated him in a campaign which centered on Jackson's image as a man of the people battling aristocracy and corruption. Jackson easily defeated Henry Clay in 1832.

Jackson's presidency defined itself in two central episodes: the nullification crisis and the "Bank War." Jackson took office amid mounting sectional acrimony over the "American System" program of fostering economic development through transportation subsidies and through protective tariffs on imports to aid American manufacturers. Many Southerners believed these policies promoted Northern growth at their expense. Jackson curbed the American System by vetoing road and canal bills beginning with the Maysville Road in 1830. However, in 1832 the state of South Carolina declared the existing tariff unconstitutional, null and void. The state took steps to block tariff collections within its borders. Though he favored a lower tariff, Jackson acted quickly to uphold federal supremacy—by force, if necessary. In a ringing proclamation, he declared the Union indivisible and branded nullification as treason. Congress reduced the tariff in 1833, defusing the crisis.

The Second Bank of the United States was a corporation chartered by Congress to provide a national paper currency and manage the government's finances. Like Thomas Jefferson, Jackson believed such a bank to be dangerous and unconstitutional. In 1832, he vetoed a bill to extend the Bank's charter beyond its scheduled expiration in 1836. Jackson's veto message counterposed the virtuous plain people against the Bank's privileged stockholders. The next year Jackson moved the federal government's deposits from the Bank to state-chartered banks, triggering a brief financial panic and prompting the Senate to censure him in 1834. Undeterred, Jackson launched a broader assault against all forms of government-granted privilege, especially corporate charters. His Farewell Address in 1837 warned of an insidious "money power."

Jackson's Bank War and its populistic, egalitarian rhetoric shaped the platform and rhetoric of his new Democratic party. (His policies also arguably helped trigger a financial panic in 1837, which deepened into a severe depression.) By casting himself as the people's tribune against the moneyed elite and their tools in government, he introduced an enduring theme in American politics.

He also carved out a stronger role for the presidency. Jackson replaced many government officials on partisan grounds, inaugurating the "spoils system." Catering to his core regional constituency of Southern planters and Western frontiersmen, he condemned antislavery agitation, favored cheaper public lands, and strong-armed Indian tribes into removing west of the Mississippi. In a confrontation between Georgia and the Cherokee Nation, Jackson backed state authority against tribal sovereignty and refused to protect Indians' treaty rights despite their recognition by the United States Supreme Court. Jackson wielded executive powers vigorously, defying Congress, vetoing more bills than all his predecessors combined, and frequently reshuffling his cabinet.

Strong-willed and sharp-tempered, a fierce patriot and rabid partisan, Jackson was always controversial, both as a general and as President. He personalized disputes and demonized opponents. In a notorious episode, Jackson broke open his first Cabinet and forced a rupture with Vice-President John C. Calhoun by championing the character of Peggy Eaton, the vivacious and controversial wife of the secretary of war. Yet behind Jackson's towering rages often lay shrewd calculation of their political effects.

Jackson secured the presidential succession in 1836 to his faithful lieutenant and second vice president, Martin Van Buren. He then retired to The Hermitage, his cotton plantation near Nashville, where he died in 1845.

8. Martin Van Buren (1837-1841)

Martin Van Buren 1837-1841

Born: December 5, 1782, Kinderhook, New York
Nickname: "The Little Magician," "The Red Fox of Kinderhook"
Education: Kinderhook Academy (graduated 1796)
Religion: Dutch Reformed
Marriage: February 21, 1807, to Hannah Hoes (1783–1819)
Children: Abraham (1807–1873), John (1810–1866), Martin (1812–1855), Winfield Scott (1813), Smith Thompson (1817–1876)
Career: Lawyer
Political Party: Democrat
Died: July 24, 1862, Kinderhook, New York

Martin Van Buren said that the two happiest days of his life were his entrance into the office of President and his surrender of the office. While his political opponents were glad to see him go - they nicknamed him "Martin Van Ruin" - many Americans were not. Even though he lost the 1840 presidential election, Van Buren received 40,000 more votes than he had in his 1836 victory. In subsequent years, historians have come to regard Van Buren as integral to the development of the American political system.

Van Buren was the first President not born a British subject, or even of British ancestry. The Van Burens were a large, struggling family of Dutch descent. Martin's father, Abraham Van Buren—a supporter of Thomas Jefferson in a region populated by supporters of Jefferson's opponents, the Federalists—ran a tavern where politicians often gathered as they traveled between New York City and Albany. This environment gave young Martin a taste for politics. Though the Van Burens could not afford to send Martin to college, he managed to get a job as a clerk in a law office where he began studying law independently. After he became a lawyer, Van Buren joined the Democratic-Republicans and began his political career, as a minor county official.

Political Savvy and Party Building

Immediately, Van Buren began showing the qualities that would eventually take him to the pinnacle of American politics—and earn him a bevy of admirers as well as critics. Unfailingly polite and thoroughly shrewd, Van Buren proved an adept politician, negotiating the fractious political environment of New York state's Democratic-Republican party. As a New York politician, he set about building a political organization of his fellow Democratic-Republicans that stressed unity, loyalty, and fealty to Jeffersonian political principles. Gradually, Van Buren moved from the New York State Senate, to the New York attorney general's office, and then to the U.S. Senate. Unhappy with the politics and policies of President John Quincy Adams, Van Buren aligned himself instead with Andrew Jackson, the immensely popular war hero who wanted a return to the Jeffersonian policies of minimalist government. In Washington, he continued his political party-building efforts, but on a national scale.

When Jackson became President, he named Van Buren secretary of state, in recognition of the New Yorker's political acumen and his service during the 1828 election. From this position, Van Buren oversaw the nation's foreign affairs. But his time in Washington was also spent cultivating political relationships and allies. Van Buren continued to build the political organization that would become the Democratic Party. Just as important, Van Buren quickly became one of Jackson's trusted advisers and friends, even though the two men's political views were not always perfectly in synch. Van Buren also skillfully navigated the tempestuous in-fighting that marked Jackson's cabinet, where Vice President John Calhoun proved more an adversary than ally of the President. Toward the end of his first term, Jackson dismissed much of his cabinet, cut his relations with Vice President Calhoun, and dispatched Van Buren to the political calm of London as U.S. minister to England. During Jackson's second term, Van Buren served as vice president.

Managing a Troubled Nation

Van Buren won the presidential election of 1836 by promising to carry on the policies of Andrew Jackson. Unfortunately, Van Buren took office as the booming U.S. economy of the early and mid-1830s began to slow down. The so-called "Panic of 1837" was followed by the worst depression yet faced by the young nation. These economic troubles quickly became President Van Buren's main concern.

Van Buren's response to the crisis revealed his belief in the principles of a limited federal government, defense of states rights, and protection of the "people" from the "powerful." Thus, Van Buren rejected his Whig opposition's suggestion that he support a National Bank, which the Whigs believed could oversee and stabilize the nation's economy. Instead, the President blamed the depression on powerful monied interests at home and abroad, and proposed that the federal government deposit its funds in an independent treasury, rather than in state banks, While Van Buren and Congress argued about the merits of the independent treasury—which Congress finally authorized in the summer of 1840—the nation's economic troubles continued.

Van Buren confronted several other potentially divisive issues while President. He managed to quiet talk of annexing Texas by steadfastly announcing his opposition to such a move. His main foreign policy concerns were the growing tensions between the United States and Great Britain over the border between the United States and Canada. Van Buren ignored calls from some Americans to respond to Canadian and British provocations with force, working instead successfully through diplomatic channels to calm tensions in the region. Van Buren's measured approach to the northern border problems, however, only earned him the enmity of those who urged a more aggressive response.

Martin Van Buren's wife, Hannah, died twelve years after their marriage, leaving him a widower with four sons to raise by himself. Though Van Buren never remarried, his eldest son's wife, Angelica Singleton Van Buren, served as official White House hostess during the last two years of his presidency. His sons, moreover, emerged as some of his father's most important aides and advisers; Abraham and Martin Jr. served as personal secretaries to their father when he was President.

Political Defeat

Facing criticism at home for both the economic depression and his handling of foreign affairs, Van Buren's re-election chances suffered even more in the face of an inspired campaign offered by the Whigs and their candidate, William Henry Harrison. In only four years, the Whig party had matched the savvy and organization of the Democrats—if not their shear numbers and ideological unity. The Whigs portrayed Harrison as the rough and tumble "Log Cabin and Hard Cider" candidate and ridiculed Van Buren as fussy, aristocratic, and unmanly. There was little truth in these images—in reality, it was Van Buren who came from a modest background, while Harrison was from a ruling-class Virginia family—but the charges, coupled with dissatisfaction over Van Buren's governance, proved too much for the sitting President to overcome. Van Buren lost the election, failing even to carry his home state of New York.

Martin Van Buren served only one term as President, and those four years were marked as much by failure and criticism as by success and popular acclaim. Van Buren's troubled presidency, though, should not overshadow his significant contributions to American political development. Van Buren played key roles in the creation of both the Democratic Party and the so-called "second party system" in which Democrats competed with their opponents, the Whigs. In these ways, Van Buren left an indelible mark on American politics.

9. WILLIAM HENRY HARRISON (1841)

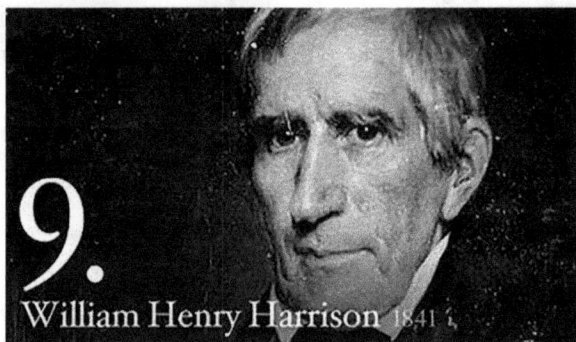
William Henry Harrison 1841

Born: February 9, 1773, Berkeley plantation, Charles City County, Virginia
Nickname: "Old Tippecanoe"; "Old Tip"
Education: Hampden-Sydney College
Marriage: November 25, 1795, to Anna Tuthill Symmes (1775–1864)
Children: Elizabeth Bassett (1796–1846), John Cleves Symmes (1798–1830), Lucy Singleton (1800–1826), William Henry (1802–1838), John Scott (1804–1878), Benjamin

(1806-1840), Mary Symmes (1809–1842), Carter Bassett (1811–1839), Anna Tuthill (1813–1865), James Findlay (1814–1817)
Religion: Episcopalian
Career: Soldier
Political Party: Whig
Died: April 4, 1841, Washington, D.C.

William Henry Harrison served the shortest time of any American President—only thirty-two days. He also was the first President from the Whig Party. He had won his nickname, "Old Tip," as the tough commanding general of American forces who defeated hostile Native Americans at the Battle of Tippecanoe in the Ohio River Valley in 1811.

Harrison, the youngest of seven children, was born on February 9, 1773, only two years before the American Revolution. His family was among the richest and the most politically prominent in the colony. Harrison's father had served three terms as governor. When young Harrison reached adulthood, he chose a career in the military, a decision that disappointed his father, who had wanted him to become a physician.

Military and Political Involvements

Serving in the Northwest Territories under General "Mad Anthony" Wayne, Harrison advanced to captain and commander of Fort Washington, near present-day Cincinnati. By the late 1790s, he enjoyed a substantial reputation among white settlers as an Indian fighter. President John Adams appointed Harrison secretary of the Northwest Territory in 1798. Two years later, Adams named him governor of the Indian Territory—present day Indiana and Illinois. Presidents Jefferson and Madison kept him in that position for twelve years.

While governor, Harrison negotiated many treaties with the Native Americans of the region, and most of them deprived the Indians of their lands for little money in return. These treaties were signed after Harrison had defeated the tribes in battle, and the peace of the victor was not gentle. For example, when Harrison signed the Treaty of Fort Wayne, the United States acquired three million acres of land with a single document. In another case, he paid the Indians one penny for each 200 acres in a deal that transferred 51 million acres to the United States. When the proud Shawnee chief Tecumseh tried to organize resistance to the advancing white settlers, Harrison led a force of 950 men against his Indian Confederacy, defeating 650 warriors at Tippecanoe Creek on November 7, 1811.

During the War of 1812, Harrison, then a general in the American army, engaged a combined British and Indian force of 1,700 men in the battle at the Thames River in 1813. When the smoke had cleared, Tecumseh, who had joined the British, lay dead. Harrison became a national hero.

After the war, Harrison served in the U.S. House of Representatives from Ohio until 1819. He supported Henry Clay's so-called "American System," which favored internal improvements funded by the federal government. When General Andrew Jackson raided Spanish Florida without specific orders in the First Seminole War (1818), Harrison joined with others in Congress in trying to censure him. This led to great animosity between the two men. Although he now lived and worked in the West, Harrison was still a southerner when it came to slavery. He consistently opposed any attempt by Congress to restrict the spread of slavery or to curtail the authority of slave masters over their slaves.

In the 1820s, Harrison served in the Ohio State Senate, as a U.S. senator from Ohio, and as U.S. minister to Colombia. With Jackson's election, Harrison lost his diplomatic position and retired to his farm in North Bend, Ohio, becoming active in organizing the Whig opposition to Jackson.

Anti-Jackson Candidate

In 1836, the opponents of Andrew Jackson desperately wanted to defeat his handpicked successor, Martin Van Buren, but they had no real party basis from which to work. The anti-Jackson forces tried a very impractical and unusual scheme. They adopted the name "Whigs" (the name of the British party opposed to the monarchy) and ran four candidates from four different regions. They hoped that this tactic would deny Van Buren a majority in the Electoral College and thus throw the election into the House of Representatives. Harrison was the Whig candidate of the West. In the election, Harrison came in second, but Van Buren won a majority of both the popular and Electoral College vote.

Four years later, the Whigs ran the first modern presidential campaign in American history, with Harrison as their presidential candidate. It was a race filled with songs, advertising, slogans, and organized rallies. In the election campaign of 1840, the Whigs handed out free hard cider in little bottles shaped like log cabins at barbecues and bonfires—and they used the slogan "Old Tippecanoe and Tyler, Too" to promote Harrison's candidacy. (John Tyler was his running mate.)

The incumbent President Martin Van Buren, who came across to the American people as a dandy, as a man who looked and acted like an aristocrat, could not overcome his image. People also held him responsible for the economic collapse in the late 1830s. Harrison won the election with 53 percent of the vote, and more people voted in 1840 than ever before.

Harrison, the oldest man at age sixty-eight (before Ronald Reagan) to be inaugurated President, died after serving only one month in office. He had become ill after delivering his inaugural address outdoors in the cold March weather without a hat or a coat and died of a respiratory infection, probably pneumonia. He was the first President to die in office. Harrison's grandson, Benjamin Harrison, would become President of the United States in 1889.

10. JOHN TYLER (1841-1845)

Born: March 29, 1790, Charles City County, Virginia
Nickname: "Accidental President;" "His Accidency"
Education: College of William and Mary (graduated 1807)
Religion: Episcopalian
Marriage: March 29, 1813, to Letitia Christian (1790–1842); June 26, 1844, to Julia Gardiner (1820–1889)
Children: Mary (1815–1848), Robert (1816–1877), John (1819–1896), Letitia (1821–1907), Elizabeth (1823–1850), Anne Contesse (1825), Alice (1827–1854), Tazewell (1830–1874), David Gardiner (1846–1927), John Alexander (1848–1883), Julia Gardiner (1849–1871), Lachlan (1851–1902), Lyon Gardiner (1853–1935), Robert Fitzwalter (1856–1927), Pearl (1860–1947)
Career: Lawyer
Political Affiliation: Democrat, Whig
Died: January 18, 1862, Richmond, Virginia

John Tyler signaled the last gasp of the Old Virginia aristocracy in the White House. Born a few years after the American Revolution in 1790 to an old family from Virginia's ruling class, Tyler graduated from the College of William and Mary at the age of seventeen, studied law, and went to work for a prestigious law firm in Richmond. At twenty-one, Tyler had used his father's contacts to gain a seat in the Virginia House of Delegates where he began immediately fighting the Bank of the United States, which he opposed as a broadening of nationalist power. After serving an uneventful stint in the military during the War of 1812, Tyler won election to the House of Representatives and quickly became a Washington insider, seen frequently at Dolly Madison's posh parties.

Champion of Southern Power

As a southern planter, Tyler bitterly opposed a strong standing army, tariffs, and extending the vote to men without property, resenting this challenge to traditional southern power. The popular Andrew Jackson of Tennessee represented everything in politics that Tyler was against, especially the new voting power of the West. When Jackson's government attempted to restrict slavery in new states west of Missouri, Tyler saw it as such an abuse of federal power that he resigned from Congress in disgust.

When he returned to Washington in 1827, Tyler reluctantly supported Jackson's reelection in 1832 but became furious when Jackson threatened to use federal force against South Carolina when the state renounced federal tariffs. Twice he stridently condemned the President on the Senate floor for what he considered the President's abuse of executive power. Disgusted with Jackson, Tyler teamed up with Henry Clay and Daniel Webster to form the new Whig Party.

Martin Van Buren's failure to alleviate the economic depression which followed Andrew Jackson's presidency

gave the Whigs the chance they needed in 1840. The Whigs'
presidential candidate, William Henry Harrison, was
marketed as a humble frontiersman, the "Log Cabin and Hard
Cider" candidate, despite the fact that he was highly
educated, wealthy, and descended from Virginia's ruling
class. John Tyler was selected as his running mate to appeal
to the South. Under the slogan, "Tippecanoe and Tyler Too,"
Harrison and Tyler won the election with broad populist
support in a backlash against Van Buren's insider ways.
Ironically, Tyler was propelled into office by the commoners
he had formerly tried so hard to lock out.

Orderly Transfer of Power

On the day of his inaugural, Harrison gave a rambling two-
hour speech outdoors in freezing weather without coat or hat.
A month later he was dead. Tyler, who had returned to his
Virginia plantation after the inaugural, was rushed to
Washington to fill the vacant presidency. Because no
President had ever died in office before, some felt that Tyler
was merely an acting or interim President. Tyler firmly
asserted that the Constitution gave him full and unqualified
powers of office and had himself sworn in immediately as
President, setting a critical precedent for an orderly transfer
of power following a President's death.

Fearing that he would alienate Harrison's supporters, Tyler
decided to keep the dead President's entire cabinet even
though several members were openly hostile to Tyler and
resented his assumption of the office. After Tyler vetoed a
bill to resurrect the Bank of the United States, his entire
cabinet resigned in protest, with the exception of Secretary of
State Webster, then in the midst of sensitive negotiations
with Great Britain. During his second year in office, the
Whigs, led by Henry Clay, expelled him from the party and
tried to have him impeached. The Whigs had to settle for one
of their committees passing a resolution of censure against
the President.

In a bid for reelection, Tyler worked to annex Texas, against the wishes of abolitionists who feared that it would become another slave state. Tyler's Democratic rival, James Polk, blunted the issue by also endorsing Texas statehood. Tyler pushed ahead though, introducing Texas annexation to Congress as a joint resolution requiring only a majority vote of each chamber of Congress, thereby dodging the two-thirds majority required to ratify a treaty. This approach succeeded in achieving Texas's incorporation into the Union.

The 1844 presidential election boiled down to a fight between Tyler, Polk, and Henry Clay. Fearing that he and Polk might split the vote, handing the election to Clay, Tyler voluntarily withdrew, consoling himself that at least he took Clay down with him. In a final insult, Congress overrode his veto of a military appropriation, marking the first override of a presidential veto in American history. The nearly bankrupt Tyler moved back to his plantation in Virginia with his second wife, Julia Gardiner Tyler. Just prior to the Civil War, Tyler chaired the Richmond Convention, which attempted to reconcile the North and South. When Lincoln rejected his proffered compromises, Tyler became a leading proponent of Southern secession.

11. JAMES K. POLK (1845-1849)

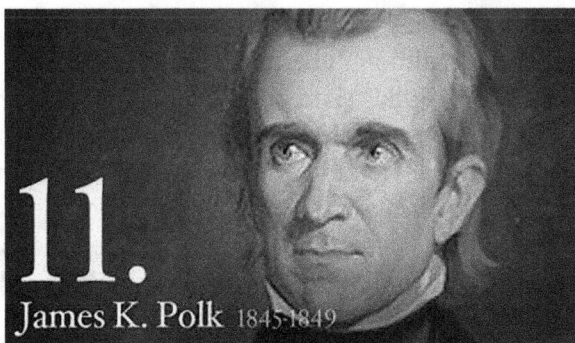

James K. Polk 1845-1849

Born: November 2, 1795, Mecklenburg County, North Carolina

Full Name: James Knox Polk
Nickname: "Young Hickory"
Full Name: James Knox Polk
Education: University of North Carolina (graduated 1818)
Religion: Presbyterian
Marriage: January 1, 1824, to Sarah Childress (1803–1891)
Children: None
Career: Lawyer
Political Party: Democrat
Died: June 15, 1849, Nashville, Tennessee

Under James Knox Polk, the United States grew by more than a million square miles, adding territory that now composes the states of Arizona, Utah, Nevada, California, Oregon, Idaho, Washington, much of New Mexico, and portions of Wyoming, Montana, and Colorado. More than any other President, Polk pursued "Manifest Destiny," a phrase coined by his fellow Jacksonian Democrat, John L. O'Sullivan, to express the conviction that Providence had foreordained the United States to spread its republican institutions across North America. He accomplished every major goal that he set for himself as President and in the process successfully waged war against Mexico, obtaining for the United States most of its present boundaries as a nation.

A man of firm personal principles, he kept his word to retire after a single term, although he easily could have won reelection. Despite Polk's accomplishments, many historians today regard him not as a great president but as one who missed opportunities. He failed to understand the depth of popular emotion over the westward expansion of the South's "peculiar institution." This failure on his part left the issue of slavery unaddressed and thus unresolved at the end of his term in 1849.

Youth and Family

Polk was born on a family farm in North Carolina. When he was ten, his family traveled by covered wagon to the frontier of Tennessee to carve a plantation out of the wilderness. The hardships of the journey damaged Polk's health for the rest of his life.

The Polk family did well financially, ultimately acquiring thousands of acres and more than fifty slaves. Polk was schooled at home and at two Presbyterian schools in Middle Tennessee. At the age of twenty, he continued his education at the University of North Carolina, graduating in 1818. He then returned home to study law under a prominent Nashville lawyer. In 1825, Polk won election to the United States House of Representatives, where he served seven terms.

Building Political Assets

Andrew Jackson enjoyed the support of Polk's father in his unsuccessful 1824 presidential campaign. When Jackson finally won the White House in 1828, Polk proved to be his closest ally in Congress. With Jackson behind him, Polk became the Speaker of the House in 1835, a position he held for four years. He so strongly supported Jackson's initiatives that his colleagues nicknamed him "Young Hickory." In 1839, he was elected governor of Tennessee.

When Polk ran for reelection in 1841, it was a bad time to be a Democrat. The country was in a severe depression, complete with bank failures and farm foreclosures, and the new Whig Party heaped blame on the party of Andrew Jackson. Polk lost the election. After a second defeat at the polls in 1843, Polk turned his attention to the family plantation.

Polk's wife, Sarah Childress, whom he married in 1824, helped him throughout his political career. A wealthy and well-educated Tennessean, she proved to be the perfect political wife of the day, entertaining and mingling easily with people—in contrast to her more reserved husband. When she settled into the life of the Polk plantation after her husband's second gubernatorial defeat, she probably had no idea that her next residence would be the White House.

Surprising Nomination and Close Election

When Democrats convened to select their presidential nominee for the election of 1844, no one expected Polk to emerge at the top of the ticket. Former President Martin Van Buren was the front-runner—but Van Buren had lost to the Whig William Henry Harrison in 1840, and many felt he was too weak a candidate. Moreover, the New Yorker had lost the support of the South due to his opposition to annexing Texas. The convention deadlocked, and prodded by Andrew Jackson, Van Buren threw his delegates behind the nation's first dark horse candidate: James Knox Polk. Opposition Whigs soon asked, "Who is James K. Polk?" In order to answer this question, Polk developed an explicit platform.

With Pennsylvania's George M. Dallas as his running mate, Polk announced his support both for the annexation of Texas and for the "reoccupation" of all of the Oregon Territory, which the United States then jointly occupied with the British between the latitudes of 42° and 54°40'. With his supporters pushing the slogan, "Fifty-Four Forty or Fight," Polk thus balanced the idea of a new slave state (Texas) with the possibility of a new free state (Oregon).

The election was vicious, with slavery and slander at its center. Both Polk and his Whig opponent, Henry Clay, owned slaves, but Clay opposed the annexation of Texas. The emergence of a third party further clouded things, and despite losing his home state of Tennessee Polk ultimately won with the thinnest margin in history.

Territory, Tariffs, and Slavery

Polk soon found himself in a crisis. After acquiring the territory containing present-day Oregon, Washington, and Idaho from the British, he turned his attention to Texas, which had been annexed by President John Tyler in his last days in office in 1845. Responding to Mexican counterclaims, Polk sent U.S. Army troops, under then-Colonel Zachary Taylor, into the disputed area on Texas' southern border. After a clash in late April 1846 between American and Mexican troops in the area, Polk requested and received a declaration of war from Congress. Within sixteen months, U.S. forces drove deep into Mexico, capturing Mexico City in September 1847. In the Treaty of Guadalupe Hidalgo, the United States imposed a Rio Grande border for Texas and paid $15 million to Mexico for the territories of California and New Mexico.

Domestically, Polk wanted to stabilize the U.S. banking system and to lower tariffs. He also found himself challenged by the Wilmot Proviso, a bill that intended to ban slavery in all territories acquired from Mexico. With fierce maneuvering on all sides, and with Polk opposed to it, the Proviso passed the House repeatedly, but the Senate never concurred. The unresolved status of slavery in the new western territories outlived disputes over banking and the tariff, becoming the most contentious issue facing the United States in the years immediately following Polk's presidency.

Polk kept his promise not to run for a second term and was succeeded in office by the hero of the Mexican War, Zachary Taylor, candidate of the opposition Whig Party and a man whom Polk despised. Less than three months later, Polk was dead, possibly of cholera contracted on a long tour of the southern states. He left most of his estate to his wife, with the request that she free their slaves upon her death. Polk left behind a country that was both larger and weaker—expanded by more than a million square miles but fatally torn over the

193

key issue these new lands had once again brought to the fore: slavery.

12. ZACHARY TAYLOR (1849-1850)

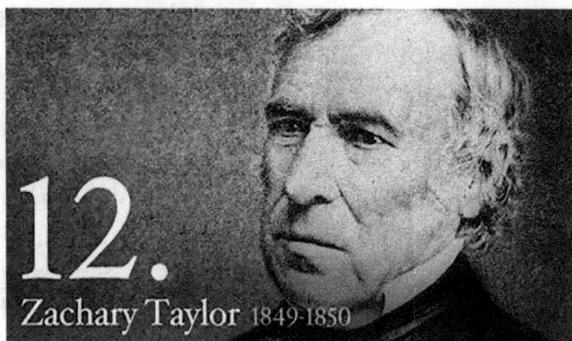

Born: November 24, 1784, near Barboursville, Virginia
Nickname: "Old Rough and Ready"
Religion: Episcopalian
Marriage: June 21, 1810, to Margaret Mackall Smith (1788–1852)
Children: Ann Margaret Mackall (1811–1875), Sarah Knox (1814–1835), Octavia Pannill (1816–1820), Margaret Smith (1819–1820), Mary Elizabeth (1824–1909), Richard (1826–1879)
Career: Soldier
Political Party: Whig
Died: July 9, 1850, Washington, D.C.

At the time he became President, Zachary Taylor was the most popular man in America, a hero of the Mexican-American War. However, at a time when Americans were confronting the explosive issue of slavery, he was probably not the right man for the job.

Taylor was a wealthy slave owner who held properties in the plantation states of Louisiana, Kentucky, and Mississippi. During his brief time in office—he died only sixteen months after his election—his presidency foundered over the question of whether the national government should permit the spread of slavery to the present-day states of California, New Mexico, and Utah, then newly won from Mexico. His sudden death put Vice President Millard Fillmore into the White House, and Fillmore promptly threw his support behind the Compromise of 1850, canceling out much of the impact of Taylor's presidency.

Career Soldier, "Indian Fighter," and War Hero

Zachary Taylor was born on November 24, 1784, to a landed family of planters. His family's fortunes grew, and by 1800, they owned 10,000 acres in Kentucky and a number of slaves. He knew as a child that he wanted a military career. In 1808, he received his first commission as an officer, becoming commander of the garrison at Fort Pickering, the site of modern-day Memphis. He was transferred from one frontier post to another in a career that built his professional reputation but made his personal life difficult.

In 1810, he married Margaret Mackall Smith, the daughter of a prominent Maryland family. She followed him from post to post as their family grew. The family finally settled in Louisiana, where Taylor assumed command of the fort at Baton Rouge. Taylor won fame as an "Indian fighter" in the present-day states of Wisconsin, Minnesota, Mississippi, Oklahoma, Kansas, Louisiana, Arkansas, Florida, and Texas. Although he frequently fought Native Americans, he also protected their lands from invading white settlers. He believed that the best solution for coexistence between settlers and Native Americans was a strong military presence to keep the two sides apart.

In 1845, Texas was granted statehood. Mexico disputed lands along the new state's border, and President James Knox Polk ordered Taylor and his troops into the contested area, a deployment that ignited the Mexican-American War. After winning two decisive encounters, Taylor, facing overwhelming odds, triumphed in a battle against the Mexican General Santa Anna at Buena Vista. When the smoke cleared, Taylor's army of 6,000 had defeated a Mexican force of 20,000, and Zachary Taylor, "Old Rough and Ready," as he was known because of his willingness to share his troops' hardships, was a national hero.

The Politics of Slavery

Although Taylor had never divulged his political preferences, after his victory, clubs sprang up to support his presidential candidacy. By then, he was a wealthy slave owner, and the South hoped he would support states' rights and the expansion of slavery into the new areas won from Mexico. The North pointed to his service on the nation's behalf and hoped fervently that he was a Union man.

In fact, Taylor thought of himself as an independent. He differed with the Democrats over the concept of a strong national bank and opposed the extension of slavery into areas where neither cotton nor sugar could be grown. He also had problems with the Whigs' support of strong protective tariffs. Most importantly, he passionately opposed secession as a means of resolving the nation's problems. In the end, he announced that he was a Whig. At their 1848 nominating convention, the Whigs named Taylor for President, adding New York's Millard Fillmore to the ticket to appease those who opposed the nomination of a slave owner and doubted Taylor's commitment to the Whig Party.

On November 7, 1848, the first time the entire nation voted on the same day, Taylor and Fillmore narrowly defeated the Democratic ticket, headed by Michigan's Lewis Cass, and the ticket of the Free-Soil Party, led by former President Martin Van Buren.

Slavery had been the driving issue of the campaign, and it would be the central challenge of Taylor's brief presidency as well. The nation was polarized over the question of whether to extend the institution to the new western territories. Taylor believed that the people of California—in which he hoped to include the Mormons around Salt Lake—and New Mexico should be allowed to decide for themselves whether or not to permit slavery by writing constitutions and applying immediately for statehood. In this way, he hoped to avoid the increasingly rancorous sectional debate over congressional prohibition of slavery in any territorial governments organized in the area. Many in the South, however, feared that the addition of two free states would upset the delicate North-South balance in the Senate.

Some southern Democrats called for a secession convention, and Taylor's reaction was a bristling statement that he would hang anyone who tried to disrupt the Union by force or by conspiracy. In this heated atmosphere, Henry Clay, Daniel Webster, and others began to cobble together a compromise in the Senate. To placate the South, they proposed the enactment of a second Fugitive Slave Law that would mandate the return of escaped slaves apprehended anywhere in the nation. This effort would become the Compromise of 1850.

The compromise legislation did not prohibit slavery in the Mexican Cession. It admitted California as a free state, and it allowed for the organization of Utah and New Mexico as formal territories, rather than as states, without any federal restrictions on slavery. This left open the possibility that any states formed from those territories could opt for slavery, and indeed the language of the compromise explicitly committed future Congresses to admit them as slave states if they so desired. Many northerners were outraged by that concession to the South, and it intensified their opposition to any further extension of slavery. This was the issue that pushed the nation down the road to Civil War.

At a time when strong leadership and party politics were absolutely essential, Taylor probably damaged his cause by refusing to engage directly with Congress or to pull together a functional coalition. He held onto his belief that the President should stand above party politics.

On July 4, 1850, after attending celebrations in Washington, D.C., Taylor contracted a virulent stomach ailment that may have been cholera. He died on July 9, and more than 100,000 people lined the funeral route to see the hero laid to rest. He left behind a country sharply divided and a vice president, Millard Fillmore, who supported the Compromise of 1850. In the end, Taylor had limited personal impact on the presidency, and his months in office did little to slow the approach of the great national tragedy of the Civil War.

13. MILLARD FILLMORE (1850-1853)

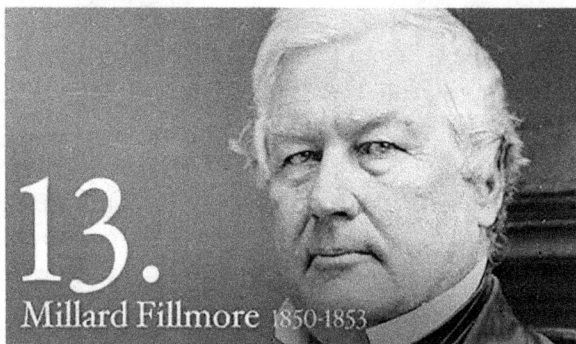

Born: January 7, 1800, Summerhill, New York
Nickname: "The American Louis Philippe"
Education: Six months of grade school; read law in 1822
Religion: Unitarian
Marriage: February 5, 1826, to Abigail Powers (1798–1853); February 10, 1858, to Caroline Carmichael McIntosh (1813–1881)
Children: Millard Powers (1828–1889), Mary Abigail (1832–1854)

Career Lawyer
Political Party: Whig
Died: March 8, 1874, Buffalo, New York

Born into desperate poverty at the dawn of the nineteenth century, Millard Fillmore climbed to the highest office in the land—and inherited a nation breaking into fragments over the question of slavery. Despite his best efforts, the lines of the future battles of the Civil War were drawn, and Fillmore found himself rejected by his own dying party and denied renomination. After almost a quarter of a century out of the White House, he died in New York state in 1874.

Fillmore, the second of eight children, was born into an impoverished family on January 7, 1800. His family's small farm in upstate Cayuga County, New York, could not support them, and Fillmore's father apprenticed his son to a clothmaker, a brutal apprenticeship that stopped just short of slavery. Fillmore taught himself to read, stealing books on occasion, and finally managed to borrow thirty dollars and pay his obligation to the clothmaker. Free, he walked one hundred miles to get back home to his family.

He was obsessed with educating himself. He pored over every book he could get his hands on and attended school in a nearby town for six months. His teacher, Abigail Powers, encouraged and helped him. She would prove to be the most influential person in his life. She was only nineteen—not even two years older than her pupil. After Fillmore received a clerkship with a local judge, he began to court Abigail Powers. The couple married in 1826.

Anti-Jackson Politics

As a young lawyer, Fillmore was approached by a fledgling political party and asked to run for the New York State Assembly. In 1829, he began the first of three terms in the assembly, where he sponsored a substantial amount of legislation. In 1832, Millard Fillmore was elected to the U.S. House of Representatives.

At that time, Andrew Jackson was President. Jackson's repeated clashes with Congress and his ambitious attempts to expand presidential power united several parties against him. Fillmore's own Anti-Masonic Party merged with the Whigs, which represented the older, more entrenched power structure and opposed everything that Jackson and the Democrats represented. In 1843, at the end of four terms in Congress, which were interrupted by one defeat, Fillmore resigned from the legislature. After unsuccessfully lobbying for the vice presidential nomination on the Whig ticket with Henry Clay and losing an election for governor of New York, both in 1844, Fillmore was elected New York state comptroller, or chief financial officer, in 1847. He won this election by such a wide margin that he was immediately considered a prospect for national office.

The Whigs selected the military hero General Zachary Taylor as their presidential nominee for the election of 1848. The nomination of a slave owner who held property in Louisiana, Kentucky, and Mississippi infuriated abolitionist Whigs from the North. The party decided to balance the ticket by putting a Northerner in the vice presidential slot. Hence, Fillmore was chosen.

The Taylor-Fillmore ticket won a bitterly fought election over the Democratic ticket led by Michigan senator Lewis Cass. Taylor and Fillmore were an odd match -- the products of very different backgrounds and educations and far apart on the issues of the day. The two men did not meet until after the election and did not hit it off when they did. In a short time, Fillmore found himself excluded from the councils of power, relegated to his role as president of the Senate.

Slavery and the Compromise of 1850

The critical issue facing President Taylor was slavery. Henry Clay had crafted a series of proposals into an omnibus bill that became known as the Compromise of 1850, a patchwork of legislation that would admit California as a new free state; organize New Mexico and Utah, the remainder of the Mexican Cession, as territories on the basis of popular sovereignty; and readjust the disputed boundary between Texas and New Mexico. The compromise also established a fugitive slave law that guaranteed that runaway slaves apprehended anywhere in the United States would be returned to their owners. Taylor refused to take a stand, and the compromise bill was stalled in endless debates in the Senate by mid-1850. But then the unthinkable happened: the President died, possibly of cholera.

As President, Fillmore strongly supported the compromise. Allying himself with the Democratic Senator Stephen Douglas and appointing the pro-compromise Whig Daniel Webster as his secretary of state, Fillmore engineered its passage. By forcing these issues, Fillmore believed he had helped to safeguard the Union, but it soon became clear that the compromise, rather than satisfying anyone, gave everyone something to hate. Under the strains of the failed agreement, the Whig Party began to come apart at the seams.

On the international stage, Fillmore dispatched Commodore Perry to "open" Japan to Western trade and worked to keep the Hawaiian Islands out of European hands. He refused to back an invasion of Cuba by a group of Southern adventurers who wanted to expand the South into a slave-based Caribbean empire. This "filibustering" expedition failed, and Fillmore took the blame from Southerners. At the same time, he offended Northerners by enforcing the Fugitive Slave Law in their region. Weary and dispirited, he tried to decline to run again but was prevailed upon to allow his name to be put forward—only to lose the nomination to General Winfield

Scott. Shortly thereafter, his beloved Abigail died, followed by his twenty-two-year-old daughter Mary.

In 1856, he ran for election as the presidential candidate of the Whig-American Party, a fusion of the remaining Whigs and the anti-immigrant American (nicknamed "Know-Nothing") Party. He won the Electoral College votes of Maryland and 21 percent of the popular vote. But the newly organized Republican Party, even in defeat, eclipsed Fillmore and the Whigs, winning 33 percent of the vote, and Fillmore's poor performance marked the end of his party. Millard Fillmore died of a stroke in March of 1874.

14. FRANKLIN PIERCE (1853-1857)

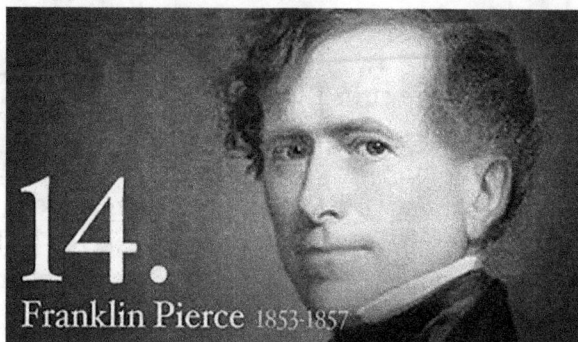

14.
Franklin Pierce 1853-1857

Born: November 23, 1804, Hillsborough (now Hillsboro), New Hampshire
Nickname: "Young Hickory of the Granite Hills"
Education: Bowdoin College (graduated 1824)
Religion: Episcopalian
Marriage: November 19, 1834, to Jane Means Appleton (1806–1863)
Children: Franklin (1836); Frank Robert (1839–1843); Benjamin (1841–1853)
Career: Lawyer, Public Official
Political Party: Democrat
Died: October 8, 1869, Concord, New Hampshire

Franklin Pierce, the 14th President of the United States, came to office during a period of growing tension between the North and South. A politician of limited ability, Pierce was behind one of the most crucial pieces of legislation in American history. Although he did not author the Kansas-Nebraska Act, he did encourage its passage by Congress. And that piece of legislation set the nation on its path to civil war.

Like many American politicians, Franklin Pierce's career was aided by his father, a two-term governor of New Hampshire. Before he was thirty, Franklin Pierce had served in the New Hampshire legislature and had been elected to the U.S. Congress where he served as both a congressman and senator. Bored and lonely in Washington, the young congressman developed a drinking problem and a reputation as a gossipy Washington insider. In an attempt to settle down, the handsome, socially gregarious Pierce married Jane Means Appleton. Jane Pierce was her husband's opposite; she was painfully shy, deeply religious, often in bad health, and a strong advocate of the temperance movement. She detested Washington and refused to live there, even after Pierce became a U.S. senator in 1837. Indeed, Jane's disgust with the political life in Washington must have been behind Pierce's decision to resign from the Senate in 1841. Subsequently, Franklin Pierce served in the Mexican-American War, and in something of a surprise was elected President in 1852. After his presidency he retired to Concord, New Hampshire, where he died in 1869.

15. James Buchanan (1857-1861)

15.
James Buchanan 1857-1861

Born: April 23, 1791, Cove Gap (near Mercersburg), Pennsylvania
Nickname: "Old Buck"
Education: Dickinson College (graduated 1809)
Religion: Presbyterian
Marriage: None
Career: Lawyer
Political Party: Democrat
Died: June 1, 1868, near Lancaster, Pennsylvania

In the 1850s, the question of slavery divided the United States. Hopes ran high that the new President, "Old Buck," might be the man to avert national crisis. He failed entirely. During his administration, the Union broke apart, and when he left office, civil war threatened.

James Buchanan was the son of Irish immigrants who had made a successful life for themselves as merchants in rural Pennsylvania. The Buchanans could afford to send James to good schools, and after graduating with honors from Dickinson College, James Buchanan studied law. His legal and political careers moved forward together. Becoming a successful attorney, he advanced from state legislator to national figure, including membership in both houses of Congress, ambassadorships, and a cabinet post. The ambitious Buchanan had his sights on the presidency for many years before he actually attained the office. He tried for the White House in 1844, 1848, and 1852 before finally achieving his goal in 1856.

A Dividing Nation

By 1856, the debates over slavery had reached an unprecedented emotional intensity, with abolitionists and proslavery forces alike openly advocating violence and at times resorting to it. A number of abolitionists had been murdered in Kansas, and a radical abolitionist named John Brown had, in retaliation, massacred five settlers loosely affiliated with the proslavery party. Southerners were enraged while many in the North lauded Brown as a hero. In this environment, Buchanan asserted that slavery should be a matter for individual states and territories to decide for themselves. This approach gained him Southern support. His opponent, Senator John C. Fremont, the first Republican presidential candidate, argued that the federal government should prevent slavery from spreading into the new western territories. Shortly before the campaign, Buchanan expressed his fears about the task ahead: "Before many years the abolitionists will bring war upon this land," he said. "It may come during the next presidential term." Buchanan won the election, and many hoped that his experience would help the nation avert war.

Two days after Buchanan's inauguration, the Supreme Court announced its decision in the Dred Scott case. Influenced by the new President, who was sympathetic to Southern interests, the Supreme Court ruled that because slaves—and even former slaves—were not citizens, they had no right to sue for their freedom in a U.S. court of law. Furthermore, the Court declared unconstitutional the Missouri Compromise of 1820, which banned slavery in the portion of the Louisiana Purchase above 36 degrees 30 minutes north latitude. Republicans denounced the decision and vowed to repudiate it. America had become a nation with a sharply divided political system: the Republicans, exclusively Northern and antislavery, and the Democrats, dominantly Southerners and their Northern allies who defended slavery and states' rights.

Political Troubles

Eager to retain the support of Southern Democrats and believing early statehood for Kansas would defuse the explosive territorial problem, Buchanan endorsed a proslavery constitution for Kansas. His fellow Democrat, Senator Stephen A. Douglas of Illinois, challenged this endorsement and instead demanded a legitimate popular vote in Kansas. These Kansas troubles, especially the break with Douglas, divided the Democratic Party and weakened Buchanan. Meanwhile, in 1859, John Brown seized the Southern town of Harpers Ferry in Virginia in a futile attempt to spark an uprising of slaves. Although Brown was captured and hanged, his action drove another wedge between North and South.

In 1860, the rift between James Buchanan and Stephen Douglas doomed the political aspirations of both. Under the strain of internal pressure and sectional tension, the Democratic Party finally snapped in two, allowing an unknown railroad lawyer from an upstart party—the Republican Abraham Lincoln—to win the White House. The election of a Northerner clearly opposed to the extension of slavery outside existing Southern states frightened the South.

Six weeks after Lincoln's election, South Carolina left the Union, and within another six weeks, six other states followed. Maintaining that he lacked power, the lame-duck Buchanan took no action to stop secession, which only emboldened the new Confederacy and gave seceding states time to set up a government. Buchanan seemed eager to get out of the White House before the real disaster ensued. He vanished from public life and retreated to his home, seeing only close friends until his death in 1868.

16. ABRAHAM LINCOLN (1861-1865)

16.
Abraham Lincoln 1861-1865

Born: February 12, 1809, Hardin (now Larue) County, Kentucky
Nickname: "Honest Abe"; "Illinois Rail-Splitter"
Religion: No formal affiliation
Marriage: November 4, 1842, to Mary Todd (1818–1882)
Children: Robert Todd (1843–1926), Edward Baker (1846–1850), William Wallace (1850–1862), Thomas "Tad" (1853–1871)
Career: Lawyer
Political Party: Whig; Republican
Died: April 15, 1865, Washington, D.C.

When Abraham Lincoln was elected President in 1860, seven slave states left the Union to form the Confederate States of America, and four more joined when hostilities began between the North and South. A bloody civil war then engulfed the nation as Lincoln vowed to preserve the Union, enforce the laws of the United States, and end the secession. The war lasted for more than four years with a staggering loss of more than 600,000 Americans dead. Midway through the war, Lincoln issued the Emancipation Proclamation, which freed all slaves within the Confederacy and changed the war from a battle to preserve the Union into a battle for freedom. He was the first Republican President, and Union victory ended forever the claim that state sovereignty superseded federal authority.

Killed by an assassin's bullet less than a week after the surrender of Confederate forces, Lincoln left the nation a more perfect Union and thereby earned the admiration of most Americans as the country's greatest President.

Born dirt-poor in a log cabin in Kentucky in 1809, Lincoln grew up in frontier Kentucky and Indiana, where he was largely self-educated, with a taste for jokes, hard work, and books. He served for a time as a soldier in the Black Hawk War, taught himself law, and held a seat in the Illinois state legislature as a Whig politician in the 1830s and 1840s. From state politics, he moved to the U.S. House of Representatives in 1847, where he voiced his opposition to the U.S. war with Mexico. In the mid-1850s, Lincoln left the Whig Party to join the new Republican Party. In 1858, he went up against one of the most popular politicians in the nation, Senator Stephen Douglas, in a contest for the U.S. Senate. Lincoln lost that election, but his spectacular performance against Douglas in a series of nationally covered debates made him a contender for the 1860 Republican presidential nomination.

Fighting for Unity and Freedom

In the 1860 campaign for President, Lincoln firmly expressed his opposition to slavery and his determination to limit the expansion of slavery westward into the new territories acquired from Mexico in 1850. His election victory created a crisis for the nation, as many southern Democrats feared that it would just be a matter of time before Lincoln would move to kill slavery in the South. Rather than face a future in which black people might become free citizens, much of the white South supported secession. This reasoning was based upon the doctrine of states' rights, which placed ultimate sovereignty with the states.

Lincoln vowed to preserve the Union even if it meant war. He eventually raised an army and navy of nearly 3 million northern men to face a southern army of over 2 million soldiers. In battles fought from Virginia to California (but mainly in Virginia, in the Mississippi River Valley, and along the border states) a great civil war tore the United States apart. In pursuing victory, Lincoln assumed extralegal powers over the press, declared martial law in areas where no military action justified it, quelled draft riots with armed soldiers, and drafted soldiers to fight for the Union cause. No President in history had ever exerted so much executive authority, but he did so not for personal power but in order to preserve the Union. In 1864, as an example of his limited personal ambitions, Lincoln refused to call off national elections, preferring to hold the election even if he lost the vote rather than destroy the democratic basis upon which he rested his authority. With the electoral support of Union soldiers, many of whom were given short leaves to return home to vote, and thanks to the spectacular victory of Union troops in General Sherman's capture of Atlanta, Lincoln was decisively reelected.

What started as a war to preserve the Union and vindicate democracy became a battle for freedom and a war to end slavery when Lincoln issued the Emancipation Proclamation in January of 1863. Although the Proclamation did not free all slaves in the nation—indeed, no slaves outside of the Confederacy were affected by the Proclamation—it was an important symbolic gesture that identified the Union with freedom and the death of slavery. As part of the Proclamation, Lincoln also urged black males to join the Union forces as soldiers and sailors. By the end of the war, nearly two hundred thousand African Americans had fought for the Union cause, and Lincoln referred to them as indispensable in ensuring Union victory.

Personal Tragedies and Triumphs

While the war raged, Lincoln also suffered great personal anguish over the death of his beloved son and the depressed mental condition of his wife, Mary. The pain of war and personal loss affected him deeply, and he often expressed his anguish by turning to humor and by speaking eloquently about the meaning of the great war which raged across the land. His Gettysburg Address, delivered after the Battle of Gettysburg, as well as his second inaugural in 1865, are acknowledged to be among the great orations in American history.

Almost all historians judge Lincoln as the greatest President in American history because of the way he exercised leadership during the war and because of the impact of that leadership on the moral and political character of the nation. He conceived of his presidential role as unique under the Constitution in times of crisis. Lincoln was convinced that within the branches of government, the presidency alone was empowered not only to uphold the Constitution, but also to preserve, protect, and defend it. In the end, however, Lincoln is measured by his most lasting accomplishments: the preservation of the Union, the vindication of democracy, and the death of slavery—accomplishments achieved by acting "with malice towards none" in the pursuit of a more perfect and equal union.

17. ANDREW JOHNSON (1865-1869)

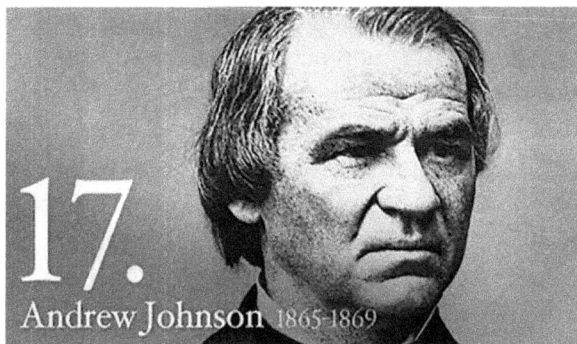

Andrew Johnson 1865-1869

Born: December 29, 1808, Raleigh, North Carolina
Nickname: None
Religion: No formal affiliation
Marriage: May 17, 1827, to Eliza McCardle (1810–1876)
Children: Martha (1828–1901), Charles (1830–1863), Mary (1832–1883), Robert (1834–1869), Andrew (1852–1879)
Career: Tailor; Public Official
Political Party: Democrat; Unionist
Died: July 31, 1875, Carter's Station, Tennessee

Andrew Johnson gives truth to the saying that in America, anyone can grow up to become President. Born in a log cabin in North Carolina to nearly illiterate parents, Andrew Johnson did not master the basics of reading, grammar, or math until he met his wife at the age of seventeen. The only other man to attain the office of President with so little formal education was Abraham Lincoln. Whereas Lincoln is esteemed as America's greatest President, Johnson, his successor, is ranked as one of the worst.

After Andrew's father died, his mother and her new husband apprenticed fourteen-year-old Andrew and his older brother William to a local tailor. After serving a number of years in this trade, the boys ran away for several years, dodging rewards for their capture placed by their former employer.

Andrew later returned to his mother, and the entire family moved west to Greeneville, Tennessee, where young Andrew set up shop as a tailor and met his wife, Eliza McCardle. Eliza educated Andrew and helped him make wise investments in town real estate and farmlands. When Johnson reached the White House, First Lady Eliza Johnson was a semi-invalid suffering from tuberculosis during her husband's term in office. She only made two public appearances during her entire stay in the executive mansion. Nevertheless, she operated behind the scenes with energy and tact and was fondly remembered by the White House staff.

Political Leanings

By 1834, the young tailor had served as town alderman and mayor of Greeneville and was fast making a name for himself as an aspiring politician. Johnson considered himself a Jacksonian Democrat, and he gained the support of local mechanics, artisans, and rural folk with his common-man tell-it-like-it-is style. He quickly moved up to serve in his state's legislature, the U.S. House of Representatives, and as governor of Tennessee. When the Civil War broke out, Johnson was a first-term U.S. senator aligned with the states' rights and proslavery wing of the Democratic Party.

However closely he identified with his fellow Southerners' views on slavery, Johnson disagreed strongly with their calls to break up the Union over the issue. When Tennessee left the Union after the election of Abraham Lincoln, Johnson broke with his home state, becoming the only Southern senator to retain his seat in the U.S. Senate. In the South, Johnson was deemed a traitor; his property was confiscated and his wife and two daughters were driven from the state. In the North, however, Johnson's stand made him an overnight hero.

Though Johnson was deeply committed to saving the Union, he did not believe in the emancipation of slaves. After

Lincoln made him the military governor of Tennessee, Johnson convinced the President to exempt Tennessee from the Emancipation Proclamation. By the summer of 1863, however, he began to favor emancipation as a war measure. Concerned about his chances for reelection, Lincoln felt that he needed a man like Johnson as his vice president to help balance the ticket in 1864. Lincoln's enemies could not easily depict him as a tool of the abolitionists with Johnson as his running mate. Together, the two won a sweeping victory against Democratic candidate General George B. McClellan and his running mate, George Pendleton.

Reconstructing the Defeated South

Tragically, Abraham Lincoln was assassinated days after the Civil War ended in 1865. Had the assassin's plot gone as planned, Johnson would have been killed along with Lincoln; instead, he became President. In a strange twist of fate, the racist Southerner Johnson was charged with the reconstruction of the defeated South, including the extension of civil rights and suffrage to black Southerners. It quickly became clear that Johnson would block efforts to force Southern states to guarantee full equality for blacks, and the stage was set for a showdown with congressional Republicans, who viewed black voting rights as crucial to their power base in the South.

During the first eight months of his term, Johnson took advantage of Congress being in recess and rushed through his own policies for Reconstruction. These included handing out thousands of pardons in routine fashion and allowing the South to set up "black codes," which essentially maintained slavery under another name. When Congress came back into session, Republicans moved to stop the President. In 1866, Congress passed the Freedmen's Bureau Bill, providing shelter and provision for former slaves and protection of their rights in court, as well as the Civil Rights Act, defining all persons born in the U.S. as citizens. Congress also passed the

Fourteenth Amendment to the Constitution, authorizing the federal government to protect the rights of all citizens. Each of these—except the Amendment—was passed over President Johnson's veto. In a final humiliating gesture, Congress passed the Tenure of Office Act, which stripped the President of the power to remove federal officials without the Senate's approval, and in 1867, established a military Reconstruction program to enforce political and social rights for Southern blacks.

Challenging Congress and Impeachment

Furious, Johnson decided to go straight to the people in an attempt to regain his stature and authority as President. During the congressional elections of 1866, he set out on a speaking tour to campaign for congressmen who would support his policies. The plan was a complete disaster. In speech after speech, Johnson personally attacked his Republican opponents in vile and abusive language. On several occasions, it appeared that the President had had too much to drink. One observer estimated that Johnson lost one million Northern votes in this debacle.

Having lost both congressional and popular support, Johnson was finished. Blocked at every turn, he felt he had no choice but to challenge the Tenure of Office Act as a blatant usurpation of presidential authority. In direct opposition to the act, he fired Secretary of War Stanton. Congress then voted to impeach Johnson by a vote of 126 to 47 in February 1868, citing his violation of the Tenure of Office Act and charging that he had brought disgrace and ridicule on Congress. By a margin of one vote, the Senate voted not to convict Johnson, and he served the duration of the term won by Lincoln.

During Johnson's term, the Reconstruction Acts of 1867 extended suffrage to formerly enslaved male African Americans, completely transforming the American electorate.

Hundreds of black delegates participated in state constitutional conventions, and from 1869 until 1877, fourteen African American men served in the U.S. House of Representatives and two were in the U.S. Senate. All of this occurred over Johnson's head, and all would change once the white Southerners regained their stranglehold on the South. In the meantime, terrorist organizations such as the KKK attacked black citizens and their supporters. In 1868, one-tenth of the black delegates to the state constitutional conventions had experienced physical abuse.

Andrew Johnson is largely viewed as the worst possible person to have been President at the end of the Civil War. He utterly failed to make a satisfying and just peace because of his racist views, his gross incompetence in federal office, and his incredible miscalculation of public support for his policies. One can only sadly speculate about how different America would have been had Lincoln lived to see the country through the critical period of Reconstruction. In the end, Johnson did more to extend the period of national strife than to heal the wounds of war.

18. Ulysses S. Grant (1869 – 1877)

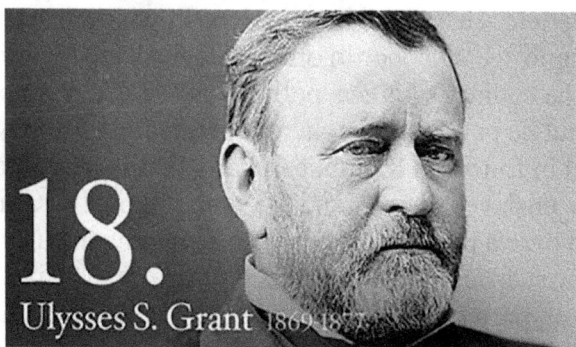

Ulysses S. Grant 1869-187..

Born: April 27, 1822, Point Pleasant, Ohio
Nickname: "Hero of Appomattox"

Education: U.S. Military Academy, West Point, New York (graduated 1843)
Religion: Methodist
Marriage: August 22, 1848, to Julia Boggs Dent (1826–1902)
Children: Frederick Dent (1850–1912), Ulysses Simpson (1852–1929), Ellen Wrenshall (1855–1922), Jesse Root (1858–1934)
Career: Soldier
Political Party: Republican
Died: July 23, 1885, Mount McGregor, New York

Ulysses S. Grant is best known as the Union general who led the United States to victory over the Confederate States of America during the American Civil War. As a two-term President, he is typically dismissed as weak and ineffective; historians have often ranked Grant's presidency near the bottom in American history. Recently, however, scholars have begun to reexamine and reassess his presidential tenure; recent rankings have reflected a significant rise.

Every President presents historians with some contradictions, but Grant might do so more than most. He was quiet and soft-spoken but able to inspire great bravery from his soldiers on the battlefield. He was an honorable man who was unable or unwilling to see dishonor in others. He disdained politics but rose to the country's highest political office. He was no great orator, but he possessed a coherent political philosophy mirrored in Lincoln's Republican Party that won the war, freed the enslaved people, and saved the Republic. Grant presided over a powerful if unstable economy unleashing productive capacities only dreamed of before the Civil War. A great supporter of the transcontinental railroads, Grant oversaw the completion of the one running from Sacramento, California, to Omaha, Nebraska, in 1869 in his first year in office. Overall, Grant's intentions were honorable, and he made efforts that few had attempted before him, especially in the areas of African American rights, Native American policy, and civil service reform. He also executed a successful foreign policy and was responsible for improving Anglo-American relations.

Early Life

Ulysses Grant was born in Ohio, the first of six children. He was small, sensitive, quiet, and well-known for his talent with horses. He attended the United States Military Academy at West Point in New York and excelled in mathematics, writing, drawing, and horsemanship. After graduating, he was assigned to an infantry company in Missouri. His company soon moved south to prepare for the conflict brewing with Mexico over disputed Texas territory. From 1846 to 1848, Grant fought in the Mexican War and was twice cited for bravery.

After the war, Grant moved to various Army postings in Detroit, New York, and the Pacific Northwest. He resigned suddenly from the Army in 1854 and returned to the Midwest to be with his family. Grant then attempted a variety of jobs, including farming and insurance sales, before finding work in his family's leather goods store in Galena, Illinois. Through these difficult times, he relied on his wife, Julia Dent Grant. The two were a devoted couple and adoring parents to their four children.

Civil War Hero

When the American Civil War began in 1861, experienced officers like Grant were in short supply. The Illinois governor assigned him to make a disciplined fighting unit out of the rebellious Twenty-First Illinois Volunteer Infantry Regiment. Lieutenant Colonel Grant drilled the men, instituted badly needed discipline, and soon earned the respect of the volunteers. The Army noted his efforts and promoted him to brigadier general.

Grant garnered attention as he led his troops to fight and win battles in the Western Theater. He captured Fort Henry and Fort Donelson in Tennessee, forced the surrender of Vicksburg, Mississippi, and defeated a larger Southern force at Chattanooga, Tennessee. In the last year of the war, he was both praised and criticized for his willingness to fight and sustain a high number of casualties. Grant helped end the bloody Civil War when he directed the Union forces to lay siege to General Robert E. Lee's Army of Northern Virginia in Petersburg, a small city south of Richmond, Virginia, forcing its surrender in April 1865. At that point, General Grant was the most revered man in the Union.

Lincoln's tragic assassination at the end of the Civil War was followed by the ineffective leadership of President Andrew Johnson, a Democrat from Tennessee. Johnson urged a moderate approach to Reconstruction that would not punish the South or protect the rights of the newly freed slaves beyond emancipation. Radical Republicans wanted to ensure the civil and political rights of African Americans. In the election of 1868, postwar social and economic policies were the major campaign issues. The Republicans backed Grant, who concluded his acceptance speech with "Let us have peace." The popular general won the election to become the nation's eighteenth President.

Presidency

Coming into office, President Grant alienated party stalwarts by rejecting party politics. When he appointed his cabinet, he did not turn to Republican leaders for their advice. Instead, he chose people he thought he could trust and to whom he could delegate responsibility. This strategy led to some good cabinet appointments but also to a number of dubious ones. Grant was also loyal out of all proportion to anyone who had helped him or worked with him. As a result, he was sometimes unwilling to remove ineffective people, and some areas of his administration suffered from incompetence and corruption.

In his first inaugural address, Grant spoke of his desire for the ratification of the Fifteenth Amendment, which sought to grant citizens the right to vote regardless of race or previous servitude. He lobbied hard to get the amendment passed, angering many Southern whites in the process. He also, on occasion, sent in the military to protect African Americans from newly formed terrorist groups, such as the Ku Klux Klan, which tried to prevent blacks from participating in society. Grant incurred the wrath of citizens who blamed him for the economic woes that plagued the nation in the aftermath of the war. In 1872, however, Grant won reelection by a landslide.

During his second term, a depression in Europe spread to the United States, resulting in high unemployment. Like so many Presidents before and after Grant, scandals tended to divert attention from the administration's policy agenda. Although Grant was never personally implicated in any of the scandals, he did not disassociate himself from the members of his administration who were guilty. His inability to clean up his administration tarnished his reputation in the eyes of the American public. In 1875, he announced that he would not seek a third term. The Republicans nominated Rutherford B. Hayes to be their standard-bearer in the 1876 election.

After his presidency, Grant found himself in economic difficulties and dying of throat cancer. He lost his money in a financial scandal, yet he was determined to provide for his family after his death. After Century Magazine approached him to write articles about his Civil War experiences, Grant discovered that he enjoyed the process and decided to compile his memoirs. He approached this last battle as he had all others—with grim and dogged determination. His final days were spent on his porch with pencil and paper in hand, wrapped in blankets and in fearsome pain, slowly scrawling out his life's epic tale. He completed the book just days before his death. It was hugely successful and provided for his family's financial security.

19. RUTHERFORD B. HAYES (1877-1881)

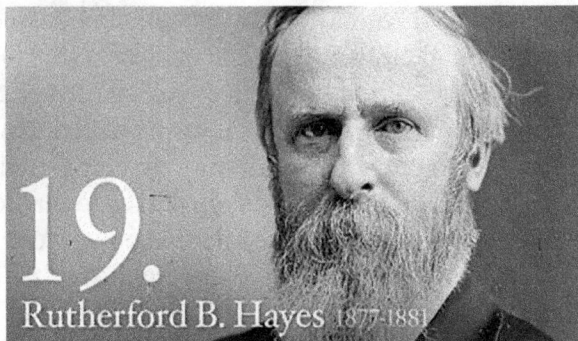

Rutherford B. Hayes 1877-1881

Born: October 4, 1822, Delaware, Ohio
Full Name: Rutherford Birchard Hayes
Nickname: "Dark-Horse President," "Rud"
Education: Kenyon College (graduated 1842), Harvard Law School (graduated 1845)
Religion: Methodist
Marriage: December 30, 1852, to Lucy Ware Webb (1831–1889)
Children: Birchard Austin (1853–1926), James Webb Cook (1856–1934), Rutherford Platt (1858–1927), Joseph Thompson (1861–1863), George Crook (1864–1866), Fanny (1867–1950), Scott Russell (1871–1923), Manning Force (1873–1874)
Career: Lawyer
Political Party: Republican
Died: January 17, 1893, Fremont, Ohio

The policies of Rutherford B. Hayes, America's nineteenth President, began to heal the nation after the ravages of the Civil War. He was well suited to the task, having earned a steadfast reputation for integrity throughout his career as a soldier and a statesman. Upstanding, moral, and honest, Hayes was elected after the most lengthy, bitterly disputed, and corrupt presidential election in history.

Hayes's father ran a successful farm and whiskey distillery in Ohio but died ten weeks before Rutherford was born. Raised by his single mother, Rud developed a very close relationship with his brilliant sister, Fanny Hayes, who encouraged him to achieve the prominent career denied to her because she was a woman. With the help of his wealthy uncle, Sardis Birchard, Hayes went to Harvard Law School and then made a name for himself as a successful criminal defense lawyer in Cincinnati. There he married Lucy Ware Webb. Lucy advocated temperance and abolition, and was a strong Methodist who placed more emphasis on good works than on being "born again." Without nagging, she influenced her husband. After marriage he became a stronger antislavery advocate and a teetotaler following his move to the White House, and he regularly attended religious services with Lucy, though he never joined a church.

Patriot of the Union

When the Civil War broke out, Hayes was already nearly forty-years old and the father of three with a fourth on the way. Nevertheless, he was one of the first three-year volunteers, stating that he would rather die in the conflict than live having done nothing for the Union. Using his political connections, Hayes was appointed a major in the 23rd Ohio Volunteers. An officer with no military experience, he learned quickly, worked hard, and with his "intense and ferocious" demeanor on the battlefield gained the respect of the enlisted men and his superiors. At the Battle of Opequon Creek, for example, Hayes led the charge through a morass that turned the tide of battle. Wounded five times in the war, Hayes kept leading his men into battle, and by the end of the conflict he was a brigadier general, and later breveted major general for "gallant and distinguished services."

While campaigning in the Shenandoah Valley in 1864 he was nominated in Cincinnati for the U.S. House of Representatives. Hayes refused to return to take to the stump, stating that "an officer fit for duty who at this crisis would abandon his post to electioneer for a seat in Congress ought to be scalped." That statement was worth all the speeches he could have made. Hayes was elected and the war was over before the first session of his Congress met on in December 1865.

Road to the White House

After the Civil War, Hayes served as member of the U.S. House of Representatives (1865-1867) and then as governor of Ohio (1868-1872, 1876-1877). By 1876, Republicans recognized that the scrupulous Hayes—a war hero from a populous swing state and a candidate acceptable to the major factions in the Republican party - was presidential material. "Availability" secured Hayes the nomination, but he faced a tough campaign. The nation was in the midst of an economic depression, the Grant administration was tarnished by scandals, and Democratic opponent Samuel J. Tilden of New York was a superb political organizer with a reform reputation. On Election Day, Tilden rolled up a plurality of 250,000 votes, but the vote in three southern states was close enough for both Republicans and Democrats to claim them and with those states the presidency. To decide who carried those states, Congress set up a special commission which awarded the disputed Electoral College votes to Hayes, making him the winner. Outraged and frustrated, Democrats dubbed Hayes "Rutherfraud" and "His Fraudulency."

The Hayes Presidency

Hayes's inaugural address was conciliatory in tone and addressed specific problems. To alleviate hard times, he backed existing legislation that called for the nation's return to the gold standard in 1879. To eliminate political corruption, he advocated a nonpartisan reformed civil service, observing that "he serves his party best who serves his country best." To conciliate the South, Hayes said it should have local self government, but that those governments must obey the entire Constitution, including the Reconstruction amendments. Perhaps because Hayes, along with his comrade in arms William McKinley, had more combat experience than other Presidents, he wished to arbitrate disputes with other nations. He also congratulated the American people for the peaceful resolution of the recent disputed election.

As President, Hayes sought to implement his inaugural address. He had supported radical Reconstruction legislation which aimed to secure the rights of black citizens, but by 1877, Hayes believed that military occupation had bred hatred among southerners and had prevented the nation from healing itself in the aftermath of war. Actually, Reconstruction was virtually over when Hayes took office in March 1877, with federal troops protecting Republican governments only in New Orleans, Louisiana, and Columbia, South Carolina. It ended completely when, within two months of his inauguration, Hayes ordered those federal troops to their barracks, but only after Louisiana and South Carolina authorities pledged to respect the civil and voting rights of blacks. These promises were soon broken and the white supremacist Democratic Party asserted total dominance of the South. By the 1890s, the Democratic hold on the South resulted in a complete denial of voting rights for blacks until the 1960s.

Hayes was a patient and a gradual reformer. He feared that sweeping changes were often not lasting and was satisfied with smaller incremental gains. He had great faith in education as the keys to prosperity and harmonious relations among diverse racial and ethnic groups. He did not attempt to reform the entire civil service, but concentrated on one major office, demonstrating that open competitive examinations did, in fact, reap better workers. He did not attack all spoils-minded senators but only the imperious and obnoxious Roscoe Conkling of New York. The death of Abraham Lincoln, the impeachment of Andrew Johnson, and the failures of Ulysses S. Grant had left the presidency in a weakened state. Hayes helped to restore prestige to the office by defeating Conkling and the idea of "senatorial courtesy," which claimed for senators the right to appoint civil servants in their states. He also defeated an attempt by the Democratic-controlled Congress to force him to accept unwanted legislation by attaching amendments - riders—to necessary appropriations bills. By the time Hayes left office, senators could suggest but not dictate the appointment of officers, nor was the President's veto power destroyed. Hayes helped restore prestige to the presidency, heal the wounds left by the Civil War, and strengthen the Republican party sufficiently to win the election of 1880.

In his very active retirement Hayes continued to struggle for equal educational opportunities for all children. He also was active in the prison reform movement.

20. James A. Garfield (1881)

Born: November 19, 1831, Orange Township, Cuyahoga County, Ohio
Full Name: James Abram Garfield
Nickname: None
Education: Western Reserve Eclectic Institute (now Hiram College), Williams College (graduated 1856)
Religion: Disciples of Christ
Marriage: November 11, 1858, to Lucretia Rudolph (1832–1918)
Children: Eliza A. (1860–1863), Harry A. (1863–1942), James R. (1865–1950), Mary (1867–1947), Irvin M. (1870–1951), Abram (1872–1958), Edward (1874–1876)
Career: Teacher, Public Official
Political Party: Republican
Died: September 19, 1881, Elberon, New Jersey

James A. Garfield is remembered as one of the four "lost Presidents" who served rather uneventfully after the Civil War. Of the four lost Presidents—Hayes, Garfield, Arthur, and Harrison—Garfield is best remembered for his dramatic assassination a mere 100 days after he assumed office.

From Poverty to Politics

The youngest of five children born on a poor farm on the outskirts of Cleveland, Ohio, Garfield is perhaps the poorest man ever to have become President. Supporting himself as a part-time teacher, a carpenter, and even a janitor through college, he was an idealistic young man who identified with the antislavery tenets of the new Republican Party. After graduating from Williams College, Garfield studied law on his own and passed the Ohio bar exams in 1861 before throwing himself into politics and winning a seat in the Ohio legislature. Garfield was a loyal Unionist who built a reputation as a Civil War hero that earned him a seat in the House of Representatives without ever having campaigned.

During Garfield's congressional terms, debates raged between legislators who demanded that all U.S. money be backed by gold and the "Silverites" and "Greenbackers," who wanted to issue paper currency and coin silver more freely in an attempt to alleviate pressing debts, especially those of struggling farmers. Garfield advocated hard money policies backed by gold, making him a favorite with eastern "Gold Bug" Republicans. He opposed cooperative farm programs such as those supported by the Grange, an agrarian organization; labor unions; the eight-hour workday; and federally funded relief projects.

Like many men in office, Garfield had a scandal to live down. He was implicated in the Credit Mobilier scandal in which congressmen who owned stock in Credit Mobilier, a construction company for the transcontinental Union Pacific Railroad, were accused of turning a blind eye to corruption in the company.

In 1876, Garfield supported the reform-minded Rutherford B. Hayes for President. To soothe Democrats who were enraged by Hayes's election after disputes about the electoral returns from several key states, he supported the Compromise of

1877, which ended the military occupation of the South. Garfield also had a talent for achieving compromise between the "Stalwart" Republicans, led by Roscoe Conkling (the New York State political boss), and an opposing faction, disparagingly called "Half-Breeds" by Conkling and his allies.

Presidential Politicking

In the election of 1880, the Republican ticket looked like it would boil down to a fight between former President Ulysses S. Grant and the more moderate James G. Blaine. Garfield surprised everyone, however, by earning an ever-increasing number of votes in the convention balloting. He won the presidential nomination and eventually the election against Democrat Winfield S. Hancock, a Union general who made his mark at Gettysburg. The election was the closest on record. Garfield won by the narrowest of margins and only with the help of the New York political boss Roscoe Conkling, with whom Garfield had agreed to consult on party appointments—had New York gone Democratic, Garfield would have lost the presidency.

Both James and Lucretia Garfield were devout members of a relatively new Protestant denomination, the Christian Church (Disciples of Christ). "Crete" devoted herself to raising the Garfield's five children, all of whom grew up to have rather distinguished careers. Though she dreamed of refurbishing the executive mansion, Mrs. Garfield caught malaria from the swamps behind the White House before she could begin the project. Eventually, she enjoyed a complete recovery and lived to the ripe old age of eighty-six.

Since Garfield was struck down four months into his term, historians can only speculate as to what his presidency might have been like. Garfield was assassinated by Charles Julius Guiteau, an emotionally disturbed man who had failed to gain an appointment in Garfield's administration. Garfield did have time to appoint his cabinet, however, and in doing so, he refused to cave in to Stalwart pressure, enraging Senator Conkling, who resigned in protest. Had Garfield served his term, historians speculate that he would have been determined to move toward civil service reform and carry on in the clean government tradition of President Hayes. He also supported education for black southerners and called for African American suffrage, as he stressed in his inaugural address. Unfortunately, he is best remembered for his assassination. And although his killer was insane, Garfield's greatest legacy was the impact of his death on moving the nation to reform government patronage.

21. CHESTER A. ARTHUR (1881-1885)

Chester Alan Arthur 1881-1885

Born October 5, 1829, Fairfield, Vermont
Full Name: Chester Alan Arthur
Nickname: "The Gentleman Boss"
Religion: Episcopalian
Marriage: October 25, 1859, to Ellen Lewis Herndon (1837–1880)
Children: William Lewis Herndon (1860–1863), Chester Alan (1864–1937), Ellen Herndon (1871–1915)
Education: Union College (graduated 1848)
Career: Lawyer
Political Party: Republican
Died: November 18, 1886, New York, New York

Chester Arthur was the fifth child of a fervent abolitionist preacher who moved his family from one Baptist parish to the next throughout New York and Vermont. Attending Union College, Arthur showed far more interest in extracurricular activities and political demonstrations than in his studies. As a young man, Arthur worked for one of the most prominent law firms in New York City. He was involved in two cases focusing on African American rights. One involved fugitive slaves while the other centered on segregated streetcars.

Political Machine Operator

Arthur also worked actively for Roscoe Conkling, a New York Republican Party boss and U.S. senator who used patronage and party discipline to advance his power. Conkling headed a major party faction, the Stalwarts. Recognizing the administrative genius that Arthur demonstrated as quartermaster general for all of New York during the Civil War and his success as a lawyer, Conkling helped Arthur get appointed as collector of the Port of New York under Republican President Ulysses S. Grant. While there is no evidence of blatant corruption on Arthur's part, the New York Customs House had close ties to Boss Conkling's political machine; Arthur routinely collected kickbacks of salary called "assessments" from customs house employees to support the Republican Party.

In 1881, Arthur became vice president under the moderate Republican candidate, James Garfield. Under President Rutherford B. Hayes's administration, there had been attempts to reform New York's corrupt civil service system, and Arthur broke with President Garfield when Garfield appointed a member of the rival Republican faction, the Half-Breeds, to the post of collector of the Port of New York. The move destroyed Conkling's power once and for all. Arthur and Garfield were nearly estranged when Garfield was assassinated and Arthur found himself President.

Reform and Refurbish President

As President, Arthur surprised everyone by acting independently, defying his state-based reputation as a slick machine politician who would advance the agenda of his own party faction and ignore the needs of the nation at-large. Domestic affairs dominated his presidency. In reforming civil service, Arthur supported the Pendleton Act, which attempted to counter patronage and cronyism by requiring competitive exams for government office.

Specifically, the law banned salary kickbacks and ensured that promotion would be based on merit, not connections. While the Republican Party usually worked to protect big business and manufacturing, Arthur pushed for tariff reduction to relieve indebted farmers and middle-class consumers. He also vetoed the notorious pork-barrel Rivers and Harbors Act of 1882, arguing that the growing surplus of federal funds should be decreased by tax reductions rather than government expenditures. After vetoing a more restrictive bill, Arthur supported the Chinese Exclusion Act of 1882, banning Chinese immigration for ten years and forbidding Chinese citizenship.

Arthur was most passionate about his project to refurbish the White House. Known as a man of elegant taste who loved to throw lavish parties, Arthur came to the presidency as "The Gentleman Boss." Disgusted with the shabby look of the executive mansion, Arthur hired the most famous designer in New York, Louis Comfort Tiffany, to transform it into a showplace befitting the office. His wife, Ellen Lewis Herndon, had died before he assumed office. And although Arthur loved to showcase his two children at White House social affairs, he much preferred fishing, feasting with his cronies, and administrative work to family life. Because he knew that he suffered from a fatal kidney disease, Arthur did not actively seek reelection for a second term and died less than two years after leaving office.

Chester A. Arthur's administration marks a period of transition in American politics. Women were beginning to take an active role, pressing strongly for women's suffrage and prohibition of alchoholic beverages. Above all, the era was characterized by civil service reform, which would eventually weaken the grip of traditional ethnic and party loyalties. Despite having advanced in his career through managing the New York political machine, Arthur showed tremendous flexibility and a willingness to embrace reform. He stands as an important transitional figure in the reunification of the nation after the bitter turmoil of the Civil War and Reconstruction.

22. GROVER CLEVELAND (1885-1889)

Born: March 18, 1837, Caldwell, New Jersey
Full Name: Stephen Grover Cleveland
Nickname: "Big Steve", "Uncle Jumbo"
Education: Some common school; Read law (1855–1859)
Religion: Presbyterian
Marriage: June 2, 1886, to Frances Folsom (1864–1947)
Children: Ruth (1891–1904), Esther (1893–1980), Marion (1895–1977), Richard Folsom (1897–1974), Francis Grover (1903–1995)
Career: Lawyer
Political Party: Democrat
Died: June 24, 1908, Princeton, New Jersey

Stephen Grover Cleveland fell into politics without really trying. In 1881, local businessmen asked Cleveland, then a young lawyer, to run for mayor of Buffalo, New York. He agreed and won the Democratic nomination and the election. As mayor, Cleveland exposed city corruption and earned such a reputation for honesty and hard work that he won the New York gubernatorial race in 1882. Governor Cleveland used his power to take on the Tammany Hall, the political machine based in New York City, even though it had supported him in the election. Within a year, the Democrats were looking to Cleveland as an important new face and pragmatic reformer who might win the presidency in 1884.

Three Campaigns for President

In the election of 1884, Cleveland appealed to middle-class voters of both parties as someone who would fight political corruption and big-money interests. Many people saw Cleveland's Republican opponent, James G. Blaine, as a puppet of Wall Street and the powerful railroads. The morally upright Mugwumps, a Republican group of reform-minded businessmen and professionals, hated Blaine and embraced Cleveland's efforts at battling corruption. Cleveland also had the popularity to carry New York, a state crucial to victory.

But Cleveland had a sex-scandal to live down: he was accused of fathering a son out of wedlock—a charge that he admitted might be true—owing to his affair with Maria Halpin in 1874. By honestly confronting the charges, Cleveland retained the loyalty of his supporters, winning the election by the narrowest of margins.

When he ran for reelection in 1888, the Republicans raised lots of money from the nation's manufacturers and spent it lavishly, helping to ensure victory for their candidate, Benjamin Harrison. The election thus marked the beginning of a new era in campaign financing. Though Cleveland actually won a larger share of the popular vote, Harrison defeated Cleveland in the Electoral College.

In 1892, however, after four years of Republican leadership, Cleveland quashed the reelection hopes of Harrison, who had alienated many in his own party. He thus became the only President to serve nonconsecutive terms, winning the office once again after losing as the incumbent.

Watchdog in the White House

Cleveland did not see himself as an activist President with his own agenda to pursue, but as a guardian or watchdog of Congress. While several important pieces of legislation became law during his terms—most notably bills controlling the railroads and distributing land to Native Americans—he did not initiate any of it.

During his second term, Cleveland also had to deal with the most severe depression the nation had ever suffered. By 1894, the U.S. economy was reeling from an 18 percent unemployment rate. When 150,000 railroad workers walked off the job in sympathy with the Pullman Car workers' strike in Illinois, Cleveland sent federal troops to crush the revolt and arrest its leaders. In this instance, he tilted toward the business community in the ongoing struggle between management and labor. This decision sparked a great deal of criticism at the time as well as later from historians.

Cleveland blamed the country's economic problems on the Sherman Silver Purchasing Act passed during the Harrison administration. His attempt to repeal the act split the Democrats, and his failure to deal with the depression ensured Republican victory in the congressional elections of 1894. He left office in 1897 feeling betrayed by his own party.

Social Issues and Foreign Affairs

Cleveland's opposition to temperence won the support of the Irish, German, and East European voters who migrated to the United States by the tens of thousands in the 1880s. He was inconsistent in his attitude toward racial issues, however. Although he spoke out against injustices being visited on the Chinese in the West, he sympathized with Southern reluctance to treat African Americans as social or political equals. Native Americans, he thought, should assimilate into white society as quickly as possible through federal aid for education and private land grants. Finally, though he was careful not to alienate women by speaking out against female suffrage, he never supported a woman's right to vote.

In foreign policy, Cleveland opposed territorial expansion and entangling alliances. His behavior was inconsistent, however, and he took a bellicose position when a dispute arose with Germany over Samoa. He adopted a similar stance with respect to Hawaii, where he believed that U.S. sugar planters had conspired in the Hawaiian revolution. His most controversial action was his interference in a boundary dispute between Venezuela and Britain. Claiming that the British were violating the Monroe Doctrine, Cleveland actually threatened London with war. While historians continue to debate the wisdom of Cleveland's action, the affair brought the Monroe Doctrine back to life as the basis of U.S. foreign policy in the Western Hemisphere.

End of Bachelorhood

After two years in office as a bachelor President, Cleveland announced his marriage to his twenty-one-year-old ward, Frances Folsom, the daughter of his former law partner. The press had a field day satirizing the relationship between the old bachelor and the recent college graduate, who quickly became the most popular first lady since Dolley Madison. Frances adhered to the prevailing ideal that separated the private lives of women from the public lives of men. Respecting the wishes of her husband, she never used her popularity to advance the political causes of the day.

Cleveland's Legacy

Cleveland will be remembered for protecting the power and autonomy of the executive branch. His record-breaking use of the presidential veto earned him the deserved moniker of the "guardian President" and helped balance the power of executive and legislative branches. But he did not think that the President should propose legislation and he disliked using legislative solutions to address America's growing social and economic difficulties.

Hard-working, honest, and independent, Cleveland nevertheless had no real vision for the future. At most, historians tend to see his presidency as strengthening the power of the executive branch in relation to Congress and leading to the emergence of the modern presidency that began with Theodore Roosevelt.

23. BENJAMIN HARRISON (1889-1893)

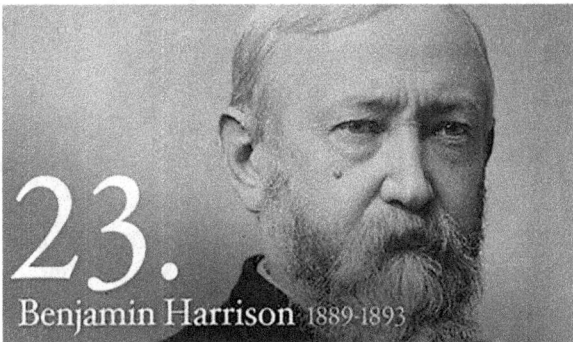

Born: August 20, 1833, North Bend, Ohio
Nickname: "Kid Gloves Harrison," "Little Ben"
Education: Miami University (Ohio), graduated 1852

Religion: Presbyterian
Marriage: October 20, 1853, to Caroline Lavinia Scott (1832–1892). April 6, 1896, to Mary Scott Lord Dimmick (1858–1948)
Children: Russell Benjamin (1854–1936), Mary Scott (1858–1930), Elizabeth (1897–1955)
Career: Lawyer
Political Party: Republican
Died: March 13, 1901, Indianapolis, Indiana

Benjamin Harrison was born in 1833 in North Bend, Ohio, to a prominent family that had a legacy of political activism. After all, he was the grandson of the nation's ninth President, William Henry Harrison. Raised on a farm adjacent to his grandfather's vast estate, Harrison believed he was destined for greatness.

He was tutored at home and read widely on his own, and he would always be more comfortable in the company of books than with other people. Over time, he developed an effective public speaking style, and he was popular among Civil War veterans because of his service as a Union general. Privately, however, Harrison was a frigid character, so stiff and aloof that he was sometimes referred to as "the human iceberg."

Political and Military Activism

Harrison graduated from Miami University in Oxford, Ohio, near the top of his class and studied law with a prominent firm in Cincinnati. In 1853, one year before he began his own law practice, Harrison married a young woman he had met while still in his teens, Caroline Lavinia Scott. They moved to Indianapolis, Indiana, in 1854. She was outgoing where he was reserved, and she loved celebrations and holidays. Eventually, she would put up the first Christmas tree ever in the White House. As a young lawyer, Harrison quickly became involved in the affairs of the new Republican Party, supporting its first presidential candidate, General John C.

Fremont in 1856 and working for Abraham Lincoln in 1860. In 1862, he joined the Seventieth Regiment of the Indiana Volunteers during the Civil War, eventually rising to the rank of brigadier general.

Following the war, Harrison returned to political life. He won the Indiana Republican gubernatorial nomination in 1876 but lost the election. He became an influential party power broker, throwing support behind the successful presidential campaigns of Rutherford B. Hayes and James A. Garfield, and in 1880, he was named to the United States Senate by the Indiana state legislature—senators were not elected by popular vote until 1913. In the Senate, he championed pensions for Civil War veterans, high protective tariffs, a modernized navy, and conservation of western lands—all issues that he would uphold as President. He also broke with his party to oppose an act designed to close America to Chinese immigrants. The Chinese Exclusion Act passed without his support.

In 1887, the Indiana state legislature had come under Democratic control, and it declined to return Harrison to the Senate. A year later, declaring himself a "rejuvenated Republican," he announced his candidacy for the party's presidential nomination. He proved to be everyone's second choice in a field of seven serious candidates. He was nominated on the eighth ballot, and New York banker Levi P. Morton was named as his running mate. The Democrats, meanwhile, nominated the incumbent President Grover Cleveland and Ohio Senator Allen G. Thurman.

It was a relatively polite campaign, with both candidates limiting their appearances and focusing primarily on the tariff and Southern problems rooted in Reconstruction. When the votes were tallied, Cleveland had received the larger number of popular votes, but Harrison had carried the Electoral College, thus giving Harrison the victory in the 1888 election.

Tough and Decisive Actions

Even though all his life he believed that he had been born to do great things, historians have traditionally not ranked Harrison as one of our most distinguished chief executives. Some historians contend that his economic policies may have contributed to the economic depression that struck America after he left office. In particular, Harrison was a protectionist who favored high tariffs. This was exemplified by his nurturing of the McKinley Tariff of 1890, which imposed high import duties to protect American corporations but had the effect of increasing prices—a stand that would cost him heavily among the voters. Harrison lobbied successfully for the passage of the Sherman Silver Purchase Act of 1890, which required that silver be used in federal coinage, a concession to the western silver interests. However, this plan was badly conceived and nearly depleted the U.S. Treasury of its gold reserves.

On the other hand, Harrison advocated the conservation of forest reserves, and he embarked on an adventurous foreign policy that included U.S. expansion in the Pacific and the building of a canal across Central America. He also supported the landmark Sherman Antitrust Act, the first bill ever to attempt to limit the power of America's giant corporations. In the area of civil rights for African Americans, Harrison endorsed two bills designed to prevent southern states from denying African Americans the vote, and he appointed the great and eloquent former slave Frederick Douglass as minister to Haiti. Recent assessments of Harrison's accomplishments give him more credit for his vision and convictions.

On the international front, Harrison was the most active President since Abraham Lincoln. He convened the first Pan-American Conference in 1889. He negotiated an American protectorate over the Samoan Islands, attempted to annex Hawaii, and continued the work of modernizing and expanding the United States Navy into a world-class fleet. He moved quickly and decisively where American interests were threatened, taking the nation to the brink of war with Chile over an assault on American sailors and standing firm against Britain and Canada to protect the overharvesting of fur seals in the Bering Sea. Perhaps most importantly, he saw trade as an essential part of the nation's foreign policy and negotiated a number of important reciprocal trade agreements that set the pattern for American trade policy in the twentieth century.

When Harrison lost his bid for reelection in 1892 to Grover Cleveland, he had himself partly to blame. He had frozen out many of those who should have been most active in his support, and his own party was lukewarm toward him. Additionally, midway through this second election, near the end of Harrison's term, his wife, Caroline, died of tuberculosis. Her illness and eventual death greatly distracted him, which accounts in part for the magnitude of his defeat. In 1892, the voters handed Cleveland the most decisive presidential victory in twenty years. Harrison told his family he felt as though he had been freed from prison.

In 1896, Benjamin Harrison married his deceased wife's niece, Mary Lord Dimmick, a widow nearly thirty years his junior. He remained active in public life until his death from pneumonia on March 13, 1901. His activism and willingness to wave a big stick in international affairs inspired Theodore Roosevelt, and years later, the American writer Henry Adams called Harrison the best President since Lincoln. Whether he deserved that high praise or not, there is little doubt that his presidency deserves the reconsideration many historians are giving it.

24. GROVER CLEVELAND (1893-1897)
(See prior entry No. 22).

25. WILLIAM McKINLEY (1897-1901)

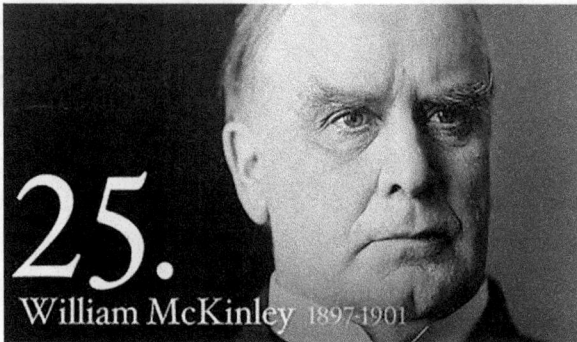

Born: January 29, 1843, Niles, Ohio
Nickname: "Idol of Ohio"
Education: Allegheny College
Religion: Methodist
Marriage: January 25, 1871, to Ida Saxton (1847–1907)
Children: Katherine (1871–1875), Ida (1873)
Career: Lawyer
Political Party: Republican
Died: September 14, 1901, Buffalo, New York

For a long time, William McKinley was considered a mediocre President, a chief executive who was controlled by his political cronies and who was pressured into war with Spain by the press. Recent historians have been kinder to McKinley, seeing him instead as a decisive President who put America on the road to world power. McKinley's difficult foreign policy decisions, especially his policy toward China and his decision to go to war with Spain over Cuban independence, helped the U.S. enter the twentieth century as a new and powerful empire on the world stage.

Political Opportunities

Born in 1843 and raised in Ohio, William McKinley planned as a young man to become a Methodist minister. When the

Civil War started, McKinley proved a valiant soldier, rising in the ranks from a private to a brevet major on the staff of Colonel Rutherford B. Hayes, who became a lifelong friend and mentor. When he returned to Ohio to practice law, he used his connections with Hayes to rise rapidly in Ohio politics. He served in Congress from 1877 to 1891 before becoming governor of Ohio. Congressman McKinley was the Republican Party's leading spokesman for protectionism in foreign trade. His McKinley Tariff of 1890 established substantially higher tariff rates on imported goods in order to protect U.S. business and manufacturing.

The nation's devastating economic collapse in 1893 turned voters against the Democratic Party's hold on the presidency, giving McKinley a good shot at the White House in 1896. McKinley argued that his commitment to protective tariffs on imported goods would cure unemployment and stimulate industrial growth. McKinley's political ally from Ohio, the industrialist Marcus Hanna, helped McKinley organize and fund his campaign. McKinley beat Democrat William Jennings Bryan in the greatest electoral sweep in twenty-five years. Four years later, the popular McKinley ran on a strong record and defeated Bryan again, by even larger margins.

Strong International Presence

McKinley led the U.S. into its first international war with a European power since the War of 1812. The decision to come to the aid of the Cubans struggling to throw off Spanish rule was hastened by reports that Spain was responsible for the explosion of the U.S. battleship Maine. On April 25, 1898, Congress declared war, promising to secure independence for Cuba once the war ended. To secure America's position in the Pacific, McKinley immediately pushed a joint resolution through Congress to annex the Hawaiian Islands. After three short months of fighting, the U.S. was victorious. The peace treaty between the United States and Spain granted Cuba its independence—although the island became a U.S.

protectorate—and gave the United States control of former Spanish colonies, the Philippines, Puerto Rico, and Guam. Practically overnight, the United States became a colonial power, but not without costs. The United States almost immediately entered into a brutal conflict with Filipino nationalists who rejected American rule.

Further asserting American power on the global scene, McKinley sent 2,000 troops to China to help the Europeans put down the Boxer Rebellion. He also intervened twice in Nicaragua to protect U.S. property interests. Both of these actions were examples of the United States as a rising hemispheric and world power.

To obtain a hold on world markets, McKinley authorized his secretary of state, John Hay, to issue the "Open Door" notes on China. These notes declared U.S. support for an independent China and expressed the American desire that all nations with commercial interests in China compete on an equal footing. The war with Spain and the Open Door strategy laid the groundwork for a new American empire.

Personal Challenges and Assassination

First Lady Ida Saxton McKinley never recovered from the devastating loss of both her infant children as well as her mother within three years of her marriage to McKinley. She developed epilepsy, a disease for which there was no treatment in the late nineteenth century. McKinley gave the First Lady his full attention, breaking White House protocol in seating her by his side at State dinners. When he was shot by an assassin in 1901, McKinley said to his personal secretary, George B. Cortelyou, "My wife, be careful, Cortelyou, how you tell her—oh, be careful." McKinley died from his wounds eight days later, on September 14, 1901.

Despite criticism from contemporaries and historians, many of whom disagreed with his policies and found his leadership wanting, McKinley was a President who acted decisively in going to war with Spain, asserted great presidential authority over his cabinet and generals, and understood the link between foreign markets and national prosperity. During his administration, the United States acquired possessions that allowed it to become a major world power.

26. THEODORE ROOSEVELT (1901-1909)

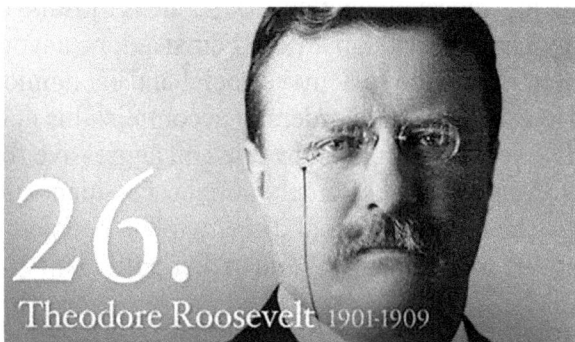

26.
Theodore Roosevelt 1901-1909

Born: October 27, 1858, New York, New York
Nickname: "TR", "Trust-Buster", "Teddy"
Education: Harvard College (graduated 1880)
Religion: Dutch Reformed
Marriage: October 27, 1880, to Alice Hathaway Lee (1861–1884), December 2, 1886, to Edith Kermit Carow (1861–1948)
Children: Alice Lee (1884–1980), Theodore (1887–1944), Kermit (1889–1943), Ethel Carow (1891–1977), Archibald Bulloch (1894–1979), Quentin (1897–1918)
Career: Author, Lawyer, Public Official
Political Party: Republican
Died: January 6, 1919, Oyster Bay, New York

Theodore Roosevelt, who came into office in 1901 and served until 1909, is considered the first modern President because he significantly expanded the influence and power of the executive office. From the Civil War to the turn of the twentieth century, the seat of power in the national government resided in the U.S. Congress. Beginning in the 1880s, the executive branch gradually increased its power. Roosevelt seized on this trend, believing that the President had the right to use all powers except those that were specifically denied him to accomplish his goals. As a result, the President, rather than Congress or the political parties, became the center of the American political arena.

As President, Roosevelt challenged the ideas of limited government and individualism. In their stead, he advocated government regulation to achieve social and economic justice. He used executive orders to accomplish his goals, especially in conservation, and waged an aggressive foreign policy. He was also an extremely popular President and the first to use the media to appeal directly to the people, bypassing the political parties and career politicians.

Early Life

Frail and sickly as a boy, "Teedie" Roosevelt developed a rugged physique as a teenager and became a lifelong advocate of exercise and the "strenuous life." After graduating from Harvard, Roosevelt married Alice Hathaway Lee and studied law at Columbia University. He dropped out after a year to pursue politics, winning a seat in the New York Assembly in 1882. A double tragedy struck Roosevelt in 1884, when his mother and his wife died in the same house on the same day. Roosevelt spent two years out West in an attempt to recover, tending cows as a rancher and busting outlaws as a frontier sheriff. In 1886, he returned to New York and married his childhood sweetheart, Edith Kermit Carow. They raised six children, including Roosevelt's daughter from his first marriage. After losing a campaign for mayor, he served as Civil Service commissioner, president of the New York City Police Board, and assistant secretary of the Navy. All the while, he demonstrated honesty in office, upsetting the party bosses who expected him to ignore the law in favor of partisan politics.

War Hero and Vice President

When the Spanish-American War broke out in 1898, Roosevelt volunteered as commander of the 1st U.S. Volunteer Cavalry, known as the Rough Riders, leading a daring charge on San Juan Hill. Returning as a war hero, he became governor of New York and began to exhibit an independence that upset the state's political machine. To stop Roosevelt's reforms, party bosses "kicked him upstairs" to the vice presidency under William McKinley, believing that in this position he would be unable to continue his progressive policies. Roosevelt campaigned vigorously for McKinley in 1900—one commentator remarked, "Tis Teddy alone that's running, an' he ain't a runnin', he's a gallopin'." Roosevelt's efforts helped ensure victory for McKinley. But his time as vice president was brief; McKinley was assassinated in 1901, making Roosevelt the President of the United States.

By the 1904 election, Roosevelt was eager to be elected President in his own right. To achieve this, he knew that he needed to work with Republican Party leaders. He promised to hold back on parts of his progressive agenda in exchange for a free hand in foreign affairs. He also got the reluctant support of wealthy capitalists, who feared his progressive measures, but feared a Democratic victory even more. TR won in a landslide, becoming the first President to be elected after gaining office due to the death of his predecessor. Upon victory, he vowed not to run for another term in 1908, a promise he came to regret.

Modern Presidency

As President, Roosevelt worked to ensure that the government improved the lives of American citizens. His "Square Deal" domestic program reflected the progressive call to reform the American workplace, initiating welfare legislation and government regulation of industry. He was also the nation's first environmentalist President, setting aside nearly 200 million acres for national forests, reserves, and wildlife refuges.

In foreign policy, Roosevelt wanted to make the United States a global power by increasing its influence worldwide. He led the effort to secure rights to build the Panama Canal, one of the greatest engineering feats at that time. He also issued his "corollary" to the Monroe Doctrine, which established the United States as the "policeman" of the Western Hemisphere. In addition, he used his position as President to help negotiate peace agreements between belligerent nations, believing that the world should settle international disputes through diplomacy rather than war.

Roosevelt is considered the first modern U.S. President because he greatly strengthened the power of the executive branch. He was also an extremely popular President—so popular after leaving office in 1909 that he was able to mount a serious run for the presidency again in 1912. Believing that his successor, William Howard Taft, had failed to continue his program of reform, TR threw his hat into the ring as a candidate for the Progressive Party. Although Roosevelt was defeated by Democrat Woodrow Wilson, his efforts resulted in the creation of one of the most significant third parties in U.S. history.

With the onset of World War I in 1914, Roosevelt advocated that the United States prepare itself for war. Accordingly, he was highly critical of Wilson's pledge of neutrality. Once the United States entered the war in 1917, all four of Roosevelt's sons volunteered to serve, which greatly pleased the former President. The death of his youngest son, Quentin, left him deeply distraught. Theodore Roosevelt died less than a year later.

27. WILLIAM HOWARD TAFT (1909-1913)

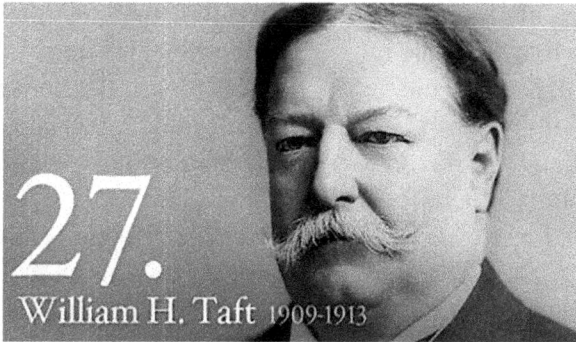

Born: September 15, 1857, Cincinnati, Ohio
Nickname: None
Education: Yale College (graduated 1878), Cincinnati Law School (LL.B., 1880)
Religion: Unitarian
Marriage: June 19, 1886, to Helen Herron (1861–1943)
Children: Robert Alphonso (1889–1953), Helen Herron (1891–1987), Charles Phelps (1897–1983)
Career: Lawyer, Public Official
Political Party: Republican
Died: March 8, 1930, Washington, D.C.

William Howard Taft faced the difficult task as President of living up to the legacy of Theodore Roosevelt. Taft so disappointed his predecessor, former mentor, and friend, that Roosevelt opposed his renomination in 1912 and bolted from the Republican Party to form his own "Bull-Moose" party, creating an opening for Democrat Woodrow Wilson in the 1912 presidential election. Taft's lifelong ambition was to serve as Chief Justice of the United States, to which he was appointed after leaving the presidency. He remains the only man in American history to have gained the highest executive and judicial positions.

Meeting Expectations

Taft, born in 1857, spent his boyhood in Cincinnati, Ohio, trying to live up to the high expectations of his demanding parents, especially his father, Alphonso Taft. Alphonso Taft was a distinguished Cincinnati attorney and a prominent Republican who served as secretary of war and then attorney general under President Ulysses Grant, and was U.S. minister (ambassador) to Austria-Hungary and Russia under President Chester Arthur. The elder Taft had also sought but lost the 1879 Republican gubernatorial nomination in Ohio.

From childhood, William Howard Taft had a weight problem, a reaction perhaps to his parents' very high expectations for him. At times during his presidency, he reached 300 pounds. He followed his father's and half-brother's path to Yale University, graduating second in his class. He studied law at the University of Cincinnati and entered private practice while also holding several local appointive positions. At age 29, Taft married an ambitious, intellectual, and independent woman, Helen "Nellie" Herron, who pushed him to strive for more than a judicial career. He held several key legal and judicial posts from 1887 to 1900, including judge of the Cincinnati Superior Court, U.S. solicitor general, and then as a member of the Sixth U.S. Circuit Court of Appeals. President William McKinley then asked Taft to serve as president of the commission to oversee the newly won Philippine Islands. Taft was disappointed, but pushed by his associates, including his wife, he took the job, with McKinley's promise of a future position on the Supreme Court upon his return.

Governor General of the Philippines

Despite his initial hesitancy about it, Taft's service in the Philippines from 1900 to 1903 was fulfilling and largely successful. While there, he twice turned down President Roosevelt's offer of a Supreme Court appointment in order to finish his work. Becoming governor of the islands in 1901, Taft abandoned the brutal and bloody tactics the U.S. military government had used to squash the nationalist rebellion. By the time he left the islands to become Roosevelt's secretary of war in 1903, Taft had constructed a functioning civil regime and pacified the islands. At the same time, Taft fully subscribed to the view that Filipinos were not capable of self-rule. He believed that independence could only come to the undeveloped nation after a long period of U.S. tutelage and protection.

As secretary of war, Taft became Roosevelt's chief emissary and confidant, assisting him in the Portsmouth Peace negotiations, and in establishing a protectorate in Cuba. Roosevelt, having sworn upon his victory in 1904 that he would not seek another term, handpicked Taft to succeed him in 1908. The public joked that T.A.F.T. stood for "take advice from Theodore." Thanks in part to Roosevelt's popularity, Taft's victory over Democrat William Jennings Bryan was decisive. Taft promised to continue Roosevelt's reform program. But Roosevelt, and many of his allies, saw Taft's administration as abandoning progressivism. The consequent animosity split the Republican Party in 1912, sweeping Woodrow Wilson into office.

A Judicial President

Taft's disposition was more prone to judicious administration than presidential activism. Though he came to the White House promising to continue Roosevelt's agenda, he was more comfortable executing the existing law than demanding new legislation from Congress. His first effort as President was to lead Congress to lower tariffs, but traditional high tariff interests dominated Congress, and Taft largely failed in his effort at legislative leadership. He also alienated Roosevelt when he attempted to break up U.S. Steel, a trust that Roosevelt had approved while President. Taft also forced Roosevelt's forestry chief to resign, jeopardizing Roosevelt's gains in the conservation of natural resources. By 1911, Taft was less active in "trust-busting," and generally seemed more conservative. In foreign affairs, Taft continued Roosevelt's goal of expanding U.S. foreign trade in South and Central America, as well as in Asia, and he termed his policy "dollar diplomacy."

President Taft's life-long dream of reaching the U.S. Supreme Court was satisfied in 1921 with his appointment as chief justice by President Warren Harding. Taft had been uncomfortable with politics. His tendency to contemplate every side of an issue served him well as chief justice but rendered him indecisive and ineffectual as President. His presidency is generally viewed as a failure, swinging as he did from a progressive program of "trust busting" to reactionary conservatism in the face of withering criticism from Roosevelt and his allies. While Taft's presidency left a mark on the organization and conduct of the executive branch, and developed the administration of anti-trust policy, his public leadership has been widely seen as below average for 20th century Presidents.

28. WOODROW WILSON (1913-1921)

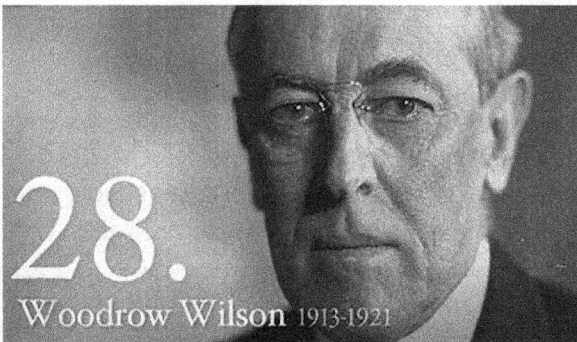

28.
Woodrow Wilson 1913-1921

Born: December 28, 1856, Staunton, Virginia
Full Name: Thomas Woodrow Wilson
Nickname: "Schoolmaster in Politics"

Education: College of New Jersey (now Princeton University), graduated 1879
Religion: Presbyterian
Marriage: June 24, 1885, to Ellen Louise Axson (1860–1914), December 18, 1915, to Edith Bolling Galt (1872–1961)
Children: Margaret Woodrow (1886–1944), Jessie Woodrow (1887–1933), Eleanor Randolph (1889–1967)
Career: Professor, College Administration, Public Official
Political Party: Democrat
Died: February 3, 1924, Washington, D.C.

Woodrow Wilson was one of America's greatest Presidents. His domestic program expanded the role of the federal government in managing the economy and protecting the interests of citizens. His foreign policy established a new vision of America's role in the world. And he helped to make the White House the center of power in Washington. Most historians rank him among the five most important American Presidents, along with Washington, Lincoln, and the two Roosevelts.

Born in Virginia in 1856 and raised in Georgia and South Carolina, Wilson's early memories included seeing Yankee soldiers marching into Augusta at the end of the Civil War. Wilson's father was a Presbyterian minister who fervently supported the South's secession from the Union. Because of the war's disruption, much of Wilson's early education came from his father at home. In 1875, he entered Princeton, graduating in 1879. After a brief period at the law school of the University of Virginia, he studied on his own and passed the Georgia bar examination. Bored as a lawyer in Atlanta, he enrolled at Johns Hopkins University, where he earned a Ph.D. in history and political science in 1886.

After a successful academic career as an author and professor at Bryn Mawr, Wesleyan, and Princeton, Wilson was elected president of Princeton in 1902. In that office, his efforts to modernize the college brought him attention as a progressive reformer, and in 1910, New Jersey Democrats approached him about running for governor. Wilson accepted, but on the condition that their support came with "no strings attached."

Rapid Rise to National Power

From this point, Wilson's rise to national power was astonishingly rapid. As governor of New Jersey, he immediately began to fight machine politics and party bosses, securing campaign finance reform, a primary law permitting voters rather than party bosses to nominate candidates, and a program to compensate workers injured on the job. In 1912, Wilson used his reputation as a progressive with strong Southern roots to run for the presidency as a Democrat. After narrowly winning the Democratic nomination, he faced a divided Republican Party. William Taft, the incumbent President, carried the official Republican nomination, but Theodore Roosevelt, believing that Taft had betrayed the cause of reform, walked out of the Republican convention and formed the short-lived Progressive or "Bull Moose" Party. Taft and Roosevelt split the Republican vote, and Wilson won the election with a little less than 42 percent of the vote.

Wilson's New Freedom platform was ambitious and thoroughly progressive. It called for tariff reduction, reform of the banking and monetary system, and new laws to weaken abusive corporations and restore economic competition. With a Presbyterian's confidence that God was guiding his course, Wilson pursued his New Freedom agenda with the zeal of a crusader, making use of his skill as an orator to galvanize the nation in support of his policies. Perhaps his greatest achievement was the passage of the Federal Reserve Act of 1913, which created the system that still provides the framework for regulating the nation's banks, credit, and money supply today. Other Wilson-backed legislation put new controls on big business and supported unions to ensure fair treatment of working Americans.

In 1914, World War I began in Europe, and with the United States trying to remain neutral, foreign policy played an important role in the 1916 presidential election. In addition to a bold program of reforms that attracted the support of farmers and laborers, Wilson's campaign slogan, "He Kept Us Out of War," helped him win reelection by a narrow margin.

Aggressive Policies

In foreign affairs, Wilson was determined to revise the imperialist practices of earlier administrations, promising independence to the Philippines and making Puerto Ricans American citizens. But Wilson's own policies could sometimes be high-handed. His administration intervened militarily more often in Latin America than any of his predecessors. In the European war, American neutrality ended when the Germans refused to suspend submarine warfare after 120 Americans were killed aboard the British liner Lusitania and a secret German offer of a military alliance with Mexico against the United States was uncovered. In 1917, Congress voted overwhelmingly to declarc war on Germany.

With the nation at war, Wilson set aside his domestic agenda to concentrate on a full-scale mobilization of the economy and industry. During the war, industrial production increased by 20 percent, daylight saving time was instituted to save fuel, the government took over the railroad system, and massive airplane and shipbuilding programs were launched. Americans began paying a new income tax and buying Liberty Bonds to pay for the war. Although most of the power the federal government acquired over the economy during the war was based on voluntary cooperation by businesses and individuals, conformity and aggressive patriotism became the order of the day. Private patriotic organizations persecuted dissenters and anyone suspected of political radicalism, and the administration sponsored Espionage and Sedition Acts that outlawed criticism of the government, the armed forces, and the war effort. Violators of the law were imprisoned or fined, and even mainstream publications were censored or banned.

League of Nations

In January 1918, Wilson made a major speech to Congress in which he laid out "Fourteen Points" that he believed would, if made the basis of a postwar peace, prevent future wars. Trade restrictions and secret alliances would be abolished, armaments would be curtailed, colonies and the national states that made up the Austro-Hungarian and Ottoman empires would be set on the road to independence, the German-occupied portions of France and Belgium would be evacuated, the revolutionary government of Russia would be welcomed into the community of nations, and a League of Nations would be created to maintain the peace. Believing that this revolutionary program required his personal support, Wilson decided that he would lead the American peace delegation to Paris, becoming the first President ever to go to Europe while in office. Despite Wilson's best efforts, however, the Treaty of Versailles, signed in June 1919, departed significantly from the Fourteen Points, leaving both the Germans and many Americans bitterly disillusioned.

Following his return to the United States in July 1919, Wilson presented the treaty to the Senate and spent much of the summer trying to build bipartisan support among senators for its approval, arguing that although imperfect, it was better than the sort of punitive treaty the British and French would have imposed on Germany. In September, having little success in winning Senate votes, Wilson began an arduous speaking tour to build public interest in the treaty and to promote U.S. participation in the new League of Nations.

Near the end of the tour, he collapsed from exhaustion, and a few days later, after returning to the White House, he suffered a massive stroke. For the last seventeen months of his term, he was an invalid, seeing almost no one except his doctors and his second wife, Edith Bolling Wilson, through whom he conducted public business. Refusing to compromise with the Senate on amendments to the treaty, Wilson eventually told his supporters to vote against it. The Senate voted twice on the treaty—in November 1919 and March 1920—defeating it both times. Thus, the United States never joined the international organization that Wilson saw as the keystone of his new world order.

Though he left office broken and defeated, Wilson believed firmly that his vision of America leading a world community of nations would eventually be embraced by the American people. Twenty-five years later, the United Nations built its headquarters in New York, a tangible symbol of the bipartisan support that Wilsonian ideals had gained after a second world war. But Wilson's legacy was not confined to foreign policy. His progressive domestic programs helped stabilize and humanize a huge industrial system, and his success in making the presidency the intellectual and political leader of the American government enabled the United States to deal effectively with the challenges and threats of the modern world.

29. WARREN G. HARDING (1921-1923)

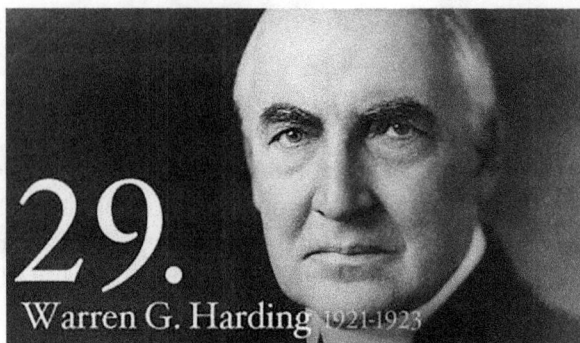

29.
Warren G. Harding 1921-1923

Born: November 2, 1865, Corsica (now Blooming Grove), Ohio
Full Name: Warren Gamaliel Harding
Nickname: None
Education: Ohio Central College (graduated 1882)
Religion: Baptist
Marriage: July 8, 1891, to Florence Kling DeWolfe (1860–1924)
Children: None
Career: Editor-Publisher
Political Party: Republican
Died: August 2, 1923, San Francisco, California

A conservative politician from Ohio, Warren G. Harding had few enemies because he rarely took a firm enough stand on an issue to make any. Who would have suspected that the man to succeed Woodrow Wilson, America's most visionary President, would be a man who saw the President's role as largely ceremonial?

Warren Harding was raised in a small town in Ohio. His wholesome and picture book childhood—farm chores, swimming in the local creek, and playing in the village band—was the basis of his down-home appeal later in life. As a young man, Harding brought a nearly bankrupt newspaper, the Marion Star, back to life. The paper became a favorite with Ohio politicians of both parties because of Harding's evenhanded reporting. Always well-liked for his good-natured manner, Harding won a seat in the Ohio State Senate, serving two terms before becoming a U.S. senator from Ohio in 1914. During his term as senator, Harding missed more sessions than he attended, being absent for key debates on prohibition and women's suffrage. Taking no stands meant making no enemies, and his fellow Republicans awarded Harding the 1920 presidential nomination, sensing the nation's fatigue with the reform agenda of Woodrow Wilson. Running with the slogan, "A Return to Normalcy," Harding beat progressive Democrat James M. Cox in a massive landslide.

Weak and Mediocre Presidency

Once in office, Harding admitted to his close friends that the job was beyond him. The capable men that Harding appointed to his cabinet included Charles Evans Hughes as secretary of state, Andrew Mellon as secretary of the treasury, and Herbert Hoover as secretary of commerce. But he also surrounded himself with dishonest cheats, who came to be known as "the Ohio gang." Many of them were later charged with defrauding the government, and some of them went to jail. Though Harding knew of the limitations of men like Harry Dougherty, the slick friend he appointed attorney general, he liked to play poker with them, drink whiskey, smoke, tell jokes, play golf, and keep late hours.

Known as a "good fellow," Harding enjoyed being liked more than he prized being a good leader. Though Harding was never linked to any crooked deals, the public was aware of his affairs with at least two women. Carrie Phillips, who had been a German sympathizer during the war, tried to blackmail Harding and was paid hush money by the Republican Party. Nan Britton, a pretty blond thirty years younger than the President, was given a job in Washington,

D.C., so that she could be near Harding. The two often met in the Oval Office, and their affair continued until Harding's death.

Decidedly conservative on trade and economic issues, Harding favored pro-business government policies. He allowed Andrew Mellon to push through tax cuts for the rich, stopped antitrust actions, and opposed organized labor.

Harding knew little about foreign affairs when he assumed office, preferring to give Secretary of State Hughes a free hand. Hughes was concerned with securing foreign markets for wealthy American banks, such as the one run by John D. Rockefeller. Hughes and Secretary of Commerce Herbert Hoover used the Fordney-McCumber Tariff to secure oil markets in the Middle East, especially in modern-day Iraq and Iran. His administration revised Germany's war debts downward through legislation, passed in 1923, known as the Dawes Plan. Hughes also called for a naval conference with nine other nations to freeze naval spending in an effort to reduce spending.

Shaken by the talk of corruption among the friends he had appointed to office, Harding and his wife, Florence "Flossie" Harding, organized a tour of the western states and Alaska in an attempt to meet people and explain his policies. After becoming ill with what was at the time attributed to ptomaine (food) poisoning, Harding had a heart attack and died quietly in his sleep. The rumors flew that Flossie had poisoned the President to save him from being engulfed in the charges of corruption that swept his administration. The Hardings never had any children; Flossie died of kidney disease in 1924.

Most historians regard Harding as the worst President in the nation's history. In the end, it was not his corrupt friends, but rather, Harding's own lack of vision that was most responsible for the tarnished legacy.

30. CALVIN COOLIDGE (1923-1929)

Born: July 4, 1872, Plymouth Notch, Vermont
Full Name: John Calvin Coolidge
Nickname: "Silent Cal"
Education: Amherst College (graduated 1895)
Religion: Congregationalist
Marriage: October 4, 1905, to Grace Anna Goodhue (1879–1957)
Children: John (1906–2000), Calvin (1908–1924)
Career: Lawyer
Political Party: Republican
Died: January 5, 1933, Northampton, Massachusetts

A quiet and somber man whose sour expression masked a dry wit, Calvin Coolidge was known as "Silent Cal." After learning of his ascendancy to the presidency following the death of Warren Harding in 1923, Coolidge was sworn in by his father, a justice of the peace, in the middle of the night and, displaying his famous "cool," promptly went back to bed.

Calvin Coolidge was born on Independence Day, 1872, and raised in Plymouth Notch, Vermont. His father was a pillar of the community, holding a variety of local offices from tax collector to constable. From him, Coolidge inherited his taciturn nature, his frugality, and his commitment to public service. The early death of his mother and sister contributed to his stoical personality.

Climbing the Political Ladder

While practicing law in Northampton, Massachusetts, Coolidge began to climb the ladder of state politics. From a spot on the City Council in 1900, he became chairman of the Northampton Republican Committee in 1904 and joined the state legislature in 1907. His term as governor of Massachusetts placed him in the national arena just in time to benefit from the return to power of the Republicans at the end of World War I. As governor, he called in the state guard to break a strike by city police in Boston, claiming that "there is no right to strike against the public safety by anybody, anywhere, anytime." This bold action won him public acclaim and swept him onto the Republican ticket as the vice presidential nominee with Warren Harding. As vice president, Coolidge kept a low profile, sitting silently during cabinet meetings and seldom speaking in his constitutional position as presiding officer of the U.S. Senate.

After Harding's death in 1923, Coolidge became President. Intent on running for reelection in 1924, he dispatched his potential Republican rivals with relative ease. He had emerged unscathed from the scandals that plagued the Harding administration, earning a reputation for being honest, direct, and hardworking. The Democrats were split in 1924, finally settling on a compromise candidate, John W. Davis of West Virginia. With a rebounding economy to help him, Coolidge won handily with the slogan "Keep Cool With Coolidge."

A Visible Yet Passive Presidency

In contrast to his disdain for small talk, Coolidge was a highly visible leader, holding press conferences, speaking on the radio, and emerging as the leader among what one survey called "the most photographed persons on earth." Reveling in what would become known as the "photo op," he posed before the cameras dressed in farmer overalls, a cowboy hat and chaps, and an Indian headdress. But his prominent profile was not matched by a commitment to activism. He believed in small government, especially at the federal level, and practiced a passive style of leadership. He saw little need to intervene in issues that Congress or the states could handle without him.

Nonetheless, Theodore Roosevelt and Woodrow Wilson had changed the presidency into an activist institution, and public opinion fairly demanded a modicum of leadership from the White House. Coolidge did have an agenda. His chief concern was economics, where he favored low taxes, reduced regulation of business, and a balanced budget. Alongside his Secretary of the Treasury Andrew Mellon, the wealthy Pittsburgh industrialist who advocated "trickle-down" economics, as critics called it, Coolidge secured reductions in rates for wealthy Americans (most citizens at the time paid little federal tax). Although many observers at the time gave the President and Secretary Mellon credit for the so-called "Coolidge Prosperity" that characterized the seven years of his presidency, in retrospect he came under criticism for having failed to try to stop the feverish stock-market speculation toward the end of his term that contributed to the stock market crash of 1929. Coolidge also fought against farm-relief legislation that might have shored up the depressed farm economy.

Like Harding, Coolidge allowed his cabinet a free hand in foreign affairs, delegating authority to Treasury Secretary Mellon, Secretary of State Charles Evans Hughes, and Commerce Secretary Herbert Hoover, all holdovers from Harding's cabinet. The President believed that the United States should seek out foreign markets and refrain from entangling alliances and participation in the League of Nations. He supported the 1928 Kellogg-Briand Pact renouncing war as a means of settling international differences, a largely symbolic pact that nonetheless became an important precedent in fostering reliance on international law. In Latin America, Coolidge's administration tended to support the interests of U.S. businesses, although the President made steps toward a less adversarial posture than his predecessors had typically maintained.

Coolidge chose not to run for a second term because his republican political philosophy led him to value highly the unwritten two-term precedent (toward which he counted the balance of Harding's term that he served). Moreover, the death of his teenage son in 1924 had taken much of the joy out of his work. True to his simple tastes, he imagined he would be happier in retirement in Northampton, Massachusetts.

First Lady Grace Coolidge was as sunny and sociable as her husband was taciturn and sardonic. The press photographed her at every opportunity, and she once joked that she was the "national hugger." Having been trained as an instructor for the deaf, Grace Coolidge brought national attention to the plight of the nation's hearing-impaired and became a close personal friend of the author and activist, Helen Keller, who was both deaf and blind.

Although the public admired Coolidge during his time in office, the Great Depression turned public opinion against him. Many linked the nation's economic collapse to Coolidge's policy decisions. He vetoed the problematic McNary-Haugen bill to aid the depressed agricultural sector while thousands of rural banks in the Midwest and South were shutting their doors and farmers were losing their land. His tax cuts worsened the maldistribution of wealth and overproduction of goods, which destabilized the economy. Although in the 1980s, conservatives, led by Ronald Reagan--who hung Coolidge's portrait in the White House--revived something of a cult of Coolidge, most historians look upon the Coolidge presidency with skepticism, considering him to have offered little in the way of a positive vision, however strong his personal integrity.

31. HERBERT HOOVER (1929-1933)

31.
Herbert Hoover 1929-1933

Born: August 10, 1874, West Branch, Iowa
Nickname: None
Full Name: Herbert Clark Hoover
Education: Stanford University (graduated 1895)
Religion: Society of Friends (Quaker)
Marriage: February 10, 1899, to Lou Henry (1875–1944)
Children: Herbert Clark (1903–1969), Allan Henry (1907–1993)
Career: Engineer
Political Party: Republican
Died: October 20, 1964, New York City, New York

Upon accepting the Republican nomination for President in 1928, Herbert Hoover predicted that "We in America today are nearer to the final triumph over poverty than ever before in the history of any land. The poorhouse is vanishing from among us." Hoover won the presidency that year, but his time in office belied his optimistic assertion. Within eight months of his inauguration, the stock market crashed, signifying the beginning of the Great Depression, the most severe economic crisis the United States had ever known. Rightly or wrongly,

Hoover's efforts to combat the Great Depression have defined his presidency and his place in American history.

Born in 1874 into a Quaker family in rural Iowa, Hoover was orphaned by the age of nine. Determined to go to the newly established Stanford University in California, Hoover worked hard to improve his mediocre grades. After graduating from Stanford with a degree in geology, Hoover became a mining engineer, traveling the world to evaluate prospective mines for potential purchase. He married the brilliant Lou Henry, the only female geology student at Stanford. Lou Hoover quickly mastered eight languages in their travels; later, she and the President would often speak Mandarin when they wanted to avoid being overheard by the White House staff. By 1914, Hoover was a millionaire, securing his wealth from high-salaried positions, his ownership of profitable Burmese silver mines, and royalties from writing the leading textbook on mining engineering.

Skilled Administrator

World War I brought Hoover to prominence in American politics and thrust him into the international spotlight. In addition to running the U.S. Food Administration, which allocated America's food resources during the conflict, Hoover organized and administered several private relief efforts before, during, and after the war. He thus became an important war-time adviser to President Woodrow Wilson even though he was a Republican. Wilson, in turn, made Hoover part of the American delegation to the Versailles peace conference that concluded the war.

During the 1920s, Hoover rose steadily in Republican politics, serving with great ability and distinction in the Harding and Coolidge administrations as secretary of commerce. Owing to his record and an effective public relations effort by his supporters, Hoover was the most prominent Republican in the United States when President

Calvin Coolidge announced, in August 1927, that he would not seek another term.

Hoover easily won the 1928 Republican nomination for President. His platform rejected farm subsidies, supported prohibition, pledged lower taxes, and promised more of the same prosperity Americans had enjoyed during the Coolidge years. Hoover's opponent in the presidential race would be Democrat Al Smith of New York, a Catholic who railed against Prohibition. Smith was a distinct underdog, however. His religion and his anti-prohibition position alienated many southern Democrats, a key constituency in the party. Hoover, on the other hand, was an extremely attractive candidate, the man who would help Americans attain new levels of prosperity—or, as a 1928 Republican slogan claimed, put "a chicken in every pot and two cars in every garage." On election day, Hoover won an overwhelming victory, claiming more than 58 percent of the vote.

Hoover and the Great Depression

Hoover came into the presidency as one of the foremost proponents of public-private cooperation—what was termed "volunterism"-- to maintain a high-growth economy. Volunterism was not premised on governmental coercion or intervention, which Hoover feared would destroy precious American ideals like individualism and self-reliance, but on cooperation among individuals and groups. Hoover did not reject government regulation out of hand, however; in fact, he supported regulating industries such as radio broadcasting and aviation that he believed served the public good. But he preferred a voluntary, non-governmental approach to economic matters, the better, he reasoned, to protect what he called the "American character."

The economic crisis that struck the United States in the late 1920s was all- encompassing, however. Having both domestic and international causes and effects, the Depression afflicted almost every sector of the American economy (although some more severely than others), revealing serious structural weaknesses that resulted in high unemployment, low economic growth, and financial instability. Most important, the Depression sapped the American people's confidence and will.

The Great Depression was a stern test for Hoover's approach and one that proved too difficult to manage. His voluntarist-inspired persuasion and programs failed to stimulate the consumption and production needed to jump-start the economy. Some policies, like the Hawley-Smoot Tariff bill that Hoover signed, retarded growth and recovery by raising tariffs (especially on agricultural products) and stifling international trade. His Agricultural Marketing Act had little impact on the prospects of American farmers.

Hoover eventually did support some interventionist government programs aimed at combating the Depression. Though undersized, the Reconstruction Finance Corporation used federal money in an ultimately unsuccessful effort to stabilize the nation's banking and financial sector. The RFC was also aimed at corporations rather than at the growing ranks of the suffering poor, a policy that reflected Hoover's own beliefs. Fearing that government aid would breed a sense of dependence among the poor, Hoover largely refused to extend such assistance to millions of the nation's unemployed and hungry who were overwhelming private relief agencies.

In the public eye, Hoover seemed uncaring, unwilling to admit that people were starving and that his ideas were failing. He lost significant public support in the summer of 1932 when General Douglas MacArthur— in defiance of Hoover's orders—removed the World War I veterans (known as Bonus Marchers) who had massed peacefully in Washington, D.C., to petition Congress for early receipt of their veterans bonuses. MacArthur was brutal in his treatment of the marchers, using cavalry, tanks, and bayonet-bearing soldiers. In the riot that followed, U.S. troops clubbed women and children, tear-gassed the marchers, burned their shacks, and forcibly drove them across the Potomac River.

Defeat

Hoover ran for reelection in 1932, anxious to prove that his policies could still ameliorate the economic crisis. Americans, though, rallied around Democrat Franklin D. Roosevelt and his "New Deal," with its vague promises of a "crusade to restore America to its own people." Roosevelt won the contest handily, ushering in decades of Democratic dominance in presidential elections. Hoover left the White House in disgrace, having incurred the public's wrath for failing to lift the nation out of the Great Depression.

Hoover in Perspective

Hoover's reputation has risen over the years. He is no longer blamed for causing the Depression; instead, scholars note that Hoover's efforts to combat its effects were extraordinary when compared to federal anti-depression measures invoked during previous economic crises. These efforts, moreover, flowed logically from the President's unique brand of social, economic, and political progressivism. Nonetheless, the nation's economy continued to sink during the Hoover presidency. With the public losing confidence in the President's abilities, leadership, and policies, Hoover paid the ultimate political price for these failures in November 1932.

32. FRANKLIN D. ROOSEVELT (1933-1945)

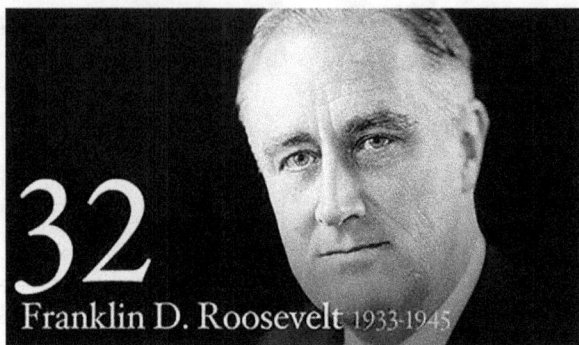

32
Franklin D. Roosevelt 1933-1945

Born: January 30, 1882, Hyde Park, New York
Full Name: Franklin Delano Roosevelt
Nickname: "FDR"
Education: Harvard College (graduated 1903), Columbia Law School
Religion: Episcopalian
Marriage: March 17, 1905, to Anna Eleanor Roosevelt (1884–1962)
Children: Anna Eleanor (1906–1975), James (1907–1991), Franklin Delano Jr. (1909), Elliott (1910–1990), Franklin Delano Jr. (1914–1988), John Aspinwall (1916–1981)
Career: Public Official, Lawyer
Political Party: Democrat
Died: April 12, 1945, Warm Springs, Georgia

Faced with the Great Depression and World War II, Franklin D. Roosevelt, nicknamed "FDR," guided America through its greatest domestic crisis, with the exception of the Civil War, and its greatest foreign crisis. His presidency—which spanned twelve years—was unparalleled, not only in length but in scope. FDR took office with the country mired in a horrible and debilitating economic depression that not only sapped its material wealth and spiritual strength, but cast a pall over its future. Roosevelt's combination of confidence, optimism, and political savvy—all of which came together in the experimental economic and social programs of the "New Deal"—helped bring about the beginnings of a national recovery.

In foreign affairs, FDR committed the United States to the defeat of the fascist powers of Germany, Japan, and Italy, and led the nation and its allies to the brink of victory. This triumph dramatically altered America's relationship with the world, guiding the United States to a position of international prominence, if not predominance. By virtue of its newfound political and economic power, as well as its political and moral leadership, the United States would play a leading role in shaping the remainder of the twentieth century.

Franklin Roosevelt also forged a domestic political revolution on several fronts. In politics, FDR and the Democratic Party built a power base which carried the party to electoral, if not ideological, dominance until the late 1960s. In governance, FDR's policies, especially those comprising the New Deal, helped redefine and strengthen both the American state and, specifically, the American presidency, expanding the political, administrative, and constitutional powers of the office.

Political Rise and Personal Tragedy

Franklin Delano Roosevelt was born in 1882 in Hyde Park, New York, to James and Sara Roosevelt. James Roosevelt was a land-owner and businessman of considerable, but not awesome, wealth. FDR grew up under the watchful eyes of his mother, whose devotion to her only child was considerable, and a host of nannies. At age 14, Franklin's parents sent him to the Groton School, a prestigious boarding school in Massachusetts. At Groton, FDR grew increasingly fond of his distant cousin, Theodore Roosevelt, a rising star in the Republican Party. FDR went on to Harvard College, where he spent more time on the college newspaper than he did on his studies. While at Harvard, FDR apparently declared himself a Democrat and began courting his distant cousin, Eleanor Roosevelt.

Franklin and Eleanor were married in New York City in 1905, a few months after FDR began law school at Columbia. Roosevelt had little interest in the law, however, and his attention soon turned to politics. He ran successfully for the New York State Senate in 1910 and was re-elected in 1912. In 1913, he joined the Wilson administration as assistant secretary of the Navy and played a key role in readying the United States for entry into the world war. FDR was roundly praised for his efforts and the leaders of the Democratic Party tabbed him as a Democrat to watch. Indeed, in 1920, the party named him its vice-presidential candidate. Although the ticket of James Cox and FDR lost, FDR's future seemed bright.

Tragedy struck, however, in 1921. Roosevelt contracted polio, a terrifying and incurable disease that left him paralyzed in his legs. Only through an arduous rehabilitation process—and with the support of his wife, his children, and his close confidantes—was FDR able to regain some use of his legs. In the 1920s, he invested a considerable part of his fortune in rehabilitating a spa in Warm Springs, Georgia, whose curative waters aided his own rehabilitation. In later years, the cottage he built there would be called "the Little White House." Though polio devastated FDR physically, his steely will seemed to grow stronger as he fought through his recovery. Eleanor later said of this time: "I know that he had real fear when he was first taken ill, but he learned to surmount it. After that I never heard him say he was afraid of anything."

Successful Governor and Presidential Candidate

FDR's political comeback began in earnest in 1928 when he won the governorship of New York. The crash of the stock market in October 1929 served as a harbinger of tougher times to come and led Governor Roosevelt to focus on combating the state's economic woes. FDR implemented a number of innovative relief and recovery initiatives— unemployment insurance, pensions for the elderly, limits on work hours, and massive public works projects—that established him as a liberal reformer. FDR's efforts also won him reelection as governor in 1930, a rare feat in the midst of depression.

By the presidential election season of 1932, the Great Depression had only worsened and showed no signs of abating. Democrats turned to FDR, a popular and successful two-term governor with a recognizable last name, to challenge President Hoover. Promising a "New Deal" for the American people, FDR was swept into office in a landslide. In his inaugural address, Roosevelt gave hope to dispirited Americans throughout the nation, assuring them that they had "nothing to fear but fear itself."

Fighting the Great Depression

President Franklin Roosevelt's "New Deal" fought the Great Depression on a number of fronts. In the famous "First Hundred Days" of his presidency, FDR pushed through legislation that reformed the banking and financial sectors, tried to cure the ills afflicting American agriculture, and attempted to resuscitate American industry. To meet the immediate crisis of starvation and the dire needs of the nation's unemployed, FDR provided direct cash relief for the poor and jobs programs. Roosevelt's reassuring "fireside chats," in which he spoke to the nation via radio about the country's predicament, calmed a worried public.

In 1935, FDR took the New Deal in a more liberal direction, overseeing the enactment of some of the most far-reaching social and economic legislation in American history. The Wagner Act allowed labor unions to organize and bargain collectively, conferring on them a new legitimacy. The Social

Security Act set up programs designed to provide for the needs of the aged, the poor, and the unemployed, establishing a social welfare net that, at least theoretically, covered all Americans. By the end of his second term, FDR and his advisers insisted that the federal government should stimulate the national economy through its spending policies, a strategy that held sway for the next thirty years.

All of these actions, though, could not end the Great Depression. Only American mobilization for war in the early 1940s brought the United States out of its economic doldrums. Nor did New Deal programs, because they reflected the biases of 1930s American politics and culture, offer the same aid to all Americans; white men generally received better benefits than women, blacks, or Latinos.

Nonetheless, FDR did much to reshape the United States. With Roosevelt as its presidential candidate, the Democratic Party won again in 1936, signaling the beginning of 30 years of political dominance that extended long after FDR's death. With FDR in the White House, the federal government played a greater role than ever before in managing the American economy and in protecting the welfare of the American people. In short, FDR oversaw major and important changes in American politics and governance that would define life in the United States for most of the twentieth century.

World War II

In addition to changing life at home, Roosevelt permanently altered America's role in the world. Hamstrung in the 1930s by domestic economic woes and a strong isolationist bloc in Congress and the public, FDR confronted Germany and Japan only tentatively as those powers looked to establish dominance in Europe and Asia, respectively. Nevertheless, Roosevelt did extend massive amounts of aid to Great Britain as that nation successfully held out against the Nazi

272

onslaught during 1940 and 1941 Working with America's allies in the Pacific, FDR also tried to contain the Japanese threat.

Japan's surprise attack on the American Navy at Pearl Harbor on December 7, 1941 officially brought the United States into World War II. FDR proved a talented war-time leader and, by 1943, the United States military, along with its allies, had turned the tide against both Germany and Japan. But Roosevelt did not live to see the war's end., In April 1945, just weeks before the German surrender, the president collapsed and died of a cerebral hemorrhage.

Under Roosevelt's leadership, the United States emerged from World War II as the world's foremost economic, political, and military power. FDR's contributions to domestic life during his presidency were just as vital. While his "New Deal" did not end the Great Depression, Roosevelt's leadership gave Americans hope and confidence in their darkest hours and fundamentally reshaped the relationship between the federal government and the American people. FDR so dominated American politics that he almost single-handedly launched the Democratic Party into a position of prolonged political dominance.. During his tenure, FDR also lifted both the standing and power of the American presidency to unprecedented heights. More broadly, however, his New Deal programs, marked a substantial turning point in the nation's political, economic, social, and cultural life.

33. HARRY S. TRUMAN (1945-1953)

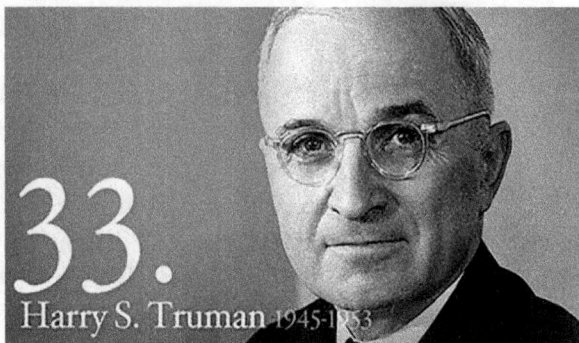

Born: May 8, 1884, Lamar, MO
Nickname: "Give 'Em Hell Harry"
Religion: Baptist
Marriage: June 28, 1919, to Elizabeth "Bess" Virginia Wallace (1885–1982)
Children: Mary Margaret (1924–2008)
Career: Farmer, Businessman, Public Official
Political Party: Democrat
Died: December 26, 1972, Kansas City, MO

Harry S. Truman became President of the United States with the death of Franklin D. Roosevelt on April 12, 1945. During his nearly eight years in office, Truman confronted enormous challenges in both foreign and domestic affairs. Truman's policies abroad, and especially toward the Soviet Union in the emerging Cold War, would become staples of American foreign policy for generations. At home, Truman protected and reinforced the New Deal reforms of his predecessor, guided the American economy from a war-time to a peace-time footing, and advanced the cause of African-American civil rights. Historians now rank Truman among the nation's best Presidents.

Student and Soldier

Harry Truman was a child of Missouri. Born on May 8, 1884, in the town of Lamar, Truman grew up in Independence, only ten miles east of Kansas City. As a child he devoured history books and literature, played the piano enthusiastically, and dreamed of becoming a great soldier. His poor eyesight made a commission to West Point impossible, however, and his family's financial problems kept him from attending a four-year college.

Truman instead worked on the family farm between 1906 and 1914. Though he detested farming, it was during this difficult time that he fell in love with Virginia "Bess" Wallace, whom he had met as a child. Bess refused Harry's marriage proposal in 1911 but the romance continued. They wed in 1919 and five years later had their first and only child, Mary Margaret.

In 1914, after his father's death, Truman tried unsuccessfully to earn a living as an owner and operator of a small mining company and oil business, all the while remaining involved with the farm. In 1917, Truman's National Guard unit shipped out to France as part of the American Expeditionary Force fighting the world war. The soldiering life suited Truman, who turned his battery—which had a reputation for unruliness and ineffectiveness—into a top-notch unit.

A Career in Politics

Back home from the war, Truman opened a men's furnishings store (shirts, ties, underwear, sock, etc.—no suits, coats, or shoes) with an army buddy. The shop failed, however, after only a few years. In 1922, Thomas J. Pendergast, the Democratic boss of Kansas City, asked Truman to run for a judgeship on the county court of Jackson County's eastern district. Truman served one term, was defeated for a second, and then became presiding judge in 1926, a position he held until 1934. As presiding judge, Truman managed the county's finances during the early years of the Great Depression. Despite his association with the corrupt Pendergast, Truman established a reputation for personal integrity, honesty, and efficiency.

In 1934, Truman was elected to the U.S. Senate with help of the Pendergast political machine. Senator Truman supported the New Deal, although he proved only a marginally important legislator. He became a national figure during World War II when he chaired the "Truman Committee" investigating government defense spending. President Franklin D. Roosevelt chose Truman as his running mate in the 1944 presidential campaign largely because the Missourian passed muster with Southern Democrats and party officials. The Roosevelt-Truman ticket won a comfortable victory over its Republican opposition, though Truman would serve only eighty-two days as vice president. With the death of FDR on April 12, 1945, Harry S. Truman became the thirty-third President of the United States.

Truman and Post-War America

Truman took office as World War II in Europe drew to a close. The German leader Adolf Hitler committed suicide in Berlin only two weeks into Truman's presidency and the allies declared victory in Europe on May 7, 1945. The war in the Pacific, however, was far from being over; most experts believed it might last another year and require an American invasion of Japan. The U.S. and British governments, though, had secretly begun to develop the world's most deadly weapon—an atomic bomb. Upon its completion and successful testing in the summer of 1945, Truman approved its use against Japan. On August 6 and 9, 1945, the U.S. Army Air Force dropped atomic bombs on two cities, Hiroshima and Nagasaki, immediately killing upwards of 100,000 people (with perhaps twice that number dying from the aftereffects of radiation poisoning). Japanese emperor

Hirohito agreed to surrender days later, bringing World War II to a close.

Truman faced unprecedented and defining challenges in international affairs during the first years of his presidency. American relations with the Soviet Union—nominal allies in the battle against Germany and Japan—began to deteriorate even before victory in World War II. Serious ideological differences—the United States supported democratic institutions and market principles, while Soviet leaders were totalitarian and ran a command economy—separated the two countries. But it was the diverging interests of the emerging superpowers in Europe and Asia which sharpened their differences.

In response to what it viewed as Soviet threats, the Truman administration constructed foreign policies to contain the Soviet Union's political power and counter its military strength. By 1949, Soviet and American policies had divided Europe into a Soviet-controlled bloc in the east and an American-supported grouping in the west. That same year, a communist government sympathetic to the Soviet Union came to power in China, the world's most populous nation. The Cold War between the United States and the Soviet Union, which would last for over forty years, had begun.

At home, President Truman presided over the difficult transition from a war-time to a peace-time economy. During World War II, the American government had intervened in the nation's economy to an unprecedented degree, controlling prices, wages, and production. Truman lobbied for a continuing government role in the immediate post-war economy and also for an expansive liberal agenda that built on the New Deal. Republicans and conservative Democrats attacked this strategy and the President mercilessly. An immediate postwar economy characterized by high inflation and consumer shortages further eroded Truman's support and contributed to the Democrats losing control of Congress in the 1946 midterm elections. Newly empowered Republicans and conservative Democrats stymied Truman's liberal proposals and began rolling back some New Deal gains, especially through the Taft-Hartley labor law moderately restricting union activity.

Election of 1948

Truman's political fortunes reached their low point in 1946 and 1947, a nadir from which few observers believed the President could recover to win a second term. Freed from shouldering primary responsibility for the nation's economy (which began to stabilize) and the nearly impossible burden of uniting the disparate Democratic party behind a progressive agenda, Truman let the Republicans try to govern. When they faltered or pushed conservative programs, Truman counterattacked with skill, fire, and wit. The President also took steps to energize his liberal Democratic base, especially blacks, unions, and urban dwellers, issuing executive orders that pushed forward the cause of African-American civil rights and vetoing (unsuccessfully) the Taft-Hartley bill.

Truman won the presidential nomination of a severely divided Democratic party in the summer of 1948 and faced New York's Republican governor Thomas Dewey in the general election. Few expected him to win, but the President waged a vigorous campaign that excoriated Republicans in Congress as much as it attacked Dewey. Truman defeated Dewey in November 1948, capping one of the most stunning political comebacks in American history.

A Troubled Second Term

Truman viewed his reelection as a mandate for a liberal agenda, which he presented under the name "The Fair Deal." The President miscalculated, however, as the American public and conservatives in both parties on Capitol Hill rejected most of his program. He did win passage of some important liberal legislation that raised the minimum wage and expanded Social Security. Moreover, the American economy began a period of sustained growth in the early 1950s that lasted for nearly two decades. Increasingly, though, his administration was buffeted by charges of corruption and being "soft on communism." The latter critique was extremely damaging as anti-communism became one of the defining characteristics of early Cold War American political culture. Some of the most virulent (and irresponsible) anti-communists, like Wisconsin's Republican senator Joseph McCarthy, lambasted the administration and the State Department, in particular.

Significant foreign policy challenges persisted into Truman's second term. The President committed the United States to the defense of South Korea in the summer of 1950 after that nation, an American ally, was invaded by its communist neighbor, North Korea. The American military launched a counterattack that pushed the North Koreans back to the Chinese border, whereupon the Chinese entered the war in the fall of 1950. The conflict settled into a bloody and grisly stalemate that would not be resolved until Truman left office in 1953. The Korean War globalized the Cold War and spurred a massive American military build-up that began the nuclear arms race in earnest.

Truman in Perspective

Truman's popularity sank during his second term, due largely to accusations of corruption, charges that the administration was "soft on communism," and the stalemated Korean War. Unsurprisingly, Truman chose not to run in 1952. The Democratic Party's candidate, Governor Adlai Stevenson, lost to war hero and Republican General Dwight D. Eisenhower in the fall election.

Truman's legacy has become clearer and more impressive in the years since he left office. Most scholars admit that the President faced enormous challenges domestically, internationally, and politically. While he occasionally failed to measure accurately the nation's political tenor and committed some significant policy blunders, Truman achieved notable successes. Domestically, he took important first steps in civil rights, protected many of the New Deal's gains, and presided over an economy that would enjoy nearly two decades of unprecedented growth. In foreign affairs, the President and his advisers established many of the basic foundations of America foreign policy, especially in American-Soviet relations, that would guide the nation in the decades ahead. On the whole, Truman is currently celebrated by the public, politicians, and scholars alike.

34. DWIGHT D. EISENHOWER (1953-1961)

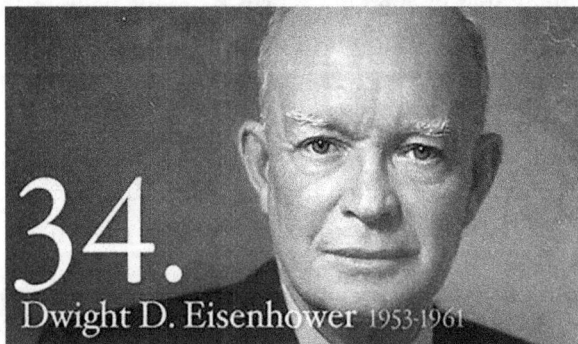
Dwight D. Eisenhower 1953-1961

Born: October 14, 1890, Denison, Texas
Full Name: Dwight David Eisenhower
Nickname: "Ike"
Education: U.S. Military Academy, West Point, New York (graduated 1915)
Religion: Presbyterian
Marriage: July 1, 1916, to Mary "Mamie" Geneva Doud (1896–1979)

Children: Doud Dwight (1917–1921); John Sheldon Doud (1922–2013)
Career: Soldier
Political Party: Republican
Died: March 28, 1969, Washington, D.C.

Born in Texas and raised in Kansas, Dwight D. Eisenhower was one of America's greatest military commanders and the thirty-fourth President of the United States. Inspired by the example of a friend who was going to the U.S. Naval Academy, Eisenhower won an appointment to the U.S. Military Academy at West Point. Although his mother had religious convictions that made her a pacifist, she did not try to stop Eisenhower from becoming a military officer.

Popular War Hero

After graduating from West Point, Eisenhower experienced several years of professional frustration and disappointment. World War I ended a week before he was scheduled to go to Europe. After peace came, his career stalled. He did enjoy the personal fulfillment that came from marrying Mamie Doud in 1916 and having a son, John, in 1922. During the 1920s, he began to get assignments that allowed him to prove his abilities. He served as a military aide to General John J. Pershing and then to General Douglas MacArthur in the Philippines. Shortly before the United States entered World War II, Eisenhower earned his first star with a promotion to brigadier general.

After the United States entered the war, Eisenhower went to Washington, D.C., to work as a planning officer. He so impressed the Army's chief of staff, General George C. Marshall, that he quickly got important command assignments. In 1944, he was Supreme Commander of Operation Overlord, the Allied assault on Nazi-occupied Europe. In only five years, Eisenhower had risen from a lowly lieutenant colonel in the Philippines to commander of the greatest invasion force in history. When he returned home in 1945 to serve as chief of staff of the Army, Eisenhower was a hero, loved and admired by the American public.

Acknowledging Eisenhower's immense popularity, President Harry Truman privately proposed to Eisenhower that they run together on the Democratic ticket in 1948—with Truman as the vice-presidential candidate. Eisenhower refused and instead became president of Columbia University and then, after the outbreak of the Korean War, the first Supreme Commander of NATO forces in Europe. In 1952, he declared that he was a Republican and returned home to win his party's presidential nomination, with Richard M. Nixon as his running mate. "Ike" endeared himself to the American people with his plain talk, charming smile, and sense of confidence. He easily beat Democrat Adlai Stevenson in 1952 and again in 1956.

Moderate Republicanism

Eisenhower was a popular President throughout his two terms in office. His moderate Republican policies helped him secure many victories in Congress, even though Democrats held the majority in both the House and the Senate during six of the eight years that Eisenhower was in the White House. Eisenhower helped strengthen established programs, such as Social Security, and launch important new ones, such as the Interstate Highway System in 1956, which became the single largest public works program in U.S. history.

Yet there were problems and failures as well as achievements. Although he secured from Congress the first civil rights legislation since the period of Reconstruction after the Civil War, he refrained from speaking out to advance the cause of racial justice. He never endorsed the Supreme Court's ruling in 1954 that racially segregated schools were unconstitutional, and he failed to use his moral authority as President to urge speedy compliance with the

282

Court's decision. In 1957, he did send federal troops to Little Rock, Arkansas, when mobs tried to block the desegregation of Central High School, but he did so because he had a constitutional obligation to uphold the law, not because he supported integration.

Eisenhower also refrained from publicly criticizing Senator Joseph R. McCarthy, who used his powers to abuse the civil liberties of dozens of citizens who he accused of anti-American activities. Eisenhower privately despised McCarthy, and he worked behind the scenes with congressional leaders to erode McCarthy's influence. Eisenhower's indirect tactics eventually worked, but they also prolonged the senator's power since many people concluded that even the President was unwilling to confront McCarthy.

Waging Cold War

Six months after he became President, Eisenhower agreed to an armistice that ended three years of fighting in Korea. Only on one other occasion—in Lebanon in 1958—did Eisenhower send combat troops into action. Yet defense spending remained high, as Eisenhower made vigorous efforts to wage the Cold War. He placed new emphasis on nuclear strength, which was popularly known as massive retaliation, to prevent the outbreak of war. He also frequently authorized the Central Intelligence Agency (CIA) to undertake covert actions—secret interventions to overthrow unfriendly governments or protect reliable anti-Communist leaders whose power was threatened. The CIA helped topple the governments of Iran in 1953 and Guatemala in 1954, but it suffered an embarrassing failure in 1958 when it intervened in Indonesia. Eisenhower avoided war in Indochina in 1954 when he decided not to authorize an air strike to rescue French troops at the crucial battle of Dienbienphu. Yet after the French granted independence to the nations of Indochina—Cambodia, Laos, and Vietnam—Eisenhower used U.S. power and prestige to help create a non-

Communist government in South Vietnam, an action that had disastrous long-term consequences. During his last years in office, Eisenhower also "waged peace," hoping to improve U.S.-Soviet relations and negotiate a treaty banning nuclear testing in the air and seas. But the Soviet downing of a U.S. reconnaissance plane—the U-2 incident of May 1, 1960— ended any hope for a treaty before Eisenhower left office.

Rising Reputation

After leaving office, Eisenhower had a mediocre reputation with most historians. Some even wondered whether a President who often made garbled public statements really understood most issues or whether staff assistants made the important decisions for this general in the White House. As time passed and more records from the Eisenhower administration became available for research, it became clear that Eisenhower was a strong leader who was very much in charge of his own administration. Historians still point to the limitations in Eisenhower's record in areas such as civil rights, and they debate the long-term consequences of his covert interventions in Third World nations. Yet his ranking is much higher, with many historians concluding that Eisenhower was a "near great" or even "great" President.

35. JOHN F. KENNEDY (1961-1963)

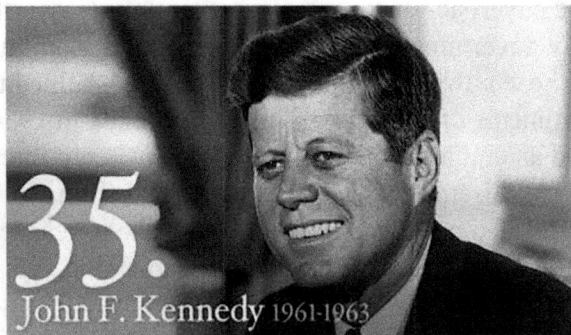

Born: May 29, 1917, Brookline, MA
Full Name: John Fitzgerald Kennedy
Nickname: "JFK," "Jack"
Education: Harvard College (graduated 1940)
Religion: Roman Catholic
Marriage: Jacqueline Lee Bouvier (1929–1994), September 12, 1953
Children: Caroline Bouvier (1957–); John Fitzgerald, Jr. (1960–1999); Patrick Bouvier (1963)
Career: Author, U.S. Navy Officer, Journalist, Public Official
Political Party: Democrat
Died: Nov. 22, 1963, Dallas, TX

John F. Kennedy was born into a rich, politically connected Boston family of Irish-Catholics. He and his eight siblings enjoyed a privileged childhood of elite private schools, sailboats, servants, and summer homes. During his childhood and youth, "Jack" Kennedy suffered frequent serious illnesses. Nevertheless, he strove to make his own way, writing a best-selling book while still in college at Harvard and volunteering for hazardous combat duty in the Pacific during World War II. Kennedy's wartime service made him a hero. After a short stint as a journalist, Kennedy entered politics, serving in the U.S. House of Representatives from 1947 to 1953 and the U.S. Senate from 1953 to 1961.

Kennedy was the youngest person elected U.S. President and the first Roman Catholic to serve in that office. For many observers, his presidency came to represent the ascendance of youthful idealism in the aftermath of World War II.

His Inaugural Address offered the memorable injunction: "Ask not what your country can do for you--ask what you can do for your country." As President, he set out to redeem his campaign pledge to get America moving again. His economic programs launched the country on its longest sustained expansion since World War II; before his death, he laid plans for a massive assault on persisting pockets of privation and poverty.

Responding to ever more urgent demands, he took vigorous action in the cause of equal rights, calling for new civil rights legislation. His vision of America extended to the quality of the national culture and the central role of the arts in a vital society.

He wished America to resume its old mission as the first nation dedicated to the revolution of human rights. With the Alliance for Progress and the Peace Corps, he brought American idealism to the aid of developing nations. But the hard reality of the Communist challenge remained.

Shortly after his inauguration, Kennedy permitted a band of Cuban exiles, already armed and trained, to invade their homeland. The attempt to overthrow the regime of Fidel Castro was a failure. Soon thereafter, the Soviet Union renewed its campaign against West Berlin. Kennedy replied by reinforcing the Berlin garrison and increasing the Nation's military strength, including new efforts in outer space. Confronted by this reaction, Moscow, after the erection of the Berlin Wall, relaxed its pressure in central Europe.

Instead, the Russians now sought to install nuclear missiles in Cuba. When this was discovered by air reconnaissance in October 1962, Kennedy imposed a quarantine on all offensive weapons bound for Cuba. While the world trembled on the brink of nuclear war, the Russians backed down and agreed to take the missiles away. The American response to the Cuban crisis evidently persuaded Moscow of the futility of nuclear blackmail.

Kennedy now contended that both sides had a vital interest in stopping the spread of nuclear weapons and slowing the arms race--a contention which led to the test ban treaty of 1963. The months after the Cuban crisis showed significant progress toward his goal of "a world of law and free choice, banishing the world of war and coercion." His administration thus saw the beginning of new hope for both the equal rights of Americans and the peace of the world.

The promise of this energetic and telegenic leader was not to be fulfilled, as he was assassinated near the end of his third year in office. For many Americans, the public murder of President Kennedy remains one of the most traumatic events in memory—countless Americans can remember exactly where they were when they heard that President Kennedy had been shot. His shocking death stood at the forefront of a period of political and social instability in the country and the world.

36. LYNDON B. JOHNSON (1963-1969)

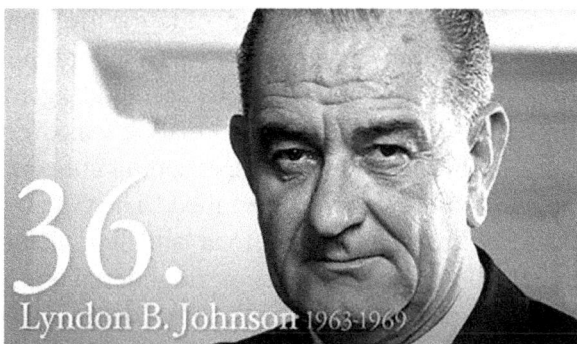

Born: August 27, 1908, near Johnson City, Texas
Full Name: Lyndon Baines Johnson
Nickname: "LBJ"
Education: Southwest Texas State Teachers College (now Texas State University), graduated 1930; Georgetown Law School, attended 1934
Religion: Disciples of Christ
Marriage: November 17, 1934, to Claudia Alta "Lady Bird" Taylor (1912–2007)
Children: Lynda Bird (1944–); Luci Baines (1947–)

Career: Teacher, Public Official
Political Party: Democrat
Died: January 22, 1973, near Stonewall, Texas

On November 22, 1963, John F. Kennedy was shot and killed in Dallas, Texas. The event thrust Lyndon Johnson into the presidency. A man widely considered to be one of the most expert and brilliant politicians of his time, Johnson would leave office a little more than five years later as one of the least popular Presidents in American history. The man who had risen from the poor Hill Country of Texas to become the acknowledged leader of the United States Senate and occupant of the Oval Office would return to Texas demoralized and discredited. He died four years later, a few hundred feet from the place of his birth.

As a man, Lyndon Johnson was obsessed with his place in history, consumed by a voracious appetite for life, and often cast between emotional extremes. He was a natural politician, and to many people who knew him, he seemed larger than life. As a President, Johnson revealed that he was even more complex and ambitious, unveiling a sweeping collection of legislative and social initiatives he called "The Great Society." Elected in his own right by a landslide victory in 1964, he seemed unsinkable but soon floundered amid the Vietnam War. Vietnam—perhaps the most divisive event in American life since the Civil War—polarized the country and transformed political, strategic, and moral debates. President Johnson was unable to devise a strategy for victory, withdrawal, or peace with honor. In 1968, facing strong opposition to his renomination, Johnson declined to seek a second term. He left to his successor the problems of Vietnam, racial unrest, and unresolved issues of income inequality and erratic economic performance.

Education and Marriage

The Johnson family had been in Texas for generations.
Farmers and ranchers, they had helped to tame the state and
had fought for the Confederacy in the Civil War. Lyndon's
father had the gregarious gifts of a politician, and three years
before Lyndon's birth, at the age of twenty-seven, he began
serving as a Texas state representative. The elder Johnson,
however, was less fortunate as a farmer and businessman.
During Lyndon's early teenage years, his father piled up
enormous debts, lost the family farm, and spiraled into
financial crisis that rarely relented the rest of his life. The
experience affected Lyndon throughout his own life and
likely contributed to his commitment to improving the lot of
the poor.

He did badly in school and was refused admission to college.
After a brief period of doing odd jobs and getting into
trouble, Johnson managed to enter Southwest Texas State
Teachers College in 1927. He taught briefly, with a stint at a
poor school in Cotulla, Texas, but his political ambitions had
already taken shape. In 1931, he won an appointment as an
aide to a congressman and left the teaching profession. The
experience was electrifying: he had found his natural
environment. He would not return to Texas full-time until
1969.

In 1934, he met Claudia Alta Taylor, "Lady Bird," and the
two were married three months later. She was a perfect
balance for him: charming and refined where he was raw and
boisterous. She also had family money, which the Johnsons
would eventually use to build a broadcasting and real estate
empire.

Fast Political Track

In 1937, Johnson resigned as the state director of the National
Youth Administration and won election to Congress,

representing his home district as an ally of President Franklin Delano Roosevelt. He was just twenty-eight years old.

He was an activist congressman, bringing electricity and other improvements to his district, but in 1941, he lost his first bid for the U.S. Senate, being defeated in an expensive and controversial election by W. Lee "Pass the Biscuits, Pappy" O'Daniel. Johnson remained in the House, and after the bombing of Pearl Harbor, President Roosevelt helped him win a commission in the Naval Reserve.

On a tour of the southern Pacific, he flew one combat mission, and it provided an ironic moment in presidential history. Before takeoff, he left one B-26 bomber, the Wabash Cannonball, to use the restroom and on his return, boarded another plane, the Heckling Hare. During the bombing mission, the Heckling Hare was forced to run back to base, while the Wabash Cannonball crashed into the sea, killing all on board. Johnson received the prestigious Silver Star for his participation. Later, when President Roosevelt insisted that members of Congress leave active service, Johnson returned to his duties in Washington. In 1948, he was finally elected to the Senate by winning the controversial Democratic primary by 87 votes. Embittered by alleged instances of voter fraud, his opponents thereafter derisively referred to him as "Landslide Lyndon."

Once in the Senate, Johnson advanced rapidly. Within two years, he was the Democratic whip; then, when the Republicans won a majority in the Senate on President Eisenhower's coattails, he became minority leader. In 1955, he was elected majority leader and transformed the position into one of the most powerful posts in American government. He worked ceaselessly and is perhaps best known for passage of the watered-down Civil Rights Act of 1957, the first such measure in almost a century. He also pushed for America's entry into what would become known as the Space Race. By

1960—after two failed attempts at the vice presidential nomination—he set his sights on the White House.

JFK and LBJ

That year, however, belonged to John Fitzgerald Kennedy. Young, handsome, rich, and witty, the Senator from Massachusetts piled up one primary win after another. Despite Johnson's announcement of his own candidacy, Kennedy was nominated on the first ballot at the Democratic convention in Los Angeles. Facing a seasoned Republican contender in Vice President Richard Nixon, Kennedy turned to Johnson to bring political and geographical balance to the ticket. Johnson delivered the South—including several states that had voted Republican during the Eisenhower years—and the team of JFK and LBJ won the election by the smallest popular margin of the century.

Although Johnson never seemed comfortable in the vice presidency, he headed the space program, oversaw a nuclear test ban treaty, and worked toward equal opportunity for members of racial minorities. He also publicly supported the young President's decision to send American military advisers to the Southeast Asian country of Vietnam, whose corrupt but friendly government was threatened by a Communist insurgency. Johnson was not, however, in Kennedy's inner circle and seemed frustrated by his lack of influence, particularly on legislative matters.

Johnson was only two cars behind Kennedy on the day the President was shot to death in Dallas. He was sworn in as President aboard Air Force One later that afternoon. A few days later, he spoke to a joint session of Congress. Seizing on Kennedy's inaugural plea to "let us begin anew," he asked Congress to "let us continue." Over the next year, he endorsed the late President's programs even as he announced his own. He pushed for passage of Kennedy's tax cut and civil rights bill and declared a "War on Poverty." When he ran for election against the Republican conservative Barry Goldwater in late 1964, he won by the biggest popular vote margin in history. During his presidency, Johnson engineered the passage of the Medicare program, poured money into education and reconstruction of the cities, and pushed through three civil rights bills that outlawed discrimination against minorities in the areas of accommodations in interstate commerce, voting, and housing.

But in the meantime, the conflict in Vietnam was intensifying. By 1965, the American "advisers" were a thing of the past as Johnson began an escalation of American commitment to more than 100,000 combat troops. Within three years, the number would swell to more than 500,000. As American casualties increased, an antiwar movement gathered momentum. The North Vietnamese and the National Liberation Front kept winning, even as Johnson poured more money, firepower, and men into the war effort. Ultimately, the President came to be identified personally with a war that seemed unwinnable. As a result, his popularity sagged drastically, dipping below 30 percent in approval ratings. Senator Eugene McCarthy, a Minnesota Democrat, announced that he would seek the Democratic nomination and did surprisingly well in the New Hampshire primary. President Kennedy's younger brother Robert also joined the race. On March 31, 1968, Johnson announced that he would neither seek nor accept the nomination. After a relatively short period in restless retirement, Lyndon Johnson died on January 22, 1973. His grave lies in a stand of live oaks along the Pedernales River at the LBJ Ranch.

37. RICHARD M. NIXON (1969-1974)

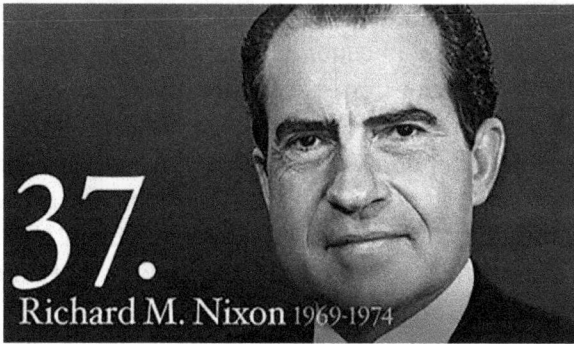

37.
Richard M. Nixon 1969-1974

Born: January 9, 1913, in Yorba Linda, California
Full Name: Richard Milhous Nixon
Nickname: None
Education: Whittier College (1934); Duke University Law School (1937)
Religion: Society of Friends (Quaker)
Marriage: Thelma "Patricia" Catherine Ryan (1912–1993), on June 21, 1940
Children: Patricia (1946–); Julie (1948–)
Career: Lawyer, Public Official
Political Party: Republican
Died: April 22, 1994, in New York, NY

Schoolchildren absorb at least one fact about Richard Milhous Nixon: He was the first and (so far) the only President of the United States to resign the office. Before the spectacular fall, there was an equally spectacular rise. In a half-dozen years, he went from obscurity to a heartbeat from the presidency, winning a congressional race (1946), national prominence in the Alger Hiss spy case (1948), a Senate seat (1950), and the vice presidency (1952). John F. Kennedy interrupted Nixon's assent in 1960, winning the presidency by the narrowest margin of the twentieth century.

After losing a 1962 race for governor of California and holding his "last press conference," Nixon patiently laid the groundwork for a comeback. In 1964, he campaigned for Republican presidential candidate Barry Goldwater at a time when other prominent Republicans were keeping their distance from the leader of the budding conservative movement. The Republican Party lost in a landslide that year but Nixon won the gratitude of conservatives, the growing power within the party. The GOP's huge losses in 1964 were offset in 1966 when two years of the Vietnam War and urban riots led to huge Republican gains in congressional elections. In 1968, Nixon won a presidential election almost as narrow as the one he had lost in 1960. He was then reelected in 1972 with a larger percentage of the votes than any other Republican during the Cold War.

Until the Watergate scandal led to his near impeachment by the House of Representatives and resignation in 1974, he was the dominant politician of the Cold War. As a Washington pundit once said, hers was not the Pepsi generation but the Nixon generation.

38. GERALD R. FORD (1974-1977)

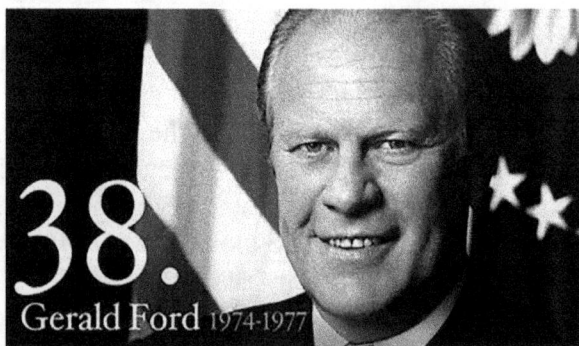

Born: July 14, 1913, in Omaha, NE
Nickname: "Jerry"
Full Name: Gerald Rudolph Ford

Education: University of Michigan (1935); Yale University Law School (1941)
Religion: Episcopalian
Marriage: Elizabeth "Betty" Bloomer Warren (1918–2011), on October 15, 1948
Children: Michael Gerald (1950–); John Gardner (1952–); Steven Meigs (1956–); Susan Elizabeth (1957–)
Career: Lawyer, Public Official
Political Party: Republican
Died: December 26, 2006, in Rancho Mirage, California

Gerald R. Ford became President of the United States on August 9, 1974, under extraordinary circumstances. Owing to the Watergate scandal, Ford's predecessor, Richard Nixon, had resigned under the threat of congressional impeachment. Ford assumed leadership of a nation whose domestic economy and international prestige—both seemingly sound in the decades after World War II—had deteriorated considerably. Just as important, Watergate, as well as the debacle of the Vietnam War, had profoundly shaken the American public's confidence in its leaders. Gerald Ford stepped into the breach opened up by these converging dynamics and achieved mixed results in addressing the twin problems of economic and geopolitical decline.

Born in Omaha, Nebraska, on July 14, 1913, Ford grew up in Grand Rapids, Michigan. He distinguished himself as both a student and football player in high school and at the University of Michigan. Ford then gained admittance to Yale University's law school, from which he graduated in 1941. Following his graduation, he returned to Grand Rapids to practice law. After the Japanese attack on Pearl Harbor officially brought the United States into World War II, Ford joined the U.S. Navy. He saw action aboard the *Monterey*, a light aircraft carrier in the South Pacific, winning ten battle stars for his service.

Politics and Marriage

After the war, Ford returned home to Grand Rapids, where he practiced law, got married, and entered politics. In 1948, he unseated Congressman Bartel (Barney) Jonkman in the Republican primary and then easily defeated Democrat Fred J. Barr, Jr., in the general election. During that same year, he married Elizabeth (Betty) Ann Bloomer, whom he had met in Grand Rapids. Ford and his new bride moved to Washington, D.C., where he would represent Michigan's Fifth Congressional District for the next twenty-four years.

In Congress, Ford's solid conservatism, his warm personality, his knowledge of the budget and appropriations process, and his willingness to accommodate his opponents propelled his rise to the Republican leadership. In 1965, Ford became Minority Leader, the highest-ranking Republican in the House of Representatives. As leader, he opposed much of President Lyndon Johnson's Great Society legislation and urged the President to prosecute the Vietnam War more vigorously. When Ford's friend and colleague Richard Nixon became President in 1969, Ford hoped for greater cooperation between Republicans in Congress and the Nixon White House. A good working relationship never came to pass, however.

Vice President and Watergate

Despite being treated as a lightweight by Nixon's staff, Ford came to the President's aid in the fall of 1973 after Vice President Spiro Agnew resigned. Nixon, who was under increasing pressure due to the Watergate scandal, surprised many by nominating Ford for the vice presidency. This was not out of any belief that Ford would play a role in policymaking that was compatible to Nixon's goals; rather, Nixon chose Ford because Congress would easily confirm him. Indeed, undertaking for the first time its confirmation role under the 25th Amendment, Congress did mount an exhaustive investigation of Ford but eventually gave the nomination its overwhelming approval. Ford took the vice presidential oath of office on December 6, 1973.

Ford traveled extensively as vice president, defending Nixon at every stop. The revelations surrounding Watergate, however, only grew more damning. During the summer of 1974, it became clear that President Nixon had grossly abused the power of his office by directing a cover-up of crimes committed by his subordinates. Nixon resigned as President on August 8, and Ford took the oath of office the next day, becoming the thirty-eighth President of the United States.

The Limits of Power

President Ford took office with the support of much of the American public, the media, and politicians from both parties. His decision—after only one month in office—to pardon former President Nixon ended this honeymoon. Domestically, Ford's greatest challenge was the country's slumping economy. The Ford administration battled repeatedly with Congress over tax cuts, federal spending, and energy policy, weakening the President politically. While the economy had begun to turn around by 1976, it still was sluggish as Ford entered the 1976 presidential election season.

In foreign affairs, Ford worked hard to maintain détente with the Soviet Union but was unable to deliver the major arms agreement he sought. Nevertheless, on Ford's watch, the United States, the Soviets, and more than thirty other nations signed the Helsinki Accords, a hallmark of détente. Ford also presided over the evacuation of Americans (and their Vietnamese allies) from defeated South Vietnam in 1975. That same year, Ford ordered the successful rescue of nearly 40 American sailors captured by Cambodia's Khmer Rouge. His biggest headaches in foreign affairs, though, often originated in domestic politics. Ford was never able to quell complaints from conservatives in the Democratic and Republican parties regarding his leadership of American foreign policy. His critics were most vocal in rejecting Ford's pursuit of détente with the Soviet Union.

1976 Election and Retirement

Ford's road to the 1976 presidential election was surprisingly difficult. Ronald Reagan, the leader of the conservative wing of the Republican Party, battled Ford throughout the primary season for the GOP presidential nomination. After surviving Reagan's challenge, Ford faced Democrat and former Georgia governor Jimmy Carter in the general election. Carter ran as a "Washington outsider" who promised to restore decency and honesty to governance in the wake of Watergate. It was an effective message and one that, along with several problems from within the Ford campaign itself, brought Carter to victory in November.

Gerald and Betty Ford retired to California after leaving the White House. The former President remained active in American political life after leaving Washington, D.C., commenting on events of the day and serving on a variety of corporate boards. Betty Ford, after battling her own problems with alcohol and pain medication, emerged as a leading advocate for the treatment of addictions. Ford died on December 26, 2006, at his home in Rancho Mirage, California.

Gerald Ford's presidency ended after only two and a half years. His record during that time was decidedly mixed; his domestic and foreign policies were neither spectacular successes nor disastrous failures. He faced considerable political opposition from Democrats in Congress and from conservative Republicans. But scholars largely agree on Ford's greatest contribution: as President, Ford's decency and honesty did much to restore the American public's faith in its political leaders.

39. JIMMY CARTER (1977-1981)

Jimmy Carter 1977-1981

Born: October 1, 1924, Plains, Georgia
Full Name: James Earl Carter, Jr.
Education: Georgia Southwestern College, 1941–1942; Georgia Institute of Technology, 1942–1943; United States Naval Academy, 1943–1946 (class of 1947); Union College, 1952–1953
Religion: Baptist
Marriage: Eleanor Rosalynn Smith (b. August 18, 1927), July 7, 1946
Children: John William (Jack) (1947–), James Earl III (Chip) (1950–), Donnel Jeffrey (Jeff) (1952–), Amy Lynn (1967–)
Career: Soldier; Farmer, Warehouseman, Public Official, Professor
Political Party: Democrat

Jimmy Carter's one-term presidency is remembered for the events that overwhelmed it—inflation, energy crisis, war in Afghanistan, and hostages in Iran. After one term in office, voters strongly rejected Jimmy Carter's honest but gloomy outlook in favor of Ronald Reagan's telegenic optimism. In the past two decades, however, there has been wider recognition that Carter, despite a lack of experience, confronted several huge problems with steadiness, courage, and idealism. Along with his predecessor Gerald Ford, Carter must be given credit for restoring the balance to the constitutional system after the excesses of the Johnson and Nixon "imperial presidency."

Carter was the first American President born in a hospital, and he was raised on his family's farm outside the small town of Plains, Georgia, where the family home lacked electricity and indoor plumbing. Jimmy was named after his father, a businessman who kept a farm and store in Plains. Carter's mother, "Miz" Lillian, a nurse by training, set a moral example for her son by crossing the strict lines of segregation in 1920s Georgia to counsel poor African American women on matters of health care.

Jimmy graduated valedictorian of the class at Plains High School. Captivated by the stories of exotic lands that his uncle visited in the U.S. Navy, Carter enrolled in the U.S. Naval Academy. He graduated in 1946 in the top tenth of his class and signed on as an officer under the tough but inspirational Captain Hyman Rickover in the Navy's first experimental nuclear submarine. (Rickover was later to become an admiral and build America's nuclear submarine force.)

Sowing Seeds of Change

In 1953, Carter and his new wife Rosalynn faced a difficult decision. His father, Earl, had died of cancer, and the family peanut farm and his mother's livelihood were in danger. Resigning from the Navy, Carter and his wife returned to Georgia to save the farm. After a difficult first few years, the farm began to prosper. He became a deacon and Sunday school teacher in the Plains Baptist Church and began serving on local civic boards before being elected to two terms in the Georgia state senate. There he earned a reputation as a tough, independent operator who attacked wasteful government practices and helped repeal laws designed to discourage African Americans from voting.

Though he had always stood up for civil rights and inclusion, and was able to win reelection to the state senate against a segregationist opponent, Carter was stung by a humiliating defeat in a run for governor of Georgia in 1966. He attributed this loss to a lack of support from segregationist whites, who had turned out in large numbers to vote for his opponent, a nationally known segregationist named Lester Maddox. In a bid to win their vote in the 1970 governor's race, Carter minimized appearances before African American groups, and even sought the endorsements of avowed segregationists, a move that some critics call deeply hypocritical. Yet after he became governor of Georgia in 1971, he surprised many Georgians by declaring that the era of segregation was over!

Presidential Politics: Scandal, Conflict, and Crisis

As Carter watched the defeat of Democratic presidential candidate George McGovern in 1972, he knew he would have to market himself as a different type of Democrat to have a shot at the White House in 1976. He was completely unknown on the national stage. In the aftermath of Nixon's Watergate scandal, however, this became an advantage. It also helped Carter that the disgraced Nixon and Vice President Spiro Agnew were replaced on the republican ticket by Gerald Ford, a political insider with no charisma and an uncanny knack for falling down stairs on camera. Despite an ill-advised interview in Playboy magazine, which plummeted his rating in the polls, Carter squeaked out a narrow victory.

Carter's newcomer status soon showed itself in his inability to make deals with Congress. Sensing his shallow public support, Congress shot down key portions of his consumer protection bill. Carter was determined to free the nation from dependency on foreign oil by encouraging alternate energy sources and deregulating domestic oil pricing. But the creation of a pricing cartel by OPEC, the oil producing countries organization, sent oil prices soaring, caused rampant inflation, and a serious recession. Carter was also deeply troubled by public scandals involving his family, including a mysterious $250,000 payment by the government of Libya to Carter's brother Billy.

Foreign affairs during the Carter administration were equally troublesome. Critics thrashed both Carter's plans to relinquish control of the Panama Canal and his response to Soviet aggression in Afghanistan by pulling out of the Olympics and ending the sale of wheat to the Russians. His recognition of communist China, which expanded on Nixon's China policy, and his negotiation of new arms control agreements with the Soviets, were both criticized by conservatives in the Republican Party. But the most serious crisis of Carter's presidency involved Iran. When the Ayatollah Khomeini seized power there, the U.S. offered sanctuary to the ailing Shah, angering the new Iranian government, which then encouraged student militants to storm the American embassy and take over fifty Americans hostage. Carter's ineffectual handling of the much-televised hostage crisis, and the disastrous failed attempt to rescue them in 1980, doomed his presidency, even though he negotiated their release shortly before leaving office.

Carter is positively remembered, however, for the historic 1978 Camp David Accords, where he mediated a historic peace agreement between Israel's Menachem Begin and Egypt's Anwar Sadat. This vital summit revived a long-dormant practice of presidential peacemaking, something every succeeding chief executive has emulated to varying degrees. Nevertheless, because of perceived weaknesses as a domestic and foreign policy leader, and because of the poor performance of the economy, Carter was easily defeated by Republican Ronald Reagan in 1980.

Since leaving office, Carter has remained active, serving as a freelance ambassador for a variety of international missions and advising presidents on Middle East and human rights issues.

40. RONALD REAGAN (1981-1989)

Ronald Reagan 1981-1989

Born: February 6, 1911, Tampico, IL
Nickname: "Dutch," "The Gipper," "The Great Communicator"
Full Name: Ronald Wilson Reagan
Education: Eureka College (1932)
Religion: Christian Church
Marriage: January 26, 1940, to Jane Wyman (1914–2007), divorced, 1948; March 4, 1952, to Nancy Davis (1923–)
Children: Maureen Elizabeth (1941–2001); Michael Edward (1945–); Patricia Ann (1952–); Ronald Prescott (1958–)
Career: Actor, Public Official
Political Party: Republican
Died: June 5, 2004

Ronald Wilson Reagan, the 40th President of the United States, followed a unique path to the White House. After successful careers as a radio sports announcer, Hollywood movie actor, and television host, he turned to politics and was elected governor of California in 1966, serving eight years. He ran unsuccessfully for President in 1968 and 1976, but in

1980, during a time of U.S. economic troubles and foreign policy difficulties, he won the Republican presidential nomination in a contest with George H.W. Bush and others and defeated President Jimmy Carter in the general election.

When Reagan took office, public confidence in government was at its lowest ebb since the Great Depression. Reagan largely succeeded in his goal of "making the American people believe in themselves again;" he called this the greatest accomplishment of his presidency. 1n 1984, Reagan was reelected to a second term in a 49-state landslide. During the eight years of his presidency, he reshaped national politics and carried out his campaign promises to cut taxes and increase the defense budget, using the latter as leverage to negotiate significant arms control agreements with the Soviet Union. Despite some setbacks, including notable budget deficits, Reagan left office in 1989 with strong approval ratings. His presidency has been ranked highly by the American people in subsequent polls. Reagan died on June 5, 2004.

Reagan Before Politics

Ronald Reagan was born on February 6, 1911, in Tampico, Illinois. His family—father Jack, mother Nelle, and older brother Neil—moved to a succession of towns in Illinois, as his nomadic father searched for sales work. In 1920, the Reagans settled in Dixon, which Ronald Reagan considered his hometown.

Ronald's gregarious father, Jack Reagan, had a grade-school education and a gift of salesmanship. He was an able salesman but was hampered by persistent alcoholism. He died in 1941. Ronald's mother, Nelle Wilson Reagan, nurtured and encouraged her sons and gave freely to charities even though the Reagans were poor. As an adult, Ronald Reagan often reminisced fondly about his mother's compassion and generosity. Nelle Reagan died in 1962.

Reagan, then known by his boyhood nickname of "Dutch," graduated in 1928 from Dixon High School, where he showed interest in dramatics, drawing, and journalism. No member of his family had any higher education, but young Ronald Reagan enrolled at Eureka College, near Peoria. He worked his way through college with dishwashing and other jobs, also sending money home and inducing his brother to enroll at Eureka. Ronald Reagan was an indifferent college student; he majored in economics and received mostly "C" grades. But Reagan threw himself into extracurricular activities, especially dramatics, and played on the football team.

Following graduation, at a time when a quarter of Americans were unemployed, Reagan found work as a radio announcer, first in Davenport, Iowa, then later Des Moines. Reagan struggled at first but in time became one of the best-known sports announcers in the Midwest. He also became a popular speaker before Des Moines service groups and enlisted as a reserve officer in the U.S. Cavalry so he could ride horses regularly. But he dreamed of bigger things. In 1937, Reagan went to California with the Chicago Cubs baseball team on spring training and arranged through a friend for a screen test at Warner Brothers. Warner Brothers offered Reagan a contract for $200 a week that launched his film career.

During the next twenty years, Reagan made 52 films, beginning with *Love Is on The Air* in 1937 and ending with *Hellcats of the Navy* in 1957. Reagan began his movie making in the B-division of Warner's, where, he said, "they didn't want [the films] good, they wanted them Thursday." His break came when his friend, the actor Pat O'Brien, recommended him for the role of doomed Notre Dame football star George Gipp in *Knute Rockne—All American* (1940), in which O'Brien had the title role. Reagan was a feature film actor from then on, receiving particularly good notices for a dramatic role in *Kings Row* (1942), which Reagan considered his best film. Overall, Reagan earned a reputation as a capable actor who did his best work in light comedies. After his film career ended, Reagan became a spokesman for General Electric, hosting the highly rated Sunday television program *General Electric Theater* and speaking to GE employees around the country.

Political Aspirations and Success

Reagan admired President Franklin D. Roosevelt, whose "New Deal for the American people" provided jobs for his father and brother during the depths of the Depression. His parents were Democrats, in a Republican area, and Ronald Reagan remained a Democrat until after he turned 50. Although he never lost his admiration for FDR, Reagan became an ardent conservative and switched his registration to Republican in 1962. Reagan's political and ideological evolution was the product of numerous factors: increased wealth, and the higher taxes that accompanied it; conflicts with leftist union leaders as an official of the Screen Actors Guild, and exposure in his General Electric days to a growing view that the federal government, epitomized by the New Deal, was stifling economic growth and individual freedom.

That view formed the essence of the speech Reagan gave on October 27, 1964, when he burst on the national political scene with a stirring televised appeal for Republican presidential candidate Barry Goldwater. Using many of the stories and statistics that had become staples of his basic GE speech, Reagan contended that government restrictions and taxation were causing the erosion of individual freedom within the United States. He also decried what he saw as the weakness of the U.S. government in the face of the expansive Soviet Union, which Reagan said was bent on world domination. His performance inspired Republicans and raised $1 million in contributions for the faltering Goldwater campaign. Although Goldwater lost the election in a landslide, conservatives had found a new standard-bearer in Reagan.

Backed by a group of wealthy Southern Californian entrepreneurs headed by auto dealer Holmes Tuttle and encouraged by Nancy Reagan, Reagan ran for governor of California in 1966 against two-term incumbent Democratic governor, Edmund G. (Pat) Brown. After defeating a well-known moderate Republican in the primary, Reagan won the governorship by nearly a million votes and was reelected for a second term in 1970. During his governorship, Reagan proved to be more pragmatic than his critics—or indeed, many of his supporters—had anticipated. Especially notable was his quick agreement to a record tax increase to solve an inherited budget deficit. Reagan also restored order on California's tumultuous university and college campuses, worked with Democrats to achieve welfare reform legislation and property tax relief, and protected the wild rivers of the state's north coast. On balance, his successes outnumbered his failures, which included a clumsy attempt to reform the state's mental hospitals and an ill-fated initiative that would have imposed a state and local government-spending cap.

Boosted by his success in California, Reagan made an abortive run for the presidency in 1968, a candidacy that divided his followers and national conservatives. Some of them wanted Reagan to seek the presidency; others believed he should prove himself longer as governor before running for higher office. Trying to please both factions, Reagan ran a half-hearted campaign that came to naught. But in 1976, with the governorship behind him, Reagan just missed wresting the Republican presidential nomination from Gerald Ford, who had become President in 1974 after the resignation of Richard Nixon. Reagan's near-miss candidacy made him the leading Republican contender in 1980, when he handily won his party's nomination and went on to defeat incumbent President Jimmy Carter by a significant margin.

Reagan's Presidency

Reagan came to the presidency with a sweeping and specific set of policy goals. In domestic affairs, he set out to revitalize the economy, reduce taxes, balance the federal budget, and reduce the size and scope of the federal government. In foreign affairs, he vowed to rebuild the American military and confront the Soviet Union and its allies with new vigor and purpose. He promised to negotiate with the Soviets from a position of strength. He feared that the accepted national policy of deterring the Soviets through a balance of nuclear terror ("mutual assured destruction") would lead to a nuclear war.

Reagan's presidency was nearly cut short by the bullet of a would-be assassin—he was shot and seriously wounded as he was leaving a Washington hotel on March 30, 1981. Reagan's brave performance in the hospital—"I hope you're all Republicans," he said to the doctors who were about to operate on him—gave him for a time a near-mythic status with the American people. With his approval ratings soaring, Reagan after his recovery won passage of much of his economic program, which featured large tax cuts and spending cuts that turned out to be smaller than advertised. Late in the year, the economy plunged into recession, reducing government revenues just as the United States was undertaking the defense buildup promised by Reagan. Taken together, the reduction in revenues and the increased military spending sent budget deficits soaring. Reagan largely ignored the deficits and focused on the recession. Many in his own party were critical of Federal Reserve chairman Paul Volcker, a Carter appointee who prescribed high interest rates to bring down inflation and crush the recession, but Reagan stuck with Volcker. Unemployment rose, but inflation subsided, and the economy turned upward in 1983, an expansion that continued throughout the Reagan presidency.

With the economy stable, Reagan turned his attention to foreign affairs; believing that the massive military buildup that Congress had approved would enable him to negotiate for reduced nuclear arsenals from a position of strength. There was little movement in this direction, however, during Reagan's first term. Soviet leaders resented Reagan's description of their country, in a March 8, 1983, speech, as "the evil empire" and in any case were preoccupied with their own leadership issues. During Reagan's first term, the Soviets went through a succession of geriatric leaders, none of whom was willing to negotiate with a U.S. President.

Americans reelected Reagan by a landslide in 1984 largely because of the economic turnaround and the perception that he was a steady leader. The nation's economy continued to expand during Reagan's second term, as did the budget deficits and the national debt. While all income levels gained from the new prosperity, Reagan's critics claimed that the wealthy were disproportionately benefited. It was in foreign affairs that Reagan had his greatest successes—and also his greatest setback. He worked diligently with the Soviet Union's new reform-minded leader, Mikhail Gorbachev, to improve superpower relations. The crucial product of their negotiations was the 1987 Intermediate Nuclear Forces (INF) treaty, the first treaty of the Cold War to reduce the number of nuclear missiles rather than stabilizing them at higher levels. The INF treat paved the way for other agreements that reduced the nuclear arsenals of the superpowers. As Gorbachev wrote, "it is difficult to overestimate the significance of this step." Gorbachev made a positive impression on Americans during a 1987 visit to the United States, and Reagan impressed the Russian people on a reciprocal 1988 trip to the Soviet Union.

Reagan's reputation was tarnished when the public learned in late 1986 that members of the President's National Security Council staff had engineered an arms sale to Iran, then involved in a bloody war with Iraq, in an ill-conceived attempt to win the release of Americans held hostage in Lebanon. Some of the proceeds from the arms sales were funneled to rebels ("Contras") opposing the Marxist government of Nicaragua. The two events became known as the Iran-Contra affair. This scandal bedeviled Reagan during the last years of his presidency, but did not overshadow his monumental accomplishments in the Cold War. Many years later, the independent counsel who had been appointed to investigate the Iran-Contra affair concluded that there was no evidence Reagan knew that proceeds from the arms sales had been diverted to the Contras.

Reagan After the Presidency

Reagan left office in January 1989, handing the presidency over to his favored successor, Vice President George H. W. Bush. Polls showed that Reagan had the highest approval rating of any departing President since Franklin D. Roosevelt.

In 1994, Reagan announced that he was suffering from Alzheimer's disease. As he battled this affliction out of the public eye, his reputation among Americans grew. It culminated in a bipartisan and international outpouring of sentiment at a state funeral after Reagan died on June 5, 2004.

41. GEORGE H.W. BUSH (1989-1993)

George H. W. Bush 1989-1993

Born: June 12, 1924, in Milton, MA
Nickname: "Poppy," "Bush 41"
Full Name: George Herbert Walker Bush
Education: Yale University (1948)
Religion: Episcopalian
Marriage: Barbara Pierce, on January 6, 1945
Children: George W. (1946–), Robin (1949–1953), John Ellis "Jeb" (1953–), Neil (1955–), Marvin (1956–), Dorothy "Doro" (1959–)
Career: Businessman, public official
Political Party: Republican

George Herbert Walker Bush belongs to a political dynasty; he sits in the middle of three generations of politicians, including his father Prescott, a senator from Connecticut; his son Jeb, former governor of Florida; and his son, George Walker, the 43rd President of the United States. In fact, George H. W. and George W. are only the second set of father and son to become President. (John Adams and John Quincy Adams were the first.)

Bush was born and raised in New England in a wealthy family. His parents valued hard work and public service and were strong influences in his life. He was educated at Phillips Academy Andover before joining the U.S. Navy and becoming a pilot, the youngest in the Navy, during World War II. After he left the Navy, he attended Yale University and received a degree in economics.

Bush decided to head out on his own after college and moved his young family to Texas, where he began to work in the oil business. He eventually relocated to Houston, Texas, and became involved in Republican Party politics, first serving as party chairman in Harris County, Texas, and then serving two terms in the U.S. House of Representatives from Houston's Seventh District.

After losing an election for a U.S. Senate seat in 1970, Bush was appointed the U.S. ambassador to the United Nations by President Richard Nixon. He went on to hold a number of positions within the presidential administrations of Nixon and Gerald Ford, including chairman of the Republican National Committee, U.S. envoy to China, and director of Central Intelligence. Bush thrived in the DCI position, and he made it clear to the incoming President, Jimmy Carter, that he would like to remain as director. Carter chose to replace him with his own nominee, so Bush reluctantly returned to Houston.

In the 1980 Republican presidential primaries, Bush ran as a moderate candidate with years of experience. However, he was quickly overwhelmed by Ronald Reagan, the former governor of California. Reagan asked Bush to be his vice president to help attract moderates and bring foreign policy experience to the ticket. The Reagan-Bush ticket won handily in both 1980 and 1984. As vice president, Bush continued to expand his foreign policy experience and traveled widely. He also became good friends with President Reagan, although he never became a close political confidant. Bush was somewhat awestruck by Reagan's political skills, and according to some observers, was mystified by the latter's hold on the public imagination.

In the 1988 presidential election, Bush's candidacy offered a continuation of the Reagan years. He wanted to soften some of Reagan's programs and promised "a kinder and gentler nation" but he did not advocate radical change or propose sweeping new legislation. Bush was the first President since Martin Van Buren to move directly from the vice presidency to the presidency through his own election, although oddly the transition was a strained one. A number of people from the Reagan administration later commented on the poor treatment they felt they had received from the incoming Bush team. Bush was sworn in as President on January 20, 1989, and with a strong team of foreign policy advisers, he helped the United States navigate the end of the Cold War and a new era in U.S.-Soviet relations. He also led an international coalition of countries which successfully forced Iraq to withdraw from Kuwait in the Persian Gulf War. Despite these successes, Bush lost reelection in 1992 when the American people, concerned about the economy, voted for change.

42. BILL CLINTON (1993-2001)

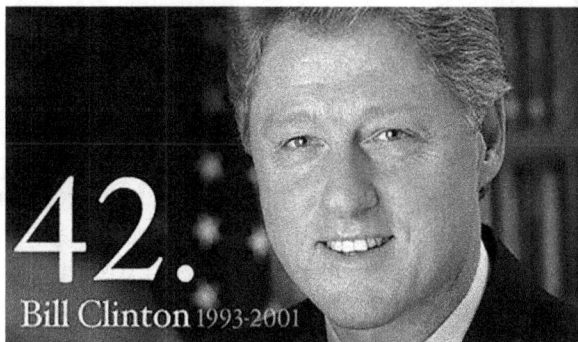

Born: August 19, 1946 in Hope, Arkansas
Full Name: William Jefferson Clinton
Education: Georgetown University (1968), attended Oxford University (1968–1970), Yale Law School (1973)
Religion: Baptist

Marriage: Hillary Rodham on October 11, 1975
Children: Chelsea Victoria (1980)
Career: Lawyer, public official
Political Party: Democrat

William Jefferson Clinton, the young President from Hope, Arkansas, succeeded where no other Democrat had since Franklin Roosevelt: he was reelected to a second term. Clinton also defied his critics by surviving an array of personal scandals, turning the greatest fiscal deficit in American history into a surplus, effectively using American force to stop the murderous "ethnic cleansing" wars in Bosnia and Kosovo, and presiding over the greatest level of economic prosperity since the early 1960s. He also endured unrelenting personal attacks from the right-wing of the Republican Party, the loss of Congress to the Republicans for the first time in forty years, and a humiliating but unsuccessful impeachment trial by the U.S. Senate. He fashioned himself as a "New Democrat" and has frequently been referred to as the "Comeback Kid." Few Presidents have both raised more questions about the standing of the presidency and simultaneously presided over a longer period of sustained prosperity.

Road to the White House

Bill Clinton, whose father died a few months before he was born, wanted to be President from a very early age. Born in 1946, he attended public schools in Hot Springs, Arkansas, after moving there from Hope. As a boy he was obsessed with politics, winning student elections at high school and later at Georgetown University in Washington, D.C. Work on a committee staff of Senator William Fulbright of Arkansas and attendance at Oxford University as a Rhodes scholar strengthened his resolve for a political career. After graduating from Yale Law School, Clinton briefly taught law at the University of Arkansas. He ran for the United States House of Representatives and lost, in 1974, and then was

314

elected state attorney general. In 1978, at the age of thirty-two, he became the youngest governor in the nation and in Arkansas history. After losing his bid for reelection, Clinton came back to win four terms, positioning himself for a shot at the Democratic nomination for President in 1992.

Clinton defeated President George H. W. Bush and upstart independent Ross Perot in 1992 after besting a large field of fellow Democrats for the nomination. As President-elect, Clinton vowed to focus on economic issues like a "laser beam," working especially to overcome the sluggish growth of the American economy. He also sought to remake the Democratic Party by focusing on issues supported by the middle class, such as government spending to stimulate the economy, tough crime laws, jobs for welfare recipients, and tax reform that shifted the burden to the rich. At the same time, Clinton stood firm on certain traditional liberal goals such as converting military expenditures to domestic purposes, gun control, legalized abortion, environmental protection, equal employment and educational opportunity, national health insurance, and gay rights.

Controversy, Scandal, and Success

Clinton stumbled badly in his first term when Congress vigorously rejected his complex health care reform initiative, spearheaded by First Lady Hillary Rodham Clinton. By 1994, Republicans had launched an aggressive attack on Clinton that delivered Republican majorities in both houses of Congress for the first time since 1955. Clinton fought back by capitalizing on Republican blunders and the nearly fanatical attacks unleashed on him by his conservative opponents. When Clinton refused to sign a highly controversial budget passed by the Republican-controlled Congress, he looked strong and resolute. Congress then generated a shut down of the federal government to pressure Clinton to back down, but Clinton remained firm, and the opposition caved in. Most Americans blamed Congress for the gridlock rather than the President, and Clinton was decisively reelected in 1996.

Clinton suffered two major setbacks during his administration. The first was his failure to obtain health care reform. The second, and much more damaging to his place in history, was his impeachment by the House of Representatives on charges of having lied under oath and having obstructed justice in the attempted cover-up of his affair with a White House intern, Monica Lewinsky. The impeachment issue grew out of an independent counsel's "Whitewater" investigation of Clinton's financial dealings in Arkansas, peaking just prior to the midterm elections in 1998. The American people evidently cared less about the President's marital affairs or his long-ago financial dealings than about his success in reducing deficits and obtaining economic prosperity, and they found the reactions of the Republican Congress to be excessive. The Republicans lost seats in the House, and the Senate thereafter failed to convict Clinton on the impeachment charges. Nor was the independent counsel able to link either the President or the First Lady to criminal activities in the Whitewater investigation.

In foreign affairs, Clinton succeeded in brokering peace negotiations in Northern Ireland between warring Catholics and Protestants, and—after a failed first attempt at ousting a military dictatorship in Haiti—in ending the murderous rule of Haitian leadership. His call for NATO bombings in Bosnia and Kosovo—following his earlier reticence at intervening in the Balkans—forced the government of Serbia to end its murderous attacks on Muslims in Bosnia, as well as on ethnic Albanians within the borders of its Kosovo region. Nevertheless, Clinton failed to mobilize support to end the genocide in Rwanda, and the peace talks he facilitated between Israel and the Palestine Liberation Organization soon devolved into a renewed and more lethal round of strife.

Political Partnership

Clinton's partner in his political career and marriage, Hillary Rodham Clinton, emerged as a key player in his administration. With a long record of professional achievement in Arkansas and beyond, Hillary's popularity had plummeted after she failed to achieve health care reform in Clinton's first term. However, she emerged from the Monica Lewinsky affair with very high popularity ratings in his second term.

Future history books may well begin by noting that Bill Clinton was the second President to have been impeached by the U.S. House of Representatives. However, they will also likely note his ability to survive and his impact on the politics, policies, and programs of the United States during the 1990s, including his presiding over a period of rapid economic growth. Clinton also had a significant influence on the direction of the Democratic Party, although it is yet unclear how lasting that legacy will be.

43. GEORGE W. BUSH (2001-2009)

43.
George W. Bush 2001-2009

Born: July 6, 1946, in New Haven, CT
Nickname: "Dubya"
Education: Yale (B.S., 1968), Harvard (M.B.A., 1975)
Religion: Methodist

Marriage: Laura Welch, on November 5, 1977
Children: Barbara (1981); Jenna (1981)
Career: Businessman, public official
Political Party: Republican

It took an extremely contentious vote recount and a 5-4 Supreme Court decision, but in January 2001, the Bush family succeeded in accomplishing that rarest of American exactas: a father and son who both served as President of the United States.

George W. Bush took the oath of office as the 43rd President twelve years after his father had done so—and 176 years after John Quincy Adams became the 6th President. The senior Bush, with a nod to history, once referred lightheartedly to his eldest son as "my boy Quincy," but within the Bush clan the first President Bush was often referred to as "Forty-One," and the second as "Forty-Three." In a nation divided bitterly along partisan lines, however, millions of Americans had other shorthand ways of referring to this polarizing President elected without a majority—or even a plurality—of the popular vote.

Despite the slender nature of his mandate, George W. Bush did not project himself as a minority President, and did not govern defensively. With the advantage of extensive pre-transition planning his administration hit the ground running. In his first six months in office, Bush had accomplished most of his 2000 campaign trail agenda.

Candidate Bush's priorities centered on two main issues, both of them domestic: First, he insisted that, with the federal budget in surplus, Americans were entitled to a significant tax cut. Second, he vowed an increase in federal funding for education as part of a sweeping plan for accountability from the states and districts. The schools would have to improve reading and math proficiency, particularly among minority students.

318

Bush almost always stressed a third issue when he ran as well, although it was more of a theme than a policy change: He promised to usher in an era of improved civility and cooperation in Washington.

His fast start notwithstanding, events intruded on this vision. And four years later, as Election Day 2004 approached, it was clear that Bush's razor-thin margin of victory and the ensuing Florida recount, a bitter fight over the makeup of the Senate, his conservative domestic policies, and the devastating attacks of September 11 and resulting war in made his four years in office far from tranquil, leaving an already evenly divided nation even more polarized than before.

Road to the White House

Born in New Haven, Connecticut, Bush moved as a toddler to West Texas and had what he has described as an idyllic upbringing in post-World War II Midland, the eldest son of Eastern establishment parents trying to carve out their own identities. This sense of serenity was broken by the death of his little sister Robin from childhood leukemia, a family tragedy that longtime friends believe had a hand in shaping Bush's personality. As he sought to console his parents, the boy became something of a ham—but he was a cut-up with a fatalistic streak. The episode also helped forge a lifelong closeness between Barbara Bush and her eldest son.

Following in the footsteps of his father and grandfather, Bush attended prep school, first in Houston, then in Andover. From there it was on to Yale, where he received a bachelor's degree in history in 1968, and Harvard Business School, where he received a master's degree in 1975. In between was a Vietnam War-era stint in the Texas Air National Guard where Bush flew F-102 fighters. This period of his life would later become controversial, but it wasn't at the time. Bush moved back to Texas in the mid-1970s and went into the oil business. After marrying and launching an unsuccessful run for Congress in 1978, he put together the partnership that acquired the Texas Rangers baseball team.

Bush was the public face of the Rangers front office until 1994, when he left that job to run for governor of Texas. He defeated popular incumbent Ann Richards that year and won re-election in 1998 with 68 percent of the vote. Already, the Republican establishment was lining up behind Bush for a possible presidential run in 2000. Bush raised so much money that he became the first major political candidate to eschew federal matching funds in the primaries. His only real competition for the GOP nomination was Sen. John McCain of Arizona, whom Bush outlasted, in part, because of his huge advantages over McCain in money, organization, activists, and fellow Republican officeholders. Positioning himself as a "compassionate conservative," Bush then squared off against Vice President Al Gore.

In a closely contested election that featured three presidential debates and a vice presidential debate, as well as two unified political conventions, no national consensus emerged; going into Election Day, polls showed Bush leading the race—but within the statistical margin of error. A fast-closing Gore caught Bush the weekend before November 7, in part because a story surfaced about an old drunk-driving arrest that Bush had never admitted previously. Gore ended up winning the popular tally by half-a-million votes, but it wasn't until the contentious Florida recount process was finally ended by the Supreme Court on December 12, 2000, that the election was decided.

Divided and United

In his first months in office, Bush got off to a solid start. He signed the broad-based tax cuts he had campaigned on and followed that success by shepherding through Congress a sweeping education bill that came to be called the No Child

Left Behind Act. The legislation was pending in a House-Senate conference committee on September 11, 2001. In fact, Bush was in Florida drumming up support for it—the photo-op of the day was to feature him reading to a group of sixth graders—when the World Trade Center was hit by two hijacked passenger airliners.

If Bush's tenure in the White House until that date had been marked by unexpected legislative success, he had not been successful in improving the civility of the political discourse. There were several reasons for this: Partly, feelings among Democrats about the Florida recount were too raw; also Bush's vision on domestic policy was so different from the Democrats' in Congress that a true détente was probably not plausible. Complicating that dichotomy was Bush's insistence that he not govern as a minority President: Just as President Clinton had done eight years before, he rammed through his tax bill with hardly any support from the opposite side of the aisle. In the midst of these budget battles, longtime liberal Republican senator James Jeffords of Vermont quit his party and threw in his lot with the Democrats, giving them a one-vote majority in the Senate. The ramifications of Jeffords' switch were enormous. The change in the leadership of the Senate Judiciary Committee meant that Bush could no longer count on getting his conservative judicial nominees confirmed; indeed, he ran into trouble even getting his cabinet confirmed. The upshot was that the new President's honeymoon, like his transition, was cut short.

All that was swept aside, at least for awhile, by the attacks of September 11, 2001. Reeling from the devastating blows to the World Trade Center and the Pentagon—and mindful that a plane that crashed in Pennsylvania was headed toward the Capitol or the White House—the nation's political leaders banded together while Americans of all political stripes rallied behind the commander-in-chief.

Bush's job-approval ratings soared as he faced this new challenge, and stayed at near-historic levels for well over a year. And the man who had sought the Oval Office without articulating clearly defined foreign policy goals suddenly found himself a wartime President, fighting a shadowy army of Islamic extremists holed up in some 60 countries under the direction of Osama bin Laden, who headed a worldwide terrorist organization called Al Qaeda. Bush almost instantly refocused his priorities, telling his aides that fighting what he called an international "War on Terror" was now the primary mission of his administration and those who worked in it.

But if the terrorists were scattered around the globe, their headquarters was Afghanistan, then under control of the reactionary Taliban movement. The Bush administration almost immediately issued an ultimatum to the Taliban to surrender bin Laden—a demand that was rebuffed. On October 7, 2001, the United States began air sorties against Al Qaeda terrorist camps in Afghanistan.

"We are supported," Bush said in an Oval Office address, "by the collective will of the world.

A War Presidency

Support for a military invasion of Afghanistan was certainly not unanimous in every world capital, but in the days after 9/11, the expressions of solidarity with the United States was a worldwide phenomenon—even in much of the Muslim world. In Pristina, where American armed forces under President Clinton had prevented genocide, some 10,000 Muslim Kosovars marched on September 12, 2001, carrying American flags and signs of support. Ethnic Albanians on the other side of the border, also Muslim, held candlelight vigils. "We are all Americans now!" declared the headline in Le Monde.

Yet already plans were being drawn up in the war councils of the White House and Pentagon to ready America's military forces for another invasion, one that would prove costly in lives, materiel, and national prestige: the invasion of Iraq.

In a lopsided and bi-partisan congressional vote on October 11, 2002, Bush received authorization to invade Iraq if it did not turn over its presumed arsenal of biological and chemical weapons, as well as what was thought to be its reconstituted nuclear weapons research. Iraq insisted it had no such weapons, and United Nations inspectors could not find them. But the President, expressing certainty that Iraq was hiding evidence and convinced that replacing the repressive and violent Baathist regime with a democracy would have positive and far-reaching implications throughout the Middle East, took the nation to war.

Iraq Pushback

On March 19, 2003, Bush informed the American people—and the world—that the invasion of Iraq was on. "We will pass through this time of peril and carry on the work of peace," he said in an Oval Office address. "We will defend our freedom. We will bring freedom to others, and we will prevail."

In less than six weeks, American troops were in control of Baghdad, early concerns about massive civilian casualties were unrealized, and Iraqi troops had been killed, had surrendered, or had melted back into the general population. On May 1, 2003—at a time when only 137 American military personnel had been killed—Bush told the American people that "major combat operations in Iraq have ended."

The early euphoria, however, proved premature. Remnants of the old regime, joined by Islamic terrorists who infiltrated the country, kept up a steady insurgency throughout the summer of 2003 and into the autumn. A war described as one of liberation took on the feeling of a war of occupation. In April 2004, 139 Americans were killed in Iraq in a single month. By July, the number of soldiers and Marines who had died there stood at more than 1,000.

By then, world opinion had shifted strongly against the United States—Le Monde had long since retracted its pro-American headline—and, at home, a strong anti-war sentiment re-energized the Democratic Party. The initial beneficiary was little known former Vermont governor Howard Dean, who spoke of "regime change" not in Iraq but in Washington. Dean fizzled in the primaries, but the Democrats' energy didn't, and the party settled on Massachusetts senator John Kerry as its presidential nominee. Kerry didn't mind reminding people that his initials, J.F.K., were the same as John F. Kennedy's, but Democratic party regulars agreed privately that the animating force in their party was A.B.B.—"anybody but Bush." Meanwhile, public opinion surveys showed Bush with near-unanimous support among Republicans. He'd run for office vowing to be "a uniter, not a divider," and he achieved that goal after a fashion: he helped each party to unite behind itself.

44. BARACK OBAMA (2009- 2017)

Born: August 4, 1961, in Honolulu, HI
Full Name: Barack Hussein Obama

Nickname: "Barry"
Education: Columbia University (B.A., 1983), Harvard (J.D., 1991)
Religion: Christian
Marriage: Michelle Robinson, on October 3, 1992
Children: Malia Ann (1998); Natasha, known as Sasha (2001)
Career: Community Organizer, Public Official
Political Party: Democrat

Barack Obama was inaugurated as the 44th President of the United States —becoming the first African American to serve in that office —on January 20, 2009.

The son of a white American mother and a black Kenyan father, Obama grew up in Hawaii. Leaving the state to attend college, he earned degrees from Columbia University and Harvard Law School. Obama worked as a community organizer in Chicago, where he met and married Michelle LaVaughn Robinson in 1992. Their two daughters, Malia Ann and Natasha (Sasha) were born in 1998 and 2001, respectively. Obama was elected to the Illinois state senate in 1996 and served there for eight years. In 2004, he was elected by a record majority to the U.S. Senate from Illinois and, in February 2007, announced his candidacy for President. After winning a closely-fought contest against New York Senator and former First Lady Hillary Rodham Clinton for the Democratic nomination, Obama handily defeated Senator John McCain of Arizona, the Republican nominee for President, in the general election.

When President Obama took office, he faced very significant challenges. The economy was officially in a recession, and the outgoing administration of George W. Bush had begun to implement a controversial "bail-out" package to try to help struggling financial institutions. In foreign affairs, the United States still had troops deployed in Iraq and Afghanistan, and warfare had broken out between Israel and Hamas in the

Gaza Strip, illustrating the ongoing instability of the Middle East.

During his first term, President Obama was able to work with Congress to improve the U.S. economy, pass health-care reform, and withdraw U.S. troops from Iraq. Still the President spent significant time and political effort negotiating, for the most part unsuccessfully, with Congressional Republicans about taxes, budgets, and the deficit. After winning reelection in 2012, Obama began his second term focused on immigration reform and gun control. However, much of the Capital's attention was focused on "sequestration," the automatic spending cuts that went into effect on March 1, 2013. Although the initial impact of sequestration was limited, Obama warned about its long-term effects on the economy. Agreement between the President and Congressional Republicans to craft a budget plan to end sequestration seemed unlikely to materialize quickly. President Obama's second term was marred by a deadlock with a Republican-controlled Congress. The last year of the Obama presidency saw him unable to fill a Supreme Court vacancy and unable to push much of any of his proposals through Congress.

Legacy

President Obama will likely be known to history for a number of things. The most obvious will of course be the fact that he is the first and so far only non-white president. The second will be his Obamacare health-care reform act. Repealing the "don't ask, don't tell" policy also allowed gay service members to serve openly in the military. Finally, President Obama gave the order to kill Osama bin Laden, the leader of Al Qaeda and mastermind of the 9/11 attacks.

President Obama's final years in office were marred by repeated attacks from conservatives in Congress critical of Obamacare, the Iran nuclear deal, the escalating civil war in

Syria and rise of the ISIS terror groups. This resulted in quite a bit of difficulty in passing any meaningful legislation. Despite this, as he left office, the economy and jobs were strong and the U.S. was not involved in any major conflicts around the world.

45. DONALD J. TRUMP (2017-)

Born: June 14, 1946, in Queens, New York City, New York
Full Name: Donald John Trump
Nickname: "The Donald"
Education: University of Pennsylvania (B.S., 1968)
Religion: Presybyterian
Marriage: Ivana Zelníčková (married from 1977-1992), Marla Maples (married from 1993-1999), Melania Knauss (married from 2005-).
Children: Donald Trump Jr. (1977), Ivanka Trump (1981), Eric Trump (1984), Tiffany Trump (1993), Barron Trump (2006)
Career: Businessman
Political Party: Republican

The 2016 presidential election saw a surprise that few anticipated. Democratic candidate Hillary Clinton was expected to win by a landslide by nearly every pundit and polling group. The reason for the unanticipated victory is complicated and not everyone agrees on what happened.

Trump was notorious for his bombastic and anti-politically correct stances. He also ran a populist campaign and made a lot of bold promises, many of which were quite unrealistic. It is widely believed that he was simply running to promote his own businesses with no intention of winning.

Clinton on the other hand marked the status quo traditional candidate. She was the most prominent female candidate who has ever run for President. Despite this, she was marred by a number of scandals, many of which have never been proven to be true. There was a lot of frustration with the state of American politics in 2016. There was also a lot of fear among US conservatives that the country was changing too quickly and their voice wasn't being heard. Regardless of why, Trump won the election to the surprise of everyone.

Trump's lack of experience caused many problems during his first two years in office (This book was edited in July 2018, only 1.5 years since the election).

It is hard to tell how history will view this presidency. Throughout the US and the rest of the world, there have been large-scale protests. His presidency has been marred with scandals regarding his prior personal and professional life. His communication strategy has been unusual and concerning. He has a habit of making offensive and concerning social media posts on his own personal thoughts.

In terms of accomplishments, he has passed some limited legislation. He has placed one Supreme Court justice on the bench with another currently pending approval. He has largely reduced Obamacare by removing the penalty for not having health insurance. He has rolled back a number of environmental policies. He has also passed some additional tax reforms.

It is too soon to see what will happen with the Trump presidency. Future editions of this book will cover the presidency in more depth.

###

www.ingramcontent.com/pod-product-compliance
Lightning Source LLC
Chambersburg PA
CBHW071938260326
41914CB00004B/671